Coming on Center

Coming on Center
Essays in English Education

Second Edition

James Moffett

BOYNTON/COOK PUBLISHERS

HEINEMANN

PORTSMOUTH, NH

Boynton/Cook Publishers
A Division of
Heinemann Educational Books, Inc.
70 Court Street, Portsmouth, NH 03801
Offices and agents throughout the world

Second Edition

The quotation from William Butler Yeats' "Oxford, Autumn 1920" on page 110 is reprinted by permission of Macmillan, Inc.

Library of Congress Cataloging-in-Publication Data

Moffett, James
    Coming on center : essays in English education / James Moffett. —
2nd ed.
      p.   cm.
    ISBN 0-86709-219-X
    1. English language—Study and teaching. 2. Language arts.
I. Title.
LB1576.M568 1988
428′ .007-dc 19
                                          87-27774
                                           CIP

Printed in the United States of America
92 91 90 89 88   6 5 4 3 2 1

Preface

Since the mid-sixties I have been a free-lance curriculum developer—or on some days, reformer. This collection of talks and articles represents my efforts during most of that period. I have updated the original book by dropping some earlier selections in favor of some pieces that appeared after the first edition. But I have retained certain of the earlier articles because, unfortunately, they have not dated. Some of the political dangers to education that others and I warned against have not been averted, whereas most of the curricular proposals have been.

Roughly in chronological order, these utterances sketch an interaction between educator and society in the crucial area of language learning. I had published at the end of the '60s two companion volumes of theory and practice about teaching English that, as methods textbooks, soon enjoyed much use and influence—*Teaching the Universe of Discourse* and (retitled slightly in its revised version) *Student-Centered Language Arts and Reading, K–13*. The first, like this present volume, was a collection of talks and articles that, though not intended to eventuate as a book, naturally cohered because of a certain unity and continuity in the author's preoccupations. But I was also responding to responses: the interaction consisted of my addressing issues I was asked to talk or write on by various professional organizations or institutions who knew of my work. I have acted in some measure as a weather vane, invited to hold forth on integration of the language arts or behavioral objectives or reading or humanities or writing or consciousness-expansion, according to current trends and funding. I tried to honor what some part or other of the society held important, all the while holding firmly to the development of my own ideas and ideals of growth. Shifts in both naturally formed a record that is part of what I have to say.

The bulk of this writing, however, comprises ideas about curriculum and methods intended to have some enduring utility—practical teacher talk or analysis of learning principles that aim to help educators think more effectively about what they are doing. I hope very much, for example, that some suggestions here may facilitate the teaching of reading and writing and that other suggestions will enlarge far beyond these activities our notion of language learning and curriculum development. In addition to weaving throughout the book a thread of personal chronicle for secondary interest and enhancement, background notes are meant to tie together somewhat the variety of learning matters dealt with at one time or another.

Robert Boynton and I have deleted some material that seemed to repeat key ideas an intolerable amount but at the same time permitted some redundance to remain as themes recurred within different frameworks. Totally eliminating all redundance seemed unwise to us on the grounds, as Editor Boynton expressed the matter in a note, "that each piece was, and is, of a piece and not simply a politician's theme mouthed on cue after the chicken and peas." I'm grateful indeed to him for being willing to help me prepare these items for publication and to let final decisions rest with me.

In selecting only those items that would balance and complement each other, I have also kept an eye out for variety of register employed, given that virtually all are expository. Some were carefully composed then delivered live or simply printed; some were extemporized from a very bare outline then transcribed and edited to tighten. Since readers interested in language teaching are usually interested also in such distinctions, background notes try to bring these out by relating certain circumstances of production.

Contents

Coming on Center

1

Coming on Center

Background

Delivered on the very eve of the '70s, at the convention of the National Council of Teachers of English in November 1969, this talk interweaves rapidly many of the themes developed by later essays in this book. So it may serve well as overture.

Convention programmers had assigned me the topic "A Student-Centered Curriculum" in reference to my methods textbook of that title published the year before. Although I appreciated this reference and this opportunity to expound my curriculum, I couldn't resist reacting to the implications of the program title under which my talk had been placed— "Alternative Centers for English Curricula"—which seemed to reflect euphemistically the traditional prejudice that a curriculum daring to center on the student was second-class. At any rate, fussing with their classification helped me organize my thoughts around notions of centering.

Behind this effort to whirl together many matters not usually dealt with as a whole lay an equal diversity of personal experience both remote and distant. I had just moved with family from east coast to west coast, Cambridge to Berkeley, after recuperating from finishing two books at once by spending a year relatively idle on a Caribbean island. From there I watched with some detachment the cresting and repression, in '68–'69, of reformative forces in my native land. Then suddenly we were in Berserkeley, as columnist Herb Caen calls this subtropically gorgeous hometown of radicalism (more deeply rooted in maverick middle-aged people than in students).

Three years before the convention, I had served as one of fifty participants in the Anglo-American Seminar on the Teaching and Learning of English, held for a month at Dartmouth in the summer of '66. This meeting had fallen in the middle of two years afforded me by a Carnegie Corporation grant to work full time at the Harvard Graduate School of Education on the development of a new English curriculum, which I was writing up as the two books of theory and practice. From many of the British at Dartmouth I received a gratifying corroboration of my approach, which included much drama and other peer interaction and which resembled the open classroom, though I had known nothing of what the British were doing. Many of the American participants were involved either in government-sponsored curriculum centers that were more often

1

than not perpetuating wrongheaded tradition or in efforts to found a new English on recent linguistic triumphs.

For ten years before that I had taught English (and for a while, French) at Phillips Exeter Academy, an old boys' boarding school in New Hampshire, where I had done everything from personal counseling in the dormitory to coaching lacrosse to directing drama and debating. During my later years there, Exeter flirted with coeducation in their summer school, which was open to public high school students. There and in the local town high school I transferred experiments in writing and in selection of literature to average students. The teacher's freedom at Exeter to experiment tempted me so deeply into curricular innovation that I left to carry my ideas out where they were needed more—in the public schools, first around Boston and then points west.

Having cleared my head underwater around the reefs of Barbados, I plunged back into the maelstrom of changing America as it emerged from the '60s and, barely uncrated in a new end of the country, tried to pack all I could into a carefully worded half-hour talk. It was published in the *English Journal,* April 1970.

————————◄●►————————

Why are you here today? What do you hope to get from me? From *any* speaker on English teaching? Bright ideas? New techniques? But is it bright ideas or new techniques you need most?

A new focus? Student-centered? What other kind of focus *can* there be, what*ever* your philosophy? Isn't the learner the active ingredient? And isn't the subject, his native language, already within the student, one functioning in fact of the student as human being? So why take an organic part of a person, thingify it, process it, package it, and lodge it back in him as a foreign object? Shall I *tell* you why? Would that be what you came to hear? Tell you why a student-centered curriculum is an "alternate" curriculum? Eccentric?

But what's the hurry? Let's take the case of the blue-eyed black, once a student of mine, hanging fire between his ghetto origin and his gentleman role in a famous prep school. When he talked, I understood him. When he wrote, I was lost in a bastard language no one ever heard before, a tortured syntax of false starts, obscure fusions, and never-ending self-collisions that perfectly uttered this Caucasian Negro of Mother Harlem and Father Exeter. E for English. So O.K., give our blue-eyed black a language-centered curriculum and show him what real sentences are like. You know, the kind his standard-dialect father would probably speak to him, had he stayed. Learn about our language heritage and how our language changes under the impact of social change. Or a literature-centered curriculum. Show him the masterpieces his "forefathers" created and how they can be reduced to a few mythic types for easy handling as he wends his way toward the white college of his mother's choice. Let him find himself in whichever literary selections the textbook adoption committees and their scared constituencies will permit publishers to put into literature series for him. It's a seller's market for black writers, but no vulgar language please, or sex, or politics, or controversy, or negative emotions— or even positive emotions if they get *too* high. I can center the curriculum wherever I like, but that student will center it where he must—somewhere between what people have been to him in the past and what I am to him in the present.

A freak case, this blue-eyed black. Yeah, sure. But every case is. Take a sophisticated WASP from New York City, *entitled* to blue eyes, of wealthy family, smarter than I, driven into schizophrenia. He communicates through double-binding messages as his parents taught him, sets traps for me in class, misreads literature despite his intelligence because every text is a pretext for his fantasies of abjection and domination. He stays furious at the rest of the class. They disagree with his readings and can't follow his themes . . . or smile at each other. Do I care enough for him, he wants to know after class, to immolate my other students for him? I ask him if that's the going price for love where he comes from, and he weeps and curses and is grateful. But the next day he sets another trap for me in class. And this goes on for a year.

He and I both came through, but if today—when he is himself teaching in Harlem—if today he can read perceptively, write clearly, and converse without trying to subjugate, it is not because I taught him those things. What I did was supply him with some real response to what he was expressing and support him when the response was too painful. He did the rest. His education was a lot more important to him than it was to me. Student-centered.

But the case is too freaky still. Forget minorites and neurotics and pick a normal kid (say from New Goshen, Indiana[1]). O.K. How about a nice, industrious, conscientious, Midwestern Scandinavian paper boy, eager to succeed, eager to please, thoroughly housebroken? He would bless me if I were to put into his hands a factual language book or a composition text with do's and dont's. If I were to give him five questions to answer about the short story for tomorrow. But I don't. I'm cruel. I ask him instead to write about his experience, and I don't grade his paper. I ask him to talk to the students across from him about anything in the short story, and I look toward them whenever he looks at me. To read their writing and tell them what he thinks and feels about it.

Problems come up fast. He tenses in discussion: who knows what'll get said next, and will I be equal to it? His fellows respond politely to his writing, and he understands that they are bored. Following the rules

[1]The home town of a young soldier who said he killed thirty to forty civilians at My Lai in Vietnam.

isn't enough. He's shaken. But he doesn't ask them, "What does he *want* anyway?" He asks me, "What do they *want* anyway?" I say I agree they're a hard lot but all they want is what any audience wants—you. He stares at me, and I can see the awful truth sinking in. He had me figured for the indefinite, permissive type who's a real pain because he won't come right out and say anything so you know where you stand. But it's much worse than that even. I really am tough. The course requires *full* attendance. He wants to send a stand-in, to *dance* attendance. And he wants me to give him something he has already, but I'm selfish—I want to give him something he doesn't have. Maybe by now he's forgiven me for being student-centered when he was authority-centered.

Not typical enough yet? An immigrant's grandson from the heartland? You're a hard lot too. So, next case. A tall pretty girl catches me before class and says her theme isn't ready yet because her period is on. She stands there forthright and looks level at me. She knows I'm no stickler for deadlines, and I know she's no whiner. There's just this fact of her womanhood that she wants established between us. Female first, student second. Fair enough. Besides, her steadfast look is rapidly convincing me. So I say all right, not to the late theme but to her womanhood. After all, teaching communication is my job.

The girl turns out to be a leader. She writes real and interesting stuff and reads it off in class without blinking. When she debates with boys, she doesn't act dumb and passive for fear of not attracting them. She doesn't need to cut down the other girls when they talk or write. She can like literature without embarrassment or apology. This kind of behavior bears looking into. The others do look into it. They see it's possible to be liked by both sexes even though involved in an adult-sponsored activity. She hasn't copped out, she's just exploiting me and my class for her own benefit. She can do that because I'm not trying to cover any material—nothing except what students bring up as they respond to each other and to books.

One of the people impressed by our young woman is a girl who dyes her hair one night with four cronies in a fit of fun but is mortified to sally forth the next morning. Who always grimaces in the prescribed ways, manipulates boys according to time-honored rules, and isn't about to risk losing status by showing interest in learning. But she gets taken off guard more and more, becomes rapt watching and listening, forgets her face until it mirrors each passing feeling. Kids are talking seriously to each other, *in a classroom,* about reality as she knows it. They've forgotten the teacher, and yet they do not speak as they speak in the gang. Or a girl is acting a role with a passion she shows nowhere else. It's awesome. Or that boy there reading his theme aloud, she never heard such intensity and sensitivity from him before. Where has *that* voice been? Then in her lovely, self-forgetting face you see it dawn: they haven't *begun* to show themselves to her, these boys, on dates, in gangs. Suddenly they're more than just objects to reflect her desired image back to her. She's caught up. Freed from the code—they can't help it if I force them to do all these weird things—they catch each other up until their group contagion works to open instead of to close them. Students center on each other.

But take the case of ourselves. You remember, I promised to tell you why a student-centered curriculum is an alternate—a fourth or fifth alternate, in fact. Well, hang on, this may be a dizzy trip. You've heard of the military-industrial complex, perpetrated by those other professionals, the wicked ones over there in the defense industry. Defense, it is true, is the nation's largest industry, but do you know which is second? Yours, my poetry-loving friends. Education. A booming business that people get rich off, nearly as dirty as the defense industry, hardly more moral when you consider that those who make war to make money are graduates of our *own* industry. We're dreadfully implicated in the very dehumanizing forces that are strangling our own profession. We *taught* those crazy people. Besides shopping the bazaars for bright ideas to take home and put into action, I suggest we take a long look at the system we're a part of, to grasp why it is we have not already had these bright ideas and done something about them.

So without further ado: the educational-industrial complex. An unsavory comparison, to be sure, but after you've finished recoiling, consider this. Both schooling and soldiering are compulsory. How differently would you teach if your students did not *have* to come to class? That question should haunt teachers. Thinking about it will give you more bright ideas than a century of NCTE conventions. Second, both are tax-supported, which means that, besides a captive clientele, we enjoy a monopoly business. Why innovate when the customers have to come and there's no competition? This would be a pretty good deal except that we are accountable to the public, which has an ignorant notion of education because it was educated by us. Now, education means of course that something in somebody gets changed, but taxpayers want their children to stay the way they made them. They didn't work on them all those years for *nothing*. So to educate really means to infantalize, to retard. Defense, too, is not what it says it is. We haven't been attacked for a long time, and the last occasion or so may have been rigged. Like education, defense is a *1984* term for its opposite. To defend means to menace the rest of the world with apocalyptic weapons. Actually, despite different window dressing, both industries have the same secret function—to solve certain economic, social, biological, and psychological problems of society that no one has had a creative enough education so far to solve any other way. Like overpopulation, employment, the need for outlets independent

of the market, civil disorder, personality disintegration in our kaleido-
scopic culture. Things like that. Cool the young and the poor in school-
room and barracks. Keep the kids out of politics, jobs, and girls. Issue a
uniform . . . thought and speech.

So much for vague resemblances. As a salute to systems-analysis, I'd
like to break these resemblances down into five components. First, the
compulsory element, the draftees or students, who do the work and in
whose name a vast quantity of equipment is purchased which they use
but do not choose. Proxy consumership (which, come to think of it, just
about describes the status of the Vietnamese at this moment). Second is
the officer class, the professionals, the teachers. For them the complex
provides employment (working on those very young people who might
otherwise compete with them in the labor market). These jobs are fairly
secure, since schooling and soldiering are too well built into the social
process to fluctuate on the market like other commodities. (Admittedly,
the military has a rougher time in this regard, foreign outlets being harder
to control than home consumption.)

A governing elite makes up the third component—the equivalent of
Pentagon and Congress—such as school superintendents, schoolboards,
education officials in state and federal government. These people usually
transcend the profession, which is to say they are administrators and have
all the power. The center of the complex—where lies the possibility of
colossal mischief—is in the overlap between this group and the next,
which is made up of the leaders of industry—builders and suppliers of
school plants, manufacturers of learning materials, educational testers and
researchers, and teacher trainers. What happens is that government officials and leaders of industry swap hats or swap favors and thus create demands which they also supply, as that radical Eisenhower was the first
to point out in his own profession. This is what a complex is all about—
the same people controlling the whole cycle of policy, procurement, production, and profits. There is no conflict of interest; left and right hands
are beautifully coordinated. In your industry too. These two power
groups, however, are dependent on the enlistees and the draftees, who
make up together the effective consumership and who keep the complex
running by playing along with it, one because he wants a job, the other
because he has to.

The whole complex is supported by, or rather bathed in, the fifth element, which I can only call a national mystique. This is a kind of body
steam given off by the mass of the taxpaying public, an aura that becomes
epitomized in certain master symbols or slogans, that is to say, certain
blank checks. The mystique that mandates the defense industry is "containing Communism." For education it's something like "speaking good
English," or as they said when I was a kid, "not talking common." Actually both are sub-mystiques of the grand mystique called "upholding

the American heritage," sometimes amended as "common" heritage or even, in Great Books fashion, "upholding the values of Western civilization." As if someone in our culture could *avoid* being an Aristotelian or Newtonian or Freudian.

The same fear behind both mystiques. Losing status, losing identity, being a nothing. "Contain Communism" means *don't let them blend with us.* "Speak good English" means *don't sound like those others.* Keep differences because differences will define us. Color. How you talk. Foreign ideology. It is indeed very American to be unsure who you are, because look where we came from. Trauma of the frontier, trauma of the melting pot.

But I digress, or as we English teachers write in the margin, "poor organization." I'm sure you're all panting to know how this systems-analysis relates to a student-centered curriculum. Well, I'll try to pull this all together in a climactic burst of incoherence. It happens like this. Let's say you want to let students talk and write and read and act in small groups. All the time, until the fantastic power of those groups is unlocked and carries those kids way beyond the paltry standards we now stretch for. To start with, you don't know anything about small-group process or dramatic improvisation and hardly anything about writing, because you never did these things. You never did them because whoever taught you to be a teacher never did them. Teacher trainers usually don't know about such things. People who do aren't in teacher-training institutions. What your teacher trainer is going to do instead is train you to center on textbooks and to be unable to teach without something in your hands, if only by default through not teaching you any alternatives. Deliberately or not, he programs you to need the kind of materials he's just been authoring. Furthermore, he's the same person who gets government funds to run experiments and set up workshops that omit, naturally enough, what he doesn't know about and that play up, naturally enough, the kinds of things his materials feature. He reads proposals and passes on them. Writes national exams. Consults for school systems, may even have worked for one once, or for a publisher. He's not an evil person probably, but by controlling both ends of the industrial cycle he plays a part in sending the whole system out of control, from the *educational* point of view.

But you're one of the happy few. You know how to set up improvisations and dramatizations, use small-group dynamics, build pre-writing into writing, and get all these processes feeding into each other. Fine! But when are you going to have the class time to do this? You'll have to throw out the spellers, grammar-language books, composition books, basal readers, skill builders—the whole mean, miserable lot of time-filling, tranquillizing commodities designed to market your own mind back to you. But we can no more throw that junk out than we can disarm. Everyone's investments are too great, including yours and even your students'. MIRVs and ABMs, composition texts, and practice readers—all discredited by practical experience but still around because once an industry winds up, it isn't fair to leave the poor fellow out on a limb. We can't afford peace, and we can't afford real education. They're too cheap.

But other rubbish has got to go. All those tests, you know. Second haunting question: How differently would you teach if you never had to test? But you don't have a choice, do you? There're not only those standardized achievement tests that test you, the school, and the curriculum while the kids are being tested, but teacher's turn to test comes around too. Besides your *candid* quizzes, you have your tests disguised as teaching—your book reports and research papers and essay questions. Oh, don't kid me now! We all know they're a check on the reading. Did he read it and if he did, did he comprehend it? Oh, if we could only look in their heads with a fluoroscope machine! Some way to monitor their minds.—Be reasonable. To evaluate you must see the results.—You might ask the student.—Too unscientific. The taxpayers, the colleges—they want body counts. Besides, the essay question kills two birds with one stone.—I agree with you there.

You yourself can't stop testing because you're impressed into the service of accountability, and standardized testing is no more easily dropped than cigarette manufacturing, however injurious to your health. It is packaged into materials and nested down in the souls of administrators. It evaluates curriculums and therefore dictates curriculums. Teachers teach toward the tests, and it's amazing how fast their good intentions dissolve about teaching anything else. All this has taken place haphazardly so far in English, but now that the behaviorists have teamed up with the Pentagon cost accountants imported from Ford and G.M., we're about to take the guesswork out of accountability, with the same efficiency that the Defense Department took the guesswork out of killing. We're writing behavioral goals in English which will become tests which will shrink the curriculum to observable behavior, only a lot of learning in English can't be seen unless you make the student do something to show it, so we can't teach for testing. But one thing we can say: the educational budget is well accounted for even if the education is of no account. Overt behavior. . . . Eight years out of high school a man understands in the master bedroom what his wife is saying to him, despite what she says. Are you and I going to be there to evaluate this effect of our teaching at the moment it becomes overt? Since few will get funds henceforth in English unless their project is behaviorally framed, it seems fair to say that the trend will be *self-reinforcing*. But this is necessary because we must be efficient and not waste money, in education. We must save our money to kill off those red yellow people.

Other examples I leave to your imagination. If, say, you wanted to make your homogeneous class heterogeneous, what obstacles would you encounter? It's time for teachers to quit playing dumb and passive, even if that *was* part of their teacher training. Again and again I have found that English teachers don't believe much in what they're doing, agree with a student-centered approach, and are really quite eager to make a change. But they feel powerless and don't trust their perceptions. These are effects of the educational-industrial complex we're embedded in.

I remember a dedication in a book I have forgotten. It read: "To So-and so, who taught me what I know." No, no, it didn't read that; my cliché-ridden mind read that. I looked again: "who taught me *that* I know." Who taught me that I know. What I know that's of use to you is that you know. Sweeping aside the intervening clutter, recall yourself as a young learner, then review those learners in front of you. You know. But you must assume the power to do what you know.

2

Misbehavioral Subjectives

Background

The following essay originated as part of a drama that says as much as
the essay itself. By 1969, enough federal funding had been channeled into
schools to raise issues of strict evaluation, supposedly to guarantee cost-
effectiveness. Faculty representatives from Purdue, Illinois, and Indiana
Universities had received a two-year grant from the U.S. Office of Education to produce "A Catalog of Representative Behavioral Objectives in
English, Grades 9-12" with built-in suggestions for evaluative procedures.
This was called the Tri-University Project in Behavioral Objectives. During its first year, a couple dozen "consultants," including me, were to con-
vene twice for a total of five days to write objectives for this catalog.
Consultants comprised some leaders in English education and administrators representing schools where the objectives were to be field-tested during the second year in a "controlled" comparison between schools not
using the objectives and those blessed with them. The latter, the ones
represented at the meetings, were called "ES 70 Schools"—"Experimental
Schools for the '70s." With this federal notion of "experimental" it's no
wonder the '70s got off to a bad start.

The Tri-University directors were to revise and edit our objectives
and, after field-testing and garnering reactions from outside readers, publish the Catalog for the profession. One of the directors was also the in-
house behavioral psychologist and was charged with visiting all school
sites. Directors worked closely with "major consultants" David Krath-
wohl, co-author of a continuation into the "affective domain" of Benja-
min Bloom's *Taxonomy of Educational Objectives, Cognitive Domain,* and Robert
Mager, author of the project bible, *Preparing Objectives for Programmed Instruction.* The very telling title of the latter had a more innocent air then than
it could possibly get by with today. The same for some statements in the
abstract of the Project's USOE proposal distributed to participants for
study before we met:

> Behavioral scientists may provide some assistance [in defining the
> subject of English]. They focus upon the learner—the learner as a
> doer, as a reactor, as a person whose behavior can be influenced in
> measurable and desirable ways by the classroom and by his reading,
> viewing, listening, speaking, reading, and reasoning.

To equate *doer* and *reactor* is symptomatic of this approach, whose advocates had not yet learned to mask the technocratic manipulation of students so well as later, after they came under fire. Admitting that English is not typing, the Proposal rationale continued:

> Nevertheless, despite the impossibility of eliciting for English many statements as exact as "type fifty words a minute," the search for behaviorally phrased statements has value because of the constant focus upon the child and upon the outcomes of instruction as reflected in what the child does.

Posing as child-centered while actually generating a very destructive "constant focus upon the child" struck me as exactly parallel to the fraudulent doublespeak claims of programmed instruction to be "individualized." No one has ever tried to measure the incalculable negative effects of keeping children perpetually under this kind of spotlight and of regarding them as score-sources while they are trying to grow up. This is not education but child molestation.

Similar efforts to manipulate the consultants themselves bothered me more and more after we arrived for three days, in October 1969, at the Speedway Motel in Indianapolis (no cheap symbolism, please). I might have been flattered to find that the handout called "Categories for Behavioral Objectives," which was used to group us into working parties, employed concepts and even specific terms from my two books published the year before, but when I tried to open some discussion during plenary sessions on the ideas and principles underlying the project, the "major consultants" became hostile and the directors (mostly English education professors) embarrassed. Clearly, we were to get out into those motel rooms in our small groups and write our objectives as directed, not question assumptions and intentions and ramifications. Some of the other consultants privately expressed misgivings or disgust, or satirized the project, but the mood seemed to be, "What can you do in the face of the feds? Better we're in on it."

For two days I was a good boy and went along; then at a cocktail party the evening before the third day I told the directors I couldn't stomach it any longer. They understood, they said, and we agreed that I would spend the last day writing a paper on my position. We did not discuss what I might do when we all reconvened for the final two days in St. Louis the following March. So in about four hours the next morning—having so much to get out in one sustained deadline session was rather like doing once again a long college bluebook exam—I wrote longhand the following statement, dictated it to the Project secretary, took one last look at the historic racing cars reposing in the Final Parking Lot of the lobby, and boarded a plane for the return to San Francisco.

I spent the flight trying to assimilate an experience I had never had before. At breakfast, one of the directors had offered me the presidency of the National Council of Teachers of English for the next available term, knowing full well that as soon as I finished my scrambled eggs I was going off to my room to write a dissenting view that, according to agreement, would be distributed to participants and included in the Project papers. Why hadn't he made this offer during the three nights and two days we had already spent together? And why was the offer never repeated for another year, as agreed when I declined? I know that the directors wanted badly to pull off the Project so that English could get federal support and to this end tried hard to accommodate consultants like me who were idealistic enough to be potential troublemakers. They no doubt felt justified because they were trying to protect our profession from our government. My purpose in relating this is not to embarrass these well-intentioned people but to point out what we very much need to face in the future— that it's better to do without funding than to become enslaved to its source. Schooling in the United States is supposed to be a function of municipal or county government, not of state or federal government, but we have sold it out to those centralized bureaucracies. More tax money should be retained locally so that the community can control its own schooling.

Under the title "Misbehaviorist English: A Position Paper," Anthony Tovatt and John Maxwell included this essay in their collection *On Writing Behavioral Objectives for English,* which the Commission on the English Curriculum of the National Council of Teachers of English published in 1970, prefaced by a resolution cautioning that "real danger to English instruction may result from definitions of English in the behavioral mode." This book includes articles by directors of the Tri-University Project, one of which replies directly to my article. While their collection was being compiled, the NCTE Director of Publications telephoned me to ask if I would be willing to delete the final sentence, to which some people involved in the book objected. Later, after he had left the Council, he told me that he had been hoping I would refuse, as I did.

Of course, the real drama at the Speedway Motel was an invasion of Tony Tovatt's room by a squad of field mice that forced him to bunk with me for a couple of nights. How could this be the same motel where, in the movie *Winning*, Paul Newman found his wife in bed with a faster racer?

——————◄●►——————

As an exercise in clear thinking, it might be a helpful thing for English teachers to write behavioral objectives—and then throw them away. We probably tend to be more fuzzy-headed about what we are doing than math or science teachers. At any rate, we often operate intuitively. As a result, a lot of research in English education has probably wasted government money. To concede all of this, however, is not to yield penitentially to cost accountants' preference for evaluation models. English is difficult and different, because a native language is enmeshed in the vast and intricate fabric of interpersonal and intrapersonal life. For this reason, to waste money on research in English may be necessary for a while before results are satisfactory. (More money is being wasted on more dubious enterprises.)

What I see as negative in the formulation of behavioral objectives for English concerns three areas: the inadequacy of such formulation to do justice to the goals of English, the unintended mischief that will almost surely result from publishing behavioral goals, and the bad precedent set for future relations between government and education.

Some goals in English imply overt behaviors and some do not. In insisting that desirable behaviors be *observable,* the behavioral approach rules out a great deal of learning—too much to merely mention in a cautionary note prefacing the goals. Consider, for example, what may be happening in a more taciturn member of a discussion group. The effects of certain reading, acting, and writing on a student's social, emotional, and cognitive growth tend of course to be long-range and inextricable. Although it helps to acknowledge that many of these effects will occur years later and often out of school, in practice these effects will either not be observed by evaluators or be falsely attributed to more recent school treatment— or, most likely, be ignored because they cannot be causally traced. The greater the time-space span, the less likely it is that effects can be ascribed to their proper causes. A behavioral approach will tend to favor short-span, well-segmented teaching fragments, because observed "responses" can then be more easily related to the applied "stimuli."

Even at short range, observed behavior can be badly misinterpreted by a psychology that in the name of objectivity refuses to infer what is going on in the black box of our head but does not refuse to infer the meaning of observed behaviors because the latter are supposedly self-evident and entail no inferences. But any observation entails inference. The claim to be an objective observer is really unscientific. The mere fact of being overt does not make a behavior objective. Einstein said that the observer is the essence of the situation. (In this regard, incidentally, the claim that the behavioral approach is centered on the learner is not very honest. A premium is placed on the favored viewpoint of the observer.)

In order to reduce the observer's inference to an "objective" level, it is necessary to control the stimulus-response situation to an extreme degree. In education this means to simulate laboratory conditions within a classroom—to systematically vary one factor at a time. For this reason, the protest that trivia need not result rings hollow; it is built into the "objective-observer" emphasis, which requires oversystematized fragmenting of learning. Without a respect for inner processes, such as genetic development, an observer can misinterpret certain confusions in the thought and speech of students as task failures when actually these confusions indicate arrival at a more complex stage of growth where more errors *can* be made. A student who describes dialectical differences very well after a session of hearing recordings of different dialects may be drawing on previous personal experience unknown to the observer.

So mainly, what is unscientific is limiting observation to the external view and repudiating all introspective statements. Since truth surely cannot inhere in one point of view alone, it must follow that an inside-outside view is more truthful. Overreacting to the mystical elements in earlier vitalist and mentalist psychologies, S–R psychology adopted another extreme in denying truth to the individual's own description of his inner life and consequently in denying his self-assessment of his learning. The only hope for truth through observation is to synthesize the totality of observations—from different times and vantage points—into a full picture. This certainly must include the student's statements about what he has or has not learned, how and when. The interior and external views correct and corroborate each other. Discrepancies stimulate new insights.

Also, because objectives determine evaluation, it is absolutely essential that the learner have a hand in formulating objectives. Otherwise, some kinds of learning behavior of value to him will never be written into the curriculum because they are not destined to be assessed. It is of course just this exclusion of students from decision-making that has helped to fire campus rebellions. One need not be sentimental about students or blind to their excesses to recognize nonetheless how wise and practical it is to include their view—in fact, to do more than that, to permit their groping for self-determination and power to become itself a driving force in their education. But S–R psychology is not inclined to champion this "vitalist" view that action originates in the individual as well as in the environment.

The kind of curriculum that I have been trying to evolve in collaboration with others could not be successfully evaluated by measures derived from behavioral goals. Not only could it not be assessed, it would never get off the ground because the amount and kind of activities that would have to be run off in the classroom in order to evaluate behavioristically would drive out and distort hopelessly the learning activities themselves. What I have proposed is to settle on a handful of general verbal processes that, if only from a purely logical standpoint, can't fail to develop the growth of thought and language because they are basic sending-and-receiving activities that can be varied in infinite ways, and to back these activities to the hilt without asking either teachers or students to engage in other activities merely or principally for the sake of evaluation. Assessment would occur in two main ways, one informal and the other formal: teachers would constantly match their observations against the statements of students about what they are learning and what they need to learn. Outside raters, experts in discursive learning, would assess samples of student discourse—tapes of discussion, finished compositions along with early drafts, tapes of rehearsed poetry readings, videotapes of acting and improvising—all taken in slice-of-life fashion from the normal learning activities. Rater evaluation acknowledges the subjectivity of any observer, but the subjectivity can be somewhat offset by quantifying and correlating rater judgments. This sort of observer can combine cues and get a total "reading" about which aspects of reading or composition or conversing a certain group is weak or strong on. This assesses the curriculum, but it does not necessarily tell which student has mastered which sentence structure or been sensitized to which dialectical differences. But to make sure that every student has mastered every specific should not be a goal anyway. Such uniformity at such a level of particularity is not desirable in itself, and, more important, can be bought only at a ruinous price that I, for one, would never be willing to pay.

To appreciate fully the price entailed in behavioral specification of English teaching, we have to envision realistically what will probably be done with such a list of objectives when promulgated by a prestigious leadership corps to the rest of the profession. First of all, I have noticed again and again that when second-level objectives are further specified as third-level objectives,[1] they not only become transformed into activities, which is necessary since this third level is the one that is actually behavioral or observable, but that at least half of these activities are ones I would consider undesirable, such as filling in cloze passages or listing the items of evidence in a speech or essay. The latter might very likely occur, and occur many times, in discussion, but I would be willing to trust that years of small-group discussion would, if teachers knew how to run the process well, naturally cause students to itemize evidence either individually or collectively. I would never be willing, however, to program a curriculum so minutely as to ensure that every student gave observable proof at every developmental stage that he could list someone else's evidence, because to ensure that, along with the myriad other mini-objectives, would pervert the curriculum into one vast testing system that would not leave enough room for something like small-group discussion even to become effective. In fact, most major drawbacks in the present curriculum stem from just this self-defeating effort at systematization. Instead of reading, talking, acting, and writing for real, students are taking comprehension tests, doing book reports, writing "critical" papers about literature, parsing sentences, filling in blanks, etc., to make their learning visible to the teacher. Thus the main impact of behavioral formulation in English will be to perfect the error of our present ways.

---

[1] According to guidelines issued at the conference, it is at the third of five levels of increasing specificity that objectives first become "behaviorally phrased."

·   It is reasonable to assume that a representative list of behavioral goals would be rather eagerly seized upon by (a) administrators at funding sources who are accountable to taxpayers (officials in state and federal education departments and school superintendents), (b) curriculum directors in school systems and all English teachers looking for guidance about how to teach the subject, (c) the testing industry, and (d) teachers of teachers, who wish to bring teacher education in line with the current notions of curriculum and methods. Despite all protestations to the contrary, the scenario will probably play like this. The third- and fourth-level objectives will almost automatically become measures of evaluation because they are, by virtue of being behavioral, almost in testing form already. Since tests are used to measure the performance of curriculum, teachers, and students, everyone concerned has an investment in doing only what can be tested. The testing industry certainly has little motive to pass on to schools the reservations and qualifications about behavioral objectives that the writers of them might feel. Cautionary notes and prefaces are virtually certain to be stripped away. In the familiar circular fashion of all state and national exams so far, these tests will act backward to determine the curriculum, and teachers will teach to them. This shrinking of the curriculum to fit the measuring standards is precisely what the Dartmouth Seminar denounced. Furthermore, only those projects whose objectives are stated in behavioral terms will stand much chance of receiving local, state, and federal money. Since this budgeting bias will bias research and experimentation, the S–R trend will be self-reinforcing, as indeed it has been for some time. After all, the essential motive behind the writing of behavioral objectives is to take the guesswork out of accountability.

Clearly, all areas of education have been advised to conform or lose out. To permit this kind of relationship between government and education is to encourage an already pernicious national trend. A marriage of convenience has taken place between the cost-accounting procedures developed in the Defense Department and the operant-conditioning principles of some behavioral scientists. What they have in common is a manipulative one-sided approach to human affairs and a rejection of two-way transactional models of action. Both gain. Cost-accounting administrators have mated with the psychology that suits their needs and problems best. It is the same psychology that the advertising industry has picked, and for the same reasons—manipulation of others toward one's own ends. The education industry has invested heavily in it by marketing teaching machines and other small-step programmed materials. To the extent that teachers and parents misunderstand what education is about, they too sometimes "buy" the operant-conditioning model of education—to remove choice from the "subjects" and make them do what teachers and parents want them to. On the other side, what the S–R school of behavioral science itself gains is a support that it has increasingly failed to get among the great leaders within its own discipline. This is an unholy wedding indeed.

English educators should have been asked to write goals according to their best lights but also in the light of an honest presentation of the government's accounting problems. We should never have been asked to fit English to a model chosen for these reasons and with this history. Losing this battle means losing a lot more in the future.

In short, we are being McNamara-ed, and we should fight it. But, I am told, if we don't write these behavioral objectives, "they" will. If this is true, then let's recognize this for just what it is—extortion. Lend your name and support to this project or else you-know-who will write these objectives instead of you. I simply cannot accept these conditions. I respect the directors of BOE, appreciate their good intentions, and sympathize with their own conflicts about possibly contradictory commitments, but with the submission of this position paper I must withdraw from the project.

3

Making Schools Pay Off
or
A Student-Centered
Language Arts Curriculum

Background

At the same time that I was being dragged by the heels into the educational politics and economics of the '70s, so thoroughly enshrined today that few struggle much anymore, I was signing on—with eyes wide open, I thought—to direct a large and intricate kindergarten-to-college language arts and reading program called *Interaction,* destined to be published in 1973. I had decided that school curriculum really issued from commercial corporations, and so that was where I was going to place myself. I became a capitalist lackey. For once, I resolved, a publisher was going to do a program the way it ought to be. Like my many brave co-authors, I knew such innovative materials would be a financial risk. (If you want to make money in textbooks, it's obvious how to do it, and if you can't see, the publisher will tell you.) For me personally, this meant becoming one of those dangerous people I had described as making the educational-industrial complex what it is. But I was going to save true language learning in this country by incarnating it in school materials that would make a revolutionary approach respectable to those outside the classroom and feasible for those in it. The real risk was that I wouldn't know until after the three or four years it would take to produce the program whether I had sold my soul or not. (Old Faust had to deal only with the Devil, whose contract stipulated very clearly in advance what you would have to pay, whereas corporation deals are more ambiguous or, if you like, more sporting.)

While I was senior-editing some 275 paperback anthologies replete with recordings and senior-authoring some 800 activity cards, two film series, and dozens of games, I was fighting alongside other English educators in California the now rapidly rolling movement toward state-leg-

From *Interaction: A Student-Centered Arts and Reading Program.* Teacher's Guides, pp. v-vii. Copyright ©
1973 by Houghton Mifflin Company. Reprinted by permission of the publisher.

islated (but federally "inspired") fiscal accountability based on locking behavioral-objectivized standardized tests directly into educational decision-making and hence into curriculum determination. We debated in special forums against proponents of PPBS (Planning, Programming, Budgeting Systems), gave talks and wrote articles on the folly of applying Detroit/Pentagon cost-benefit systems approaches to human learning, and even presented our cause before the State Board of Education, which didn't know much about how the state legislature's commission on school evaluation was, in effect, taking curriculum sovereignty away from districts through "accountability" bills. I was rewarded for addressing the Board on this by having my hand shaken afterwards by the rascally Max Rafferty, who was still California's Commissioner of Education and who opposed accountability for reasons very different, I suspect, from ours. Soon I found myself on mailing lists for right-wing groups in Southern California who believed not only in curbing centralized government, as I did, but also in militarism, abolition of sex education, phonics, and "literal" interpretation of the Bible.

We won the battles but lost the war. PPBS as such was never adopted in California and hence nowhere else in the nation, and before the end of the '70s we ceased hearing much about behavioral objectives. But only the names changed. PPBS took other forms. Behavioral objectives became performance objectives, and the whole movement goes today by the labels of "minimal criteria," "competencies," or "proficiency standards." The more educators combated the virus, the more virulent a strain of it evolved. It was hellbent, and nothing ever stopped it, because too many forces in government and industry wanted it and could exploit for their own motives the public's cry to make schools pay off better.

The following article says nothing directly about any of this struggle. Rather, it's about the kind of learning I was trying to protect, make a way for, keep a door open on. Essentially a nonpolitical person, I had lobbied and jousted only because I knew the curriculum that I had developed and that *Interaction* embodied was headed on a collision course with the technocratic management of youth being railroaded through schools over the heads and behind the backs of teachers. I wrote this piece as the lead statement of the curriculum in the *Interaction* teacher's guides at all four levels of the program. I entitled it "Making Schools Pay Off" to connect the philosophy of the program as directly as possible with the chief educational issue of that day, 1973, as it still is today. While writing it, I was invited to address in Miami a joint conference of the Florida Association of Teachers of English and the Florida affiliate of the International Reading Association. Many educators there knew that *Interaction* was about to appear, in time to be a candidate for upcoming state adoptions in language arts and reading, so in assigning me the topic "A Student-Centered Language Arts Curriculum" they were asking me to present the philosophy underlying the program. Under this title the *Florida English Journal* published the piece in the issue of Spring, 1973. To retain the original connection I affix both titles here.

Children do their most difficult and important learning before they come to school. Researchers constantly tell us this, but we can also see it for ourselves. Learning language, for example, is not new to the child entering kindergarten or first grade. In learning to speak, he or she has already accomplished a feat far surpassing learning to read or write, or any other task attempted in schools.

Speech occurs during the first year of life, with no specialized teacher, no curriculum and methods, no planning, and without even a fully developed nervous system—and also with no failures, no dropouts, and no underachievers. This marvel happens simply because the child is human and is therefore especially gifted for making sense of the kaleidoscope of life. From the crib on, this organism is busily processing data—classifying, relating, inferring generalizations. If it did not, it would never speak; for in order to speak, the child must: perceive and classify in the chaos around him those things to which words refer; discriminate human speech from other sound and one vocal sound from another; match these classified vocal sounds with the things they stand for; infer from dialogue all the basic grammatical rules that enable him to interpret and make up sentences he has never heard before. Motivation is the best ever—to join the human race and survive.

Preschool children have already done superbly some of the very things that we in schools arrogantly list as our goals for them. We are going to teach them all about auditory and visual discrimination, comprehension, composition, how to classify, how to draw conclusions, how to think. The fact is that we cannot teach any of these faculties, because they are part of being human and account for evolutionary survival. It helps not at all to play God. We would do very well just to avoid playing the Devil. What schools *can* do is open up all the ways and means by which a child can *continue* to exercise these faculties.

This view of children is not romantic or sentimental or permissive. Both homely observation and the best scientific findings fairly shout at us to abandon, once and for all, the notion that children come to school as empty vessels to be poured into, blank clay to be imprinted, or passive products outputted by a programmed assembly line. The real truth, as everybody knows, is that students are entirely too full of themselves for schools to bear. Instead of trying to make kids do something different from what they have been doing, we should be helping them to carry to maturity the very successful, if limited, knowledge structures they have already evolved. Instead of making them shut up in school, we should show them more ways to talk and more things to talk about. Children have been comprehending and composing all their lives. Quite literally, to comprehend and to compose mean to "take together" and to "put together." They are two sides of humanity's chief talent, which is to make sense of things by selecting and ordering experience into useful symbols.

If schools have too much ignored what the students are and what they know in favor of other, nearly disastrous approaches, the reason may lie less in some lack of insight than in some classic problems of institutions that hamstring and blindfold their staffs. As an institution, a school has an honest problem of numbers. As a *public* institution, it also has some not-so-honest problems of tampering by selfish or unthinking interests in government, industry, and community. If you multiply one set of problems by the other, you get a curriculum determined by mere standardization and politics, not by the practical realities of learning. So it fails, the public cries that it is not getting its money's worth, tighter accountability systems are installed, the original problems of standardization and politics are thereby worsened; and so the cycle goes. You do not solve a problem of numbers by playing numbers games. You solve it by *offsetting* quantification with qualification, mechanization with humanization. The great irony of performance-contracting was that school systems paid outsiders to do what they did not permit their own personnel to do—get out from under their own institutionalism.

Long analysis with many other educators has thoroughly convinced me that the famous problems of learning to read and write so plaguing public schools are not *learning* problems at all, but *institutional* problems. Learning to read and write is far easier than learning to speak, being merely a media shift from ear to eye, but *appears* much more difficult when attempted in school. Kids for whom, in fact, literacy is no problem learn it mostly at home. Those students unsuccessful at it are mainly those dependent on school for literacy. In other words, the most effective language learning requires precisely the spontaneous, responsive, personal, small-group circumstances of the home that seem impossible in any institution.

But such favorable circumstances are not impossible. Furthermore, numbers are not all bad. School has one great advantage over the home— more people and other resources. After basic speech has been acquired, a youngster can develop language power better outside the home, by communicating with a variety of people. Also, where numbers congregate, there also can be assembled more media and materials than at home. So an institution is not a hopeless place to learn in: the trick is to make numbers work for us instead of against us. This is, after all, the original purpose of any institution.

So far, public schools have been losing this struggle. In a nutshell, we have drastically overcontrolled the learning resources, in an effort to simplify management. We should *use* numbers to generate the vast quantities of practice that kids require in order to continue to develop language. The result of tidy uniformity is only chaos, of course, because everybody is prevented from doing what the institution exists to do. When reading has to be chosen, administered, and monitored by the teacher, students cannot read nearly enough, and furthermore they dislike reading. When the teacher has to process all the writing, students cannot write nearly enough, and furthermore hate to write. When speaking is outlawed as bad behavior or restricted to "class discussion" led by the teacher, students can't exercise the chief means of developing both oral and written expression. The more these target activities thus stagnate or regress, the more we feel we have to look for new methods, or ride herd on accountability. But the real problem is that making the teacher the center makes the teacher a stumbling block.

Programmed materials do not solve the problem, because, for one thing, they shunt the teachers aside instead of allotting them a more creative role. Programmed learning utilizes new technology and managerial ideas to cinch up old failures. It flies banners of "individualization," but it is merely *isolated* learning. Like other traditional approaches, it tries to wish away numbers instead of capitalizing on them. That is, it resorts to standardization. Students all do virtually the same things, and in the same order, but at somewhat different speeds. To vary pace alone is to trivialize the idea of individualization, which, to mean anything, must mean that students pursue different and unpredictable courses. What is efficient is to accommodate *all* individual differences in background and in makeup, not just speed. Furthermore, language is so thoroughly social in origin and function that it cannot be learned without interaction. We can capitalize on numbers only by making full use of people resources—the teacher, other students, and other adults—and by making the classroom a cornucopia of ways and means to learn.

Trends toward the open classroom in elementary school and elective courses in secondary school show that many people are trying to make school adjustable to individual differences in motivation and modes of learning. These individual differences derive largely from out-of-school learning of some sort; so any efforts to individualize schooling will strengthen continuity between life in and outside the classroom. The same rich variety of materials, methods, modes, and media needed to ensure each learner's finding his right way will also permit him to keep his life whole.

As variety must offset an institution's natural drift toward uniformity, wholeness must offset the tendency to fragmentation. Again, to simplify management, many schools have broken down learning into unreal units that nobody can learn. Each long-vowel spelling is made a teaching target for beginning reading, even though we know that learning to read often happens with no phonics instruction at all. Or, even with phonics instruction, it happens by *pulling together* different phonetic understandings. Later reading is broken down into scores of "skills," such as "singling out details," that are psychologically meaningless. Composition is decomposed into artificial particles like "transitions" or "topic sentences" or "paragraph structures" that can no more be factored out of the total composing act and separately taught and tested than the pound of flesh can be cut out of the body without killing both. After all, we are not dealing with carburetors or mufflers that can be taken out, fixed up, and replaced without damage to anything. Learning is organic in the true sense of being a live organization, a system of interrelationships. Further learning is *reorganization*. It may be handy to *speak* of parts of an organism, but to try to isolate them out *in actual practice* is a mad scientist's kind of fatal play.

The fragmentation of reading and writing cuts in several deadly ways. It cuts at the roots of language learning by separating reading from "language arts" and both from "oral skills," "creative writing," and "drama." "English" becomes just literature and therefore rules out huge areas of reading and writing treated nowhere else in the school curriculum. Because isolated words and sentences are easy to check out, vocabulary is thought to be learned by memorizing words out of context, and sentence structure is thought to be learned by analyzing separate sentences, whereas in truth vocabulary and sentence structure are expanded far better by pulling out all the stops on talking, reading, and writing. To atomize reading into "skill-building" passages, or composition into "practice paragraphs" simply severs action from motivation, because purpose and meaning have only wholes as goals. If these unreal units must, in addition, be sequenced, the unreality is multiplied. Although done in the name of scientific objectivity, this way of proceeding is thoroughly unscientific. All that results is a self-defeating overcontrol.

Again, we really know better, but the institutional need to monitor and account for itself pushes schools to such excesses. It seems easier to check out and report on what's going on if the action is chopped up fine. But this is the tail wagging the dog, in the worst way. Ironically, the public, in whose name these vivisections are committeed, does not assess schools in this mincing fashion but rather in a gross-gauge, rule-of-thumb way. "Can my child read?" "What does he read?" "Can he express himself well?" "Does he talk the right way for getting a job?" "Does he like to write?" etc. When parents talk accountability, they do not mean what management-by-objectives, cost-effectiveness specialists mean by it. Parents, in fact, clamor about their money's worth, but their goals are wholes—broad and humanistic—like students', and like most perceptive and experienced teachers'. Schools would do well to assess on the basis of goals as whole, motivated acts.

The program I have been working on attempts to restore wholeness—whether it is the totality of the writing act, the interrelation of reading with speaking and writing, the continuity of personal life with school life, the unity of will and action, or the integrity of individual growth. What can make this possible is a classroom array of materials and activities that are themselves wholes—that is, complete acts for common language motives. Second, each learner sequences these activities and materials differently according to the interplay of forces acting in and on him as he or she goes about evolving his or her own knowledge structures. So what this program does is set up such a powerful field that virtually anything that happens in it produces language-learning.

Personal choice is at the center, not only so that the learner *cares* about what he is doing, but so that good judgment will develop—whether the option is which book to turn to next, which activity card to select, which medium to say something in, whom to ask for help, which phrasing to express an idea in, or which way to interpret a line of poetry. But personal choice does not operate in a vacuum; in this program it operates as elsewhere, influenced by peers, elders, alluring variety in the environmental array, and intrinsic connections among things and actions. Thus, the student-centered curriculum is never "permissive" or "unstructured." It is not based on some empty and faddish notion of "doing your own thing." An individual is always a force in a field of other forces and very hard-put indeed to tell inside from outside.

Nothing can be "unstructured"; when we say that, we mean that we don't *recognize* the structure of what we're looking at. The word only expresses our ignorance. A bystander, observing a truly individualized classroom in action, may be tempted to call it "chaotic," because it is impossible for him to know what each student is doing, what he has been doing, and what knowledge structure he is building within. But any learner using this program will be learning to exercise language choices wisely, which has surely been the main goal of any traditional curriculum. The wisest decision for educators to make is to stock a classroom with as many things as possible to *choose among.* The traditional classroom has not had *enough* structures. This is one way in which it has been over-controlled. One lesson plan for all each day, one sequence for all for the year—that is not to structure *more;* it is simply to let a single structure monopolize the learning field. This monopoly rules out any real possibility of learning to develop judgment, which requires that the learner be structur*ing* in school, not structur*ed* by the school. Structuring is choosing. Comprehending, composing, making sense of the world—these are structuring. School should be harder and more fun. It should be a place where youngsters can structure for themselves, not have it done for them before they arrive. For one thing, we can't *stop* a child from structuring. For another, we have already tried that way.

The classroom should be a microcosm of what is most positive about America—its diversity and flexibility. The hybrid strength that comes from continued synthesis seems to be humanity's chief adaptation for survival in a very rapidly changing world. And the youth of the nation that serves as the growing edge of this world cannot afford to be hung up by false problems at our present rudimentary level of language teaching. There are simply too many other things schools must start teaching that we don't now have time for because language learning gets stalled in institutional problems. The future will require that children not only learn language well and fast but that they *transcend* language, liberate themselves from it, that is, go all the way through and out the other side to subtler, more powerful ways of proving and communicating that lie beyond and beneath language.

4

Teaching Literacy

Background

Although pre-service teacher training relies too much on unwise conventional wisdom and commercial materials, and seldom affords experience in such things as small-group process, writing, or drama, an encouraging trend among both districts and colleges partly compensates for this through in-service institutes, workshops, and conferences that go beyond the limitations of regular training. These are usually regional, and some fine ones I was invited to participate in exemplified a very valuable collaboration between colleges and school districts. The address coming up here was elicited from me by a very high-caliber reading institute called *The Reading Experience: Social Dimensions of Language and Reading Development,* given in the summer of 1976 by the School of Education at Fordham University's Lincoln Center campus in New York City. Although I have expounded to many groups my approach to reading, I felt this effort was especially clear, coherent, and complete, partly, I believe, because the institute had created a good situation for me by emphasizing the *contexts* of reading, the social and psychological dimensions that make it an intricate process and are too often stripped off in the hurly-burly of school life.

To say that I never had any formal preparation in the teaching of reading is simply to say that I've never taken training in *any* area of teaching. Such innocence amounts to a real advantage in the field of reading, I realized, because it's a battlefield, and the smoke of war obscures it so badly that you have to step outside to perceive anything. I never had to strive to be broadminded and overcome the partisanship of being professionally brought up a certain way. I came upon the phonics approach, look-say, and "reading for meaning" as an astonished outsider who couldn't believe that the nurses were all fighting among themselves while the baby was crying untended. I never had to learn to integrate reading with the other language arts, because for me it has never been a separate subject. At first, I did take too seriously the research in comparing reading methods that Jeanne Chall reported in *Learning to Read: The Great Debate,* before I realized such research omitted or slighted some means to literacy and reflected what schools do and publishers put out, not what schools might do or ought to do. But I always assumed that literacy learning, as I prefer to call it to include beginning writing as well, occurs as an organic part of total language experience.

If I have been able to contribute to reading—or any other language art, for that matter—it has been more from working with teachers than with children. There's a good reason for this. Most problems children have learning literacy in school are artificial and unnecessary, but it's very difficult for teachers, caught in a frenetic world they never made, to see how much these problems are school- or teacher-induced. My approach is to try to restore learning conditions in school to something like what they might be naturally, i.e., when no professional is trying to teach at a special learning site. I'm not worried about children learning to read and write when only that is involved. If I can clear up the teachers' problems, I know the children will have trouble only if they're clearly damaged in some way. Most of my ideas about literacy come from listening to teachers talk about their problems with it and from matching what I know of children's general learning processes against the materials and methods schools offer. I've also learned a lot from reading with my own children when they were small and from working on literacy materials for the *Interaction* program, which contained no textbooks, only reading selections. When you have to commit yourself to definite school materials but repudiate basal readers and programmed "skill-builders," you start really thinking about the basic nature of literacy acquisition. Mainly, I felt I had to shun convention and reconceive the two R's, to create a perspective on reading within which problems looked different and would become soluble. I've met countless reading specialists and teachers in reading labs who, despite working for years with kids, were so blinded by conventions not founded on actual learning processes that they really could not see the issues well enough to troubleshoot for themselves. Sometimes I feel embarrassed telling grown-ups things that seem obvious or commonsensical to me, but I think that schooling has operated for so long on undetected irrelevance that teachers can be at least partly excused for not being able to have the needed insights. So for me, an institute like the one at Fordham offers a fine chance to help teachers raise the quality of their thinking, so that even if they reject some of my practical suggestions, they'll be better able to see the way to go.

The text here is an edited transcription, in which I tried to retain as much of the flavor of the original as possible, consistent with reading ease. Illustrations recapitulate the transparencies referred to during the talk. I used these visuals also as cues to supplement some sparse notes.

LITERACY
GOALS

*I. To sound out with normal intonation
any text one could understand
if heard.*

*II. To write down with correct spelling
and punctuation anything one
could say.*

———◄●►———

I find it's very important to have a certain theoretical underpinning for teaching practices in literacy because I think there's tremendous confusion in the field and has been for some time due partly to an ambiguity in the term "reading." It really means two things at once in speaking of school learning. The same thing is true of writing. I could put it this way. A friend of mine in the Boston area, Joel Weinberg, a reading specialist at Simmons College, said, "I can read Hebrew aloud faultlessly, but I don't understand a word of it. Friends of mine who do can understand perfectly well without looking at the text what I am saying." There are two very different meanings of reading right there. This duality is commonly recognized in the field of reading by referring to decoding versus comprehension.

The decoding is the part that Joel was doing, that is, translating the words right off the page into vocal sounds. That's often referred to also as word attack. The other is the comprehension aspect; his friends would be listening and not looking at the text but would understand it. Now, the same thing occurs with people reading to the blind, for example, or reading aloud to a sick person, where you split these dual functions of reading off from each other. These examples dramatize what is always true of any reader. In solo silent reading, the same thing is true. The two totally different processes are going on at the same time. Now, as teachers, we have the problem of confusing these. Though fused in the mind of the reader, they should not be confused in the minds—as I think they traditionally are—of people in the teaching profession. So, I'd like to disengage a bit these two different activities. It's true that, functionally, when one reads, one does everything at once and that's the way it should be, but I think as teachers we have to separate these functions in order to understand them more clearly.

Decoding is a term borrowed from communication engineers, who speak generally of coding, which subdivides into decoding as the receptive, and encoding as the writing, end of literacy. You don't hear much about encoding in school because we're more interested in passive, receptive activity, but literacy should be symmetrical. At any rate, I start with the engineer's term "coding" and recognize three levels of coding—putting raw experience into thought, then thought into speech, and then speech into print (see Fig. 1). I think it's important to distinguish these three levels that, in a certain sense, lead in an order; that is, each presupposes the prerequisite of the one before. Before speech can be encoded into print or decoded from print, there must be the prior level of the thought-speech relationship, thought into speech, and, before that, the prerequisite of experience into thought. I'm going to translate those three levels into somewhat different terms here to develop the idea.

The experience-into-thought level is the nonverbal level of *conceptualization,* where experience is first coded into concepts. We speak of concept formation. The second level is the level of *verbalization.* To verbalize is to put thought into speech. That's the oral level. The last—and we note— the most dependent, the most derived level is speech-into-print, the written level of *literacy* (see Fig. 2). Now, we are speaking of two-way coding, encoding and decoding. Nonverbal, oral, written—literacy being the two R's, reading and writing.

LEVELS OF
CODING

• *Experience into thought*

• *Thought into speech*

• *Speech into print*   Figure 1

LEVELS OF
CODING

- *Experience into thought*
-NON-VERBAL-
Conceptualization

- *Thought into speech*
—ORAL—
Verbalization

- *Speech into print*
-WRITTEN-
Literacy

Figure 2

Let me translate these a little further. On the left of Fig. 3 are the three levels I just mentioned. I want to translate them over to the right into skills. So, reading down the left is the conceptualization level, which, when translated into school skills, let's say, comes out as the thinking skills—again, concept formation. The level of verbalization comes out as the speaking skills or oral language skills, as schools will call them, and then I have a very heavy bar down here to distinguish those two levels from the third, the literacy level or the two R's. That translates in school terms into the skills of word attack—that is to say, decoding and spelling, depending on whether one is talking about the reading direction or the writing direction.

Now, those traditionally are called the basic skills, but what justifies calling the most derived, the most dependent level, *basic* skills? Two other levels have to exist before that level can exist. We hear talk constantly about the two R's, word attack and spelling, as the basic skills. Well, from my point of view, there is kind of a misnomer involved. Those two skills are basic to literacy only. They are basic to that level, but, in the broader perspective of the total development of the learner, they are derived rather than basic. The real basic skills are thinking and speaking, right? Those are the really basic ones. So, I use "basic skills" always in quotation marks. You're not going to have basic skills in the sense of two R's until the true basic skills of thinking and speaking are thoroughly developed.

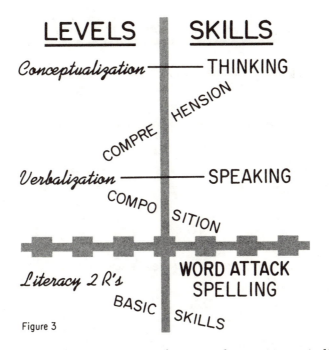

Figure 3

So I have written across Fig. 3 *comprehension* and *composition* to indicate that those first two levels cover a tremendous amount that is truly basic.

I want to continue translating those levels into other terms. Let's take just the literacy level for a while because teaching the basic skills, so-called, the two R's, tends to be such a tremendous problem in this country. I don't think it should be, but it is, and I hope I can indicate some of the reasons why it is when it should not be. So let me translate those levels now for purposes of getting just literacy for the moment into reading methods as they are practiced or could be practiced in school. In other words, we are getting into professional terms here. I say that any reading method is one or some combination of the four main reading methods listed in Fig. 4. I don't think this is my own invention, but it's my own way of codifying, if you like, what is done or talked about professionally in the field of reading, and there's a purpose to the order here.

Let me preface this first by saying that at the literacy level the learning task is essentially a paired association, as they say in psychology; that is, the learner is matching off vocal sounds he already knows with something new, which is the sights of the language—right?—the spelling. So, what we're into with the teaching of literacy is an audio-visual shift, a shift from an oral-aural medium to a visual medium, and that media shift is essentially what is called the two R's, or literacy. Anything that allows the learner to see and hear English at the same time, in some synchronized fashion, will teach reading in the basic sense of literacy. And anything

The Four Main Reading Methods

① Matching single sound with letter (s).

② Matching single spoken word with its written equivalent.

③ Watching one's oral sentences being written down.

④ Watching a text while hearing it read.   Figure 4

that does not will not. I don't think this is true because I say so; I think you should test it for yourself, but, if literacy is basically a media shift, then you have to have both media represented. The student is going to have to hear the sounds of the language, which he knows already, at the same time he sees how those sounds are written or spelled and, if he has enough of that, he will learn to read. So the methods, in a sense, necessarily, logically, must break down into something like what follows here.

One way of providing this audio-visual matching is matching single sounds with letters; that is, match each of the forty-odd phonemes of English, the basic sounds, with its spellings, and most have more than one spelling. For example, as the learner is presented with a letter or spelling, he is told how to pronounce it, or he is given the sound and shown how it is spelled. But we are below the word level. This is like subatomic physics here, particles. The second method focuses on a larger unit. This method matches a single spoken word with its written equivalent. Here we deal with single whole words rather than with word particles. The third focuses on a larger language unit and consists of the learner watching his oral sentences being written down, so that he can see how what he says looks like when it's spelled. The last method also involves whole sentences and the continuity of whole sentences. It consists of watching a text while hearing it read. What I'm saying is that any way of successfully teaching reading, in the sense of literacy, is bound to be one or more of these methods. This is my way of breaking it down. You'll have to test the truth of it yourself.

To translate these four methods into more or less traditional professional school terms, the first one would be "phonics," the level of word particles. (See Fig. 5, which moves from small unit to large unit.) Matching a single spoken word with its written equivalent has gone by the name of "look-say" or "sight word." The classic example would be flash cards. A card having one word written on it is flashed and then someone says the word so that the learner can see and hear the word at the same time. That is a larger learning unit, the whole word.

The third goes under the name of "language experience approach," done generally in primary school; no reason not to do it at later ages. It consists of the learner dictating, in effect, a story of some sort to someone who is literate, who writes down what he says—again, so that the learner can see his own speech written down and thus make the paired associ-

The Four Main Reading Methods

(1) Matching single sound with letter(s).

"PHONICS"——————— Word Particles

(2) Matching single spoken word with its written equivalent.

"LOOK-SAY," "SIGHT-WORD"——————— Words

(3) Watching one's oral sentences being written down.

"LANGUAGE EXPERIENCE"——— Phrases, Sentences

(4) Watching a text while hearing it read.

"READ-ALONG," "LAP METHOD"——— Sentences

Figure 5

ation. The last one, interestingly enough, has not been dignified as a reading method, and thereby hangs a long tale and tremendous difficulties. Most reading research will not include it, and therefore I think most reading research having to do with methodology is perhaps for that reason alone not very valid. Watching a text while hearing it read aloud, to the extent it is now beginning to be recognized as a reading method in the field, is often called "read-along." I prefer my own term, the "lap method." I deliberately make it folksy to indicate that it has been done at home and not in school. The prototype of that is a bedtime situation in which the child is sitting on the parent's lap, looking at and perhaps holding the book himself and getting the audio in his ear from the parent. The child is seeing the text while hearing it read aloud. For a number of interesting reasons, schools have virtually ignored this, have never considered this a reading method. Anyway, these are the four.

Today there's a tendency to be somewhat eclectic and mix approaches. I doubt if anyone is so diehard as to say she can do it with phonics alone or look-say alone and absolutely nothing else. In any case, if there's anything at all going on realistically in the classroom, the last two methods are bound to be represented to some extent. A person is going to be hearing something read aloud while he's watching the text.

O.K., these are in a progression going, as I said, from the smallest unit of language to the largest. The issue here is what size shall the learning unit be? What language unit shall be the learning unit? Phonics focuses on the particles that make up words. Look-say, or sight word, focuses on single, isolated, whole words, and three and four focus on sentences and sentence continuity.

The other issue is who or what supplies the audio. Given that literacy is a media shift and both media have to be present simultaneously in a synchronized fashion, where does the audio come from? Does it come from the teacher? If so, the teacher is tied up with the whole class at once, and there is no opportunity to individualize. Shall the voice be recorded? Shall the voice be the learner's own voice, as it is in number three, the language experience approach, where individual learners or a small group of kids, let's say, who have been on a trip or following a project, dictate and the teacher writes this down? The audio is then supplied by the learner himself. Students might supply the audio for each other in group exchanges. These are the main issues I think we should think about—who supplies the audio and how large shall the learning unit be.

Now, I think that covered in this scale are the kinds of controversies that have ripped apart the field of reading with arguing about one or another of these things, and I think the fights are unnecessary. What we should do is think of these as an array or progression and understand the differences among them and try to exploit those differences. Properly individualized programs, for example, would help each student find which of these or which combinations he needs. We know, for example, that many, many students have learned to read and write extremely well without any phonics at all. Other students, we know from experience, seem to have difficulty without some explicit instruction by the first method, but it's hard to judge because there has not been enough emphasis on three and four in schools, for the most part, to know what the real power and impact of that would be, whether those students who seemed to have needed phonics, because they never quite generalized the phonetic relationships and therefore were memorizing words and could not attack new words, would have been able to attack new words had they had some of three and four. Do you see what I mean? The only way you're really going to know is to have all of these in play and find out.

I think I would say generally that we should emphasize the larger units more, put most of our force, and our faith, behind them on the principle, which I think is sound, that the wholes teach the parts, not the other way around, because the whole is larger and contains the parts, and in general the larger the context, the safer you are. Just for one example, there's no way to teach the reading and writing of punctuation if you don't have whole sentences, so that rules out methods one and two. Think about that for a moment. Without whole sentences, there's no way to deal with punctuation.

Much more important, I believe, is that the larger the context, the larger the unit you're working with, the more opportunity there is for meaning and, therefore, for motivation. How much motivation or meaning is there in the syllable "ap", A–P, or "tee", or just a single consonant, the K sound, for example? No meaning and, therefore, no motivation. When you get to the whole-word level, O.K., there is *some* more meaning. You know, single words have meaning, like the word "poison" on a medicine bottle and environmental writing, signs, and captions, and so on, that deal with single words. You may know the Sylvia Ashton-Warner approach, which she described in the book *Teacher*. She tells of working with Maori children in New Zealand, of having them ask for words that were of great emotional interest to them and then writing these down on a piece of tagboard so they would build up a little word-card collection of words they were motivated to learn. O.K., that's a very creative way to work with what is not a very powerful level, that is, the isolated-word level.

Then you move on up to three and four, where kids are dictating high-interest material because it's coming from them, whole sentences, a whole story, and then listening to a text while watching it, number four; you're in again to whole pieces of real writing, real reading. Therefore, you have more meaning and motivation. Generally, as you go from one to four, you increase the amount of meaning and you decrease the problem of how to motivate. So, strictly as a strategy, I would say the safest thing to do, the most powerful approach, is to work as much as possible with the larger units and bring in the smaller units only to the extent that you feel they are warranted by practical experience. That is, phonics is only a means. Working with whole words and whole sentences . . . those are, to some extent, ends, goals—to be able to read those—but it's not a learning goal, I think, to be able to read "ap" or "tee" or anything like that. It's strictly a means. Logically, you want to focus on the goals, and when something is a means only, like phonics, then use it as little as possible and only when it justifies itself.

I'd like to use now a passage I picked from a comic strip as an example of what I think actually happens in the reading process, let's say, of a learner who knows, who has generalized for himself or had taught explicitly to him, some phonics, some of the phonetic regularities of English, but is still a very shaky or weak reader or perhaps, left to his own motivation, a nonreader. Here is what I think happens and why it is that the larger context can teach the particles, the wholes teach the parts. Figure 6 is from the comic strip, *Miss Peach.* I don't know, I guess I picked that unconsciously, being a teacher; it often focuses on the classroom. A boy there had set up a little booth as a psychiatrist, and he hung out his headshrinker's shingle and was giving advice on one thing or another, counseling, and some girl had come back to complain to him. I guess he was acting as data mates, too. She said, "That boy you sent me is a real dud, and you told me our relationship would rapidly grow and blossom into something beautiful." I picked this really very much at random, but it seemed to me the sort of reading matter that would appeal to a kid in upper elementary or junior high who is having trouble and that might provide us with a very good sample to work with. Incidentally, his response to her complaint was, "Did you water it?" It threw a little of the responsibility back to her.

I have underlined those spellings that would pose problems for many shaky or weak readers—the OY ending, the *oi* sound—that diphthong—when it has a Y instead of an I at the end of the word; or notice the OU in *you, our,* and *would.* Again, I just picked this at random, but it's typical of English that you can have three different sounds for the same spelling

Figure 6

in a passage as short as that. The *sh* sound in *relationship*, spelled with TI rather than SH or CH. The word *beautiful*, very irregular because of its French derivation, *beau*; and *grow*, the long *o* sound, is one of many spellings with the long *o* sound—O, OE, OUGH, OW, right? The long-vowel spellings are particularly difficult. *Real*—again, the long *e* is spelled many, many ways—E, EE, EA, EI, et cetera. O.K., what I think happens is this: let's say we have a ... O.K., now, a learner, a blooming reader who is very weak, but he knows some of the sound-spelling relationships. What happens is that he does use context to figure out those phonic relationships he does not know yet, that is, has not been taught or has not generalized for himself. Now, if these were isolated, he would not be able to do it. Do you see what I mean? Even the isolated word perhaps he would not get, not to mention the OU all by itself—simply no context. You don't know how to sound OU by itself or even OUGH without the rest of the word.

What the context supplies are cues or clues of essentially three sorts. Any native speakers of English, by the time they enter school, really know the basic grammar, the syntax; that is, they know the proper order of words. Of course, they have no idea what the names are, the nomenclature about nouns and adverbial clauses and determiners and modifiers. But never mind. They know how to use these. They know those slots in the sentence. No child says, "Hat blue my." He says, "My blue hat." Whether he knows a possessive adjective from a doorknob doesn't make any difference. He knows the syntax of those words, and he decodes sentences he has never heard before, and he invents or formulates sentences he has never heard before. So, the psycholinguists are quite right in praising the tremendous learning that has already gone on before children get to school in generalizing for themselves the syntactic rules of the language. They know their grammar. When we speak of teaching grammar in school, again it is kind of a misnomer. We mean we are now going to ticket, to label, all the things that they already know in a functional, operational way. O.K., drawing on that knowledge, which goes with the *oral* language skills, a reader, an incipient or weak reader, can figure out what certain words must be; that is, there are only certain things that can go after "a" in "is a real dud." After the article, you know there's going to have to be a noun coming somewhere in there, or let's say, after "real," after the modifier, there's got to be a noun. Now, he doesn't formulate that for himself, but his experience of the language tells him that. Certain slots in the sentence can be filled only with certain types of words, so that narrows down which words come up there. If winter comes, can spring be far behind? If you get a determiner, can the noun be far behind? Or predicates: "Our relationship would rapidly grow." Now, any speaker of the language who hits the word "would" knows, in most situations, that the other shoe is going to fall soon, the other part of the predicate. They don't know anything about auxiliaries in an intellectual way, but they know that there has to be the other part of the predicate coming along, so they are waiting for it. Again, that reduces the possibilities for the "grow" slot. See what I mean? The use of syntactic cues—and any proficient reader, of course, is doing this very successfully. This all goes on at computer speed, in the old biocomputer here, as John Lilly calls it. That's one set of cues.

Another is the sense, the meaning, the ongoing meaning. Now, if there isn't any meaning, of course, that rules these cues out, just as, if you don't have whole sentences, syntactic cues are ruled out. Terrible losses, because even the proficient reader requires them, and the less proficient a reader is, the more he is going to rely on those clues. All right, following the meaning, that is, the drift, of what is being said here, you can guess, you can predict what certain words will be. For example, "beautiful," isolated by itself, might be a difficult word to figure out, but, given the context, if the kid has been following the sentence so far, he can make a good guess about "beautiful." He is apt to know B; the B sound-spelling is one of the earlier ones and easier ones to learn, and the T and perhaps the L. In other words, the consonants are generally fairly easy and, knowing those, knowing that that has to be an adjective in that slot, knowing what the sense of the whole passage is, "beautiful" . . . he can figure it out. This is going on all the time in any authentic instance of someone reading or trying to read. Of course, if they do not care, none of this will work. The will must be behind the old biocomputer or you get nothing, and this is why the motivation is absolutely essential. Without it you don't even have a basis on which to think about the problem.

The third source of cues is, of course, the actual spellings, the letter knowledge that the student does have so far, whether from explicit phonics or from his own generalization. Sense, syntax, and sound-spellings are, in compact form, the three main sources of cues with which to figure out a passage (see Fig. 7). Two of these are the ideas or the ongoing sense and the vocabulary/grammar, syntax having to do with the word endings, the word order, the relationships among words. Vocabulary/grammar goes with the syntax . . . is the second source; and then comes the final one, the sound-spellings or the phonics, the phonetic relationships, how all the forty-odd phonemes in English are actually spelled in various situations.

Now, again to speak just of the literacy level, we do best, I think, to bank heavily on the larger context. The larger the language unit that is used as the learning unit, the better off we are. Count on the wholes to teach the parts, that is, the ongoing meaning, the sense, the syntax, and so on, to bring along the sound-spellings. This is how a kid who has been presented only a few of the sound-spellings, through phonics, can learn the rest on his own . . . because he can use the little letter knowledge he

KINDS OF CUES

- SENSE — *Ideas*

  −NON-VERBAL−

  Conceptualization

- SYNTAX — *Vocabulary, grammar*

  —ORAL—

  Verbalization

- SOUND — *Phonics*

  −WRITTEN−

  Literacy

Figure 7

has. He can get a lot of mileage out of the little visual knowledge he has so far accumulated by using the oral knowledge he already has, preschool and out of school, the oral knowledge being the meanings that attach to the words and his knowledge of the grammar and oral vocabulary.

I have been dwelling just on the decoding aspect. I want to shift now to comprehension. If literacy is concerned only with the overlay, the last level of coding, in Fig. 1, then what about those first two levels? They are also part of the definition of reading. Remember, I began by saying that it's a word that has a double meaning. The person who is listening to something being read aloud is doing all the comprehending, in the case, let's say, of the Hebrew being read aloud, and the person who is reading it but does not understand it is doing the decoding. What *about* the comprehending? One of the main things, it seems to me, that this kind of analysis shows is that two-thirds, at least, of learning to read does not necessarily have anything to do with books or letters, print. In other words, the audio-visual shift, from the medium of the ear to the medium of the eye, is only the tip of the iceberg. Before that can have any meaning, utility, or motivational force, we have to have developed and continue to develop in students the thinking and speaking skills represented in Fig. 1 by "conceptualization" and "verbalization."

What teaches those things? Well, a million things teach them, right? All of the accumulating experience that a learner acquires from many, many sources, through many, many media, methods, and materials, is teaching reading. Part of our difficulty, I believe, is in considering reading as a kind of isolated specialty and as a sort of technical problem concerning books. I think often a student's difficulty with reading does not have to do with the speech-to-print shift, or, at least, that in order to handle that, they have to develop the others. In other words, you learn to read from talking, from getting the kinds of experience that develop the intellect, that develop concepts, logic, much of which can be done orally.

Comprehension, in other words, is not simply connected with reading. In nonliterate or preliterate cultures, everybody is comprehending all the time. You read the environment, you read other people, you listen to what other people say. There is oral comprehension and, if this is highly developed, I think there'll be no problem of reading comprehension, given, of course, that students do make the media shift. We have to think of the teaching of reading as comprising—I think this is the only realistic way to consider it—as comprising the whole mental and verbal life of the student, so that anything that develops thinking and speaking is going to have big payoffs for reading, as well as motivating the desire to read. It's possible to teach, I think, all levels at once to some extent, and this is highly desirable for reasons that I've been suggesting and that have to do with banking more heavily on methods three and four—the whole-sentence, whole-continuity methods that teach the parts through the wholes.

Let me describe a little more fully the method I call the lap method, number four or read-along, the one that has not been generally recognized as a method. Now, never mind that you may be interested in older students—this applies at any level. You say, well, how can they really learn the basic skills, word attack and spelling, by just listening to whole texts like that without isolating particular phonemes. How are they ever going to learn those details . . . really nitty-gritty details? I will try to explain how I think that happens; it has to do with the whole issue of wholes teaching parts.

Traditionally, what happens with preschool children and the bedtime story? They are following the text with their eyes, let's say, and they hear the parent reading in their ear. There's not too much text on a page, and often the typography is such that certain words stand out—end positions, different type, enlarged, and so on . . . often they are connected with pictures, a lot of picture cues. And there's a lot of repetition—the format of the stories has repetition—so that the children recognize certain words coming up again and again and, at the same time, they hear the sound of the word. Well, what happens at first is that they memorize whole pages. If you've read many bedtime stories to children, you know that they memorize the story after a while and, if you get anything the least bit out of order, they really raise hell about it. They won't let you omit anything and get things out of order, and they can turn the pages for you after a while. Okay, you say, well, that's not really reading, and it's true, because if you took the same words on that page and wrote another text with them, the children would not be able to read that yet. Fine. They have begun the reading process in this sense, though: they are turning pages, they have the whole idea that there are ideas in the book, locked into the pages, that you open the book, you turn the pages, the ideas unfold, the story ideas, the images, that there is *pleasure* connected with this, that there are goodies locked in the book, that it's very positive, it's unthreatening, it's something one wants to do. Furthermore, they've got the synchronization to some extent. They're now synchronizing large blocks, by memorizing the pages, let's say.

O.K., to pursue this, though, what happens if they're read to very regularly—and it takes a lot of it—the same text sometimes, a new text sometimes, so that there is some old, some new? What happens eventually is that their focus gets finer and finer and finer and, instead of just the gross blocks of whole pages, it gets down to certain sentences, phrases, certain words they recognize, the number two level there of sight words—again, the repeated words, the words that are made to stand out and so on—but also they're getting down to the phonics level of number one. With enough quantity, they begin to recognize that the WH, for example, that little configuration there, appears wherever they hear the "wh—" sound—*which, what, why, where* sounds; it's in the initial position. So, after a while, they generalize for themselves that WH spells that sound, and that is learning to read, to become literate. They do this gradually—no doubt, with the easier things first, the consonants, then the short vowels and so on, then long vowels—and they begin, in other words, to infer for themselves the regularities of English spelling in exactly the same way they did this for the grammar of the language in learning to speak. The old biocomputer that does this sort of thing, that is part of human functioning, is doing this generalizing in there, and it got well exercised before the children came to school. They have already learned some of the basic concepts and vocabulary so that all they are trying to do now is to attach those things that they already know to the new medium of print, using all of these cues.

I think this is what happens, then, in the read-along or lap method, seeing and hearing language at the same time. It gradually refines down, down, down, and the children get very specific and they learn phonics from that, and this is how many, many students have learned word attack beautifully, and spelling, without any phonics. But this has not been considered a school method, and I'm obviously making a very strong pitch for it, partly because of the problem of righting an imbalance; it has been virtually omitted so far.

Practically speaking, of course, you do not have to have a lap and, if you are teaching secondary students, a little face-saving has got to go on. You use other students perhaps who are more advanced, who are able to decode well. They might even rehearse a little first and then read to the weaker readers. Older students with younger . . . I have been involved in experiments in elementary school where fifth and sixth graders come in and pair off with primary or first grade kids. Both like their relationship and, with just a little coaching, the older kids can do this very well. It does not take a teacher, it only takes someone who is literate and who is interested in doing it. So, parents, aides, older students all could do this, provide a live voice, a live audio, for the beginning or weak reader.

In addition to a live voice of this sort, you can, of course, have a recorded voice. In the *Interaction* program I referred to earlier, we recorded eighty hours of the texts. You don't have to buy the recordings. You could make the recordings yourself, have other people do it, have students do it after they have rehearsed, but I would suggest recording a lot of the texts you are using in the classroom, or if you're working with other people in the classroom, you might recommend this to them. I have even recommended this at the college level. An economics professor says that his students cannot read or do not understand the text. And I say, "Well, if you read it to them, do they get it?" And he says, "Well, it goes a lot better that way." I say, "Okay, then record it." So, they go get the recording *and* the book. The illiteracy problem is so bad in this country that it's rising through the grades and is now a serious problem in many colleges. For older students, at any rate, a recording of the text so they can do read-along or the equivalent of lap method is an excellent way, I think, for taking a person who is dependent and not proficient and helping him to become independent and proficient without loss of face, without a tremendous sort of ego ordeal, of putting self-esteem on the line, because it's really fairly easy.

To get on to other recommendations I would make for creative programs in reading, I think it's essential to integrate reading with the other language arts. This is implied in what I've been saying so far. The larger the context, the easier the learning is. The more you isolate reading from the other language arts, the harder it is to teach, just as the more you isolate phonemes from the normal language context, the harder it is actually to teach them. We have a technical approach; we think if you isolate something out and drill on that, students will learn that and then they'll put it back together with the rest. That doesn't happen. Reading itself includes that hidden part of the iceberg that doesn't have to do with books, the thinking and speaking skills. For this reason, it develops better if it's connected with all the content areas. Fortunately, there's an emphasis today on reading in the content areas, I think partly because students read so badly that the problem of literacy has spread across the board now in schools as well as up the grades. At any rate, a positive effect has been to help integrate reading with the other language arts. By "integrate," I mean that reading tasks or assignments should be, I think, tied in to little series of activities, such, for example, that a student writes something, discusses, reads, acts out, and so on . . . various interweaving of the language arts with each other and with the graphic arts, the combining of reading with photos in the forms of captions and labels, maps, charts, graphs, where words are combined with graphics. This does a number of things at once. It teaches students to use one of the language arts or one of the graphic arts to get a leverage on reading, but it also *interests* them in reading. It has a motivational payoff. The larger the context, the more meaning, the more motivation.

Now for some of the kinds of reading matter that I think it would help to introduce into the classroom. I mentioned charts, graphs, maps, and captioned photographs—graphics combined with words. In the *Interaction* program, we put out whole booklets of nothing but those, so that they'd be legitimized as reading matter. We didn't care about whether this was language arts, social studies, science, because when you get into things like that, they cut scross the different disciplines. The use of transcripts . . . a tremendous amount of really interesting material covering any kind of subject matter students might be interested in is purveyed or appears in our society in the form of transcripts. Interviews, talk shows, hearings, court trials—a lot of this really interests students and, because it's oral transcription, the speech sounds natural, not so foreign to them. Yet, in these interviews or talk shows or trials, the content can be quite deep and can cover any kind of interest.

Again, the problem with meaning is in a way the biggest one. If you do integrate reading with the language arts and with the other arts so that reading has warm-ups and follow-ups, you'll find that it's tremendously powerful. For example, students reading a few fables together . . . a small group reading a few fables together, then writing their own, 'iscussing fables without the moral until they try to agree on what the moral of the fable is and then looking to see what the moral is and then maybe writing some more fables of their own, and distributing these to other students who would then use that as reading material. Do you see what I mean? Interweaving the language arts.

I would recommend partner reading. This presupposes a system of small groups reading different kinds of reading material at the same time. I think it's self-defeating—and almost too negative to work with—to have an entire class read the same thing at the same time. I know this is standard procedure in most U.S. schools, but it's also one of the main reasons why we are having trouble with literacy. It's a gamble that you're bound to lose. The spread within any grade—third grade, tenth grade, it doesn't make any difference—the spread of interest, subject matter, content, of reading difficulty, of style, of individual and ethnic variation is so great, even in a so-called homogeneous classroom that, in effect, you have a spread of grades anywhere from four, six, eight to ten years within any one year, so that to assign the same text to a class at the same time is very self-defeating. I think there's no way to win that one. I realize this indicates a different kind of classroom organization, but that is precisely what I'm recommending. If we're serious about beating the reading problems in this country now, I think it means we have to individualize the reading from first grade on, but by "individualize" I don't mean programmed materials, that's for certain. I do mean students choosing their own reading material, given a very wide array of subject matter and difficulty, but this doesn't mean working alone. I think, on the contrary, most students, particularly if they're weak readers, will prefer to read something in company with a few partners. So what I recommend is a small-group process where students choose their reading material in combination with a few partners who are also interested in the same content, let's say, the same form, or read at about the same level of difficulty, enough to get along anyway.

So there are a number of things that go along with this approach. One is that you have to have a far wider array of reading materials in any one classroom than is customary; otherwise, individualizing is just a hollow slogan, as, indeed, it usually is. If there's no opportunity for the individual to find something of his own level to really interest him, then nothing else will work, and learning to read will seem the technical matter that you have to solve with a lot of expensive gear in a language lab, a reading lab, when actually it isn't. But the small groups choosing together the reading materials—this means, for one thing, you don't need whole-class sets of any text. What you need is to trade off the number of copies for the number of titles, get more titles in a classroom, but only a handful of copies for each, in some cases maybe only one or two. So an individual with a partner, or maybe in a small group of four, five, or six, can get both the advantages of individualization—that is, finding something that's really matched to them—and at the same time the advantages of cooperation and socializing. This is very, very powerful—different groups reading different things at the same time. I would recommend this also in a high school social studies or science course. We're rapidly losing students in the content areas in secondary school because the textbooks are just so hard for them to read or so uninteresting that we don't know how much is reading difficulty or how much is just indifference. The new math textbooks are virtually unreadable for most students. Again, we don't know how much the problem is simply motivational, because math is a dehumanized subject as it is generally presented in textbooks. So we have to get off the gold standard of the uniform textbook and, I think, get into something else, into what I'm describing.

Now, a way to facilitate this is to have a very varied, wide classroom library and to have the books cross-referenced to recordings of those texts, when you have recorded them, so the students can get the text and the recording and, as a group or alone, go off and play those. Have the books also cross-referenced to other materials that might be used in connection with them, such as graphic materials, or to activity cards that give the students follow-up activities to do in the way I was describing earlier, the interweaving.

So solving the problem of reading, I think, very much involves fairly drastic changes in reading materials and in classroom management to allow more powerful methods to operate. The same for number three, the language-experience approach of the learner dictating his own content and having somebody else write it down. That is usually done in primary school, but there's no reason not to do it in secondary. Although the teacher cannot, as with the read-along method, employ a machine, I recommend a kind of buddy system of more proficient students taking down the speech of the less proficient or—this may be most appropriate for secondary—having students talk into a tape recorder (again, maybe as a small group) or improvise a scene with a tape recorder going and then, together, transcribe their own words. This is very popular with many secondary students. It does not look babyish. It's really a language-experience method done in a more practical way for secondary. Together, with the teacher's help and with each other's help, collectively, they can transcribe their own speech and then read this back, read it to other people, or pass it on for someone else to read. It's a good use of the tape recorder, I think.

In general, I think the voice has to act as an intermediary for the beginning or weak reader between his oral language, his nonverbal experience, and books. The voice has to be the intermediary, in a progression somewhat like this: First, he has to hear some literate person sound the language while he sees it, to get the pairing of language sounds with spellings, or his own voice in the case of language experience; but there has to be an external voice to provide that intermediary in the beginning. Then what happens is that he internalizes gradually the aide's role so that he begins to be able to read solo silent more, and he is subvocalizing. The progression is: somebody else reads to you, then you begin to read out loud with partners taking turns reading the same book to each other in a small group, and then you shift the voice inside and subvocalize. The final stage—and this involves speed reading for those who are very proficient already—is that the voice disappears completely, even the inner voice, so there is a direct connection between *thought* and *sight* that bypasses the intermediary of vocalization, even subvocalization. At that point we are not talking about the kind of learners that most of us are involved with; we are talking about someone who has learned literacy so well that he can now read at the speed of sight rather than at the speed at which he can read a text aloud, and that is where you get into the Evelyn Wood type of speed reading for those for whom it works.[1]

This dissolving of the intermediary is equivalent to how, I am told, the Balinese teach their children to do their traditional dances. The adult stands behind the child and moves his body in the way the dance is made to move, and the child just moves with him by being receptive. They continue to move together like this until eventually the adult simply steps back and the child continues to move on his own. The supplying of the audio is like that, of live or recorded voice. It has to supply that kind of intermediary until the student can take off on his own. Solo silent reading may be the goal, but it's not the means. The means are social, interactive, and external until the process is learned, and then they can go on internally.

The final point I want to make is that I think the teaching of reading today, the main trends of it, are negative and going in the wrong direction, for some reasons that have to do with orientation of the whole culture, which at the moment is, in its materialism, directed toward the analytic and the particle, to breakdowns, to disintegration. The computer—which is not in itself anything bad—the computer can, in a way, symbolize this, in the way we have used it. The computer needs fine breakdowns. Programmed materials need fine breakdowns. Managerial technocrats, who want finely sliced instructional objectives, want fine breakdowns. The whole of the educational–industrial complex in this country now is pushing hard toward breaking reading and all other learning into very fine units, which is disintegrative.

As I say, it's part and parcel of a general materialistic trend that follows the lead of the federal government, which has had an extremely negative influence through its funding programs. State legislatures have followed in turn, and now it's very difficult to get support for a realistic kind of approach to reading because the trends in political and economic and legislative circles are going the other way. I say this not as a matter merely of complaint but in a positive sense. I think if as people involved in the teaching of reading you believe some of what I'm saying—you have similar insights, or this makes sense to you, or you want to test it out for yourself—you're going to have to lobby for it. I think corrective action is very much needed. The diverting of huge numbers of secondary students into labs of programmed materials where they're run through

[1]I did not mean to imply by this pragmatic line of reasoning for schools that people cannot in some circumstances connect thought to sight directly or initially. Deaf people frequently bypass oral speech in learning literacy, and to learn an oral symbol system before a visual symbol system is only a cultural convention, not a biological necessity. Preschool children's drawings and much of the world's graphic art also connect sight directly to thought.

phonic sequences they had over and over again in elementary school where it did not work the first time—this is a tremendously negative thing.

In this connection, standardized tests, I think, have been misleading us greatly, because they have no audio component. The use of cheap standardized paper and pencil tests—and that characterizes all of the ones we go by—misleads us because, without a vocal, audio component, there is no way to distinguish between decoding and comprehension problems. If a student scores low on a standardized test, *we do not know what it means.* It's generally assumed that because the test is called a reading test it's in the decoding sense that the student is failing. Most often, I would say, that is not the case. The older the student, the less true it is. More true, I think, is that his problem is in the oral language realm of thinking and speaking—what I have called the real basics. He simply doesn't know the vocabulary, he can't use the cues of sentences, the meaning, to figure out a text. But it's assumed he has a decoding problem, so he's shunted into some government-funded reading laboratory that has a lot of expensive material that isn't going to help him. If it worked, we would know by now. So I think the drift is the other way and we are engaged in trying to right that imbalance and we may have to fight for it.

5

Going with Growth: Fitting Schools to the Facts of Language Life

Background

This talk sketches some connections among cognitive growth, holistic learning, and vocal interaction. It has never been easy for me to explain how peer talk can further the most serious kinds of mental and verbal development. Few people believe it, even some who profess to, because very rarely, if ever, has a wave of students had a chance to benefit from even a whole year, much less several years' running, of good, sustained small-group vocal interaction in school. Most teachers who try it are quickly put off by such initial problems as kids fooling around and are discouraged from developing it by district insistence on teaching to tests on other things (usually language particles). So the evidence to convince is scarce. Without evidence, no conviction; without conviction, no evidence. This vicious circle makes it necessary, I feel, to combine any discussion of actual growth processes and suitable methods with remarks that bring out into the open this conflict between the political facts of life and the learning facts of life.

I doubt that I succeeded any more on this occasion than on others, but I was provided an excellent setting by another high-quality gathering, the Third Annual Conference on Language Arts Education, sponsored by the Department of Elementary and Remedial Education of the State University of New York at Buffalo in 1977. The topic helped—*Facilitating Language Development, Preschool through Adolescence*—and the emphasis that many of the following speakers gave to the *learner's* production of language, oral and written, supported well what I had to say. In 1978, the University published a report of the conference (bearing the title above and edited by Patrick Finn and Walter Petty) that produced the talks, including a transcription of mine with some following questions and answers. I was speaking from a brief outline.

A word about what is not in this talk but perhaps should be, at least in the future. In it I refer tangentially to Rudolf Steiner while mentioning developmentalists Piaget, Werner, and Erickson. Though the founder of a still-thriving international chain of Waldorf Schools, Steiner is virtually unknown among U.S. educators, most of whom would probably be

48

astonished to read some of his statements on human growth. (See Steiner's *The Kingdom of Childhood*, Rudolf Steiner Press, London, 1974, and *The Recovery of Man in Childhood*, A.C. Harwood, Hodder and Stoughton, London and Toronto, 1958.) Though not necessarily an advocate of what Waldorf Schools do, I feel almost guilty to speak, as I did here, as if I think human growth comprises only what these excellent material scientists describe. My English confreres often say that I base my work on Piaget, whereas I have always worked much more intuitively than that. As with notions of inner speech, which came to me before reading Piaget or Vygotsky or Mead, I cite these figures to gain credibility with a society that believes only authorities in white lab jackets. Piaget was the most useful for getting a curriculum across because his concepts of egocentricity, logical development, and inner speech all certified, and extended, perceptions I was operating on but needed sanctioning of.

Steiner's ideas do not so much conflict with the developmental models of Piaget, Werner, Bruner, and Erickson as they subsume them. It is, in fact, fascinating to see how, although he died in 1925, he had already described mental growth very much as they did later (and also very much as Whitehead did in *The Aims of Education*):

> ... the child up to its ninth or tenth year is really demanding that the whole world of external nature shall be made alive, because he does not yet see himself as separate from this external nature; therefore we shall tell the child fairy tales, myths, and legends.

> . . .

> It is only toward the twelfth year that the child is ready to hear causes and effects spoken of.

—pp. 63 and 65, *The Kingdom of Childhood*

Fine, that won't jar anyone today, but look further into *The Kingdom of Childhood* for a perspective far broader than that of contemporary psychology. In addition to having a strong scientific and mathematical bent and demonstrating a very accomplished intellectual scholarship (he was entrusted as a young man with the editing of Goethe's scientific writings), he was also spiritually gifted and employed these gifts in his researches. This extraordinary combination of faculties places his work, in my mind, above that of Piaget, Bruner, and Werner, who are indeed perceptive themselves but whose professional framework and affiliations would prevent them from saying what Steiner said even if they were seeing as he did (a problem of staying respectable that I think Jung and even Freud had, Freud having said in a letter that if he had it all to do over, he would go into parapsychology, and Jung having openly gone into it as well as having described an "out-of-body" experience in his autobiography).

I believe we'll soon have to expand our ideas of human growth beyond the ordinarily visible world until they embrace the full evolution of consciousness that we're really involved in. But so far I haven't felt free in such talks to do more than hint at spiritual growth, because many people turn off at what seems to them spooky or religious, especially when earning their daily bread means getting kids to score well on tests of meaningless fragments. I have tried to keep credibility so that an already difficult job of convincing will not become hopeless, while at the same time testing the upper edges of the audience to keep my own sense of integrity.

————————◄●►————————

The title of my presentation, "Going with Growth: Fitting Schools to the Facts of Language Life," does imply a discrepancy. That is, learning goes one way—the real authentic organic facts of learning—and institutionalism has a way of going its own way; so it's a perennial problem to get the two matched up and to *keep* the two matched up. I think we are in an era where they are particularly divergent, for a number of reasons.

We don't have a lot of time and I want to leave some time for questioning because this is a very mixed audience with different backgrounds and different concerns—I guess you go from nursery to college—so what I will say will be very sketchy and very suggestive and not very detailed or documented. I'll leave some of that to questioning.

Let me try to describe the growth of thought and speech in a general way as I see it. I think what can depict growth of thought and speech rather effectively is the series of pictures or photos that depict stages of growth of the embryo (or the human fetus). They used to draw these; now they have actual photographs of the embryo in different stages at several weeks, several months, and so on, *in utero*. What you see in these depictions is a whole. This whole begins with a very simple single cell that begins to divide and to differentiate into parts within itself. So if you look at depictions of the embryo at different stages you will see this whole becomes complicated within and yet—and this is my main point— it never ceases being a whole no matter what stage of development it is at. You will see the development of a cardiovascular system and a network of veins, of nerves, of various organs forming, and the limbs, but at no point is any of this separated. It is always a whole. In other words, it does not follow the industrial model of the assembly line, where the carburetor is sent in from Toledo to Detroit, and this sub-assembly is attached to other assemblies, and finally something plops off the end of the assembly line. This kind of model has been brought into education, rather inappropriately, and I think it misleads us in many ways. The growth of thought and speech does not proceed by the assembling of sub-assemblies. The teaching of tiny parts in the hopes that some day these will all get put together in the mind of a learner doesn't work. What happens is students go out of school and somehow the parts—isolated phonemes, isolated words, isolated sentences and isolated paragraphs—never get put together.

The main movement of growth is differentiation within an integrated whole. The whole is always there. Humpty Dumpty was an egg, you know, and he fell down and broke himself up, which is a kind of metaphor for the differentiating process that goes on in growth. The reason all the king's horses and all the king's men couldn't put him back together is that they couldn't put him back together as an *egg*. He is going to be something else after that, something more complex. You don't go back to being simple. There is a double process then of differentiation within a constant reintegrating. You have to keep both of those to maintain balance, and if we go too far one way or the other, growth is going to go very badly. These processes correspond to analysis and synthesis. To break the wholes down into parts corresponds to what was just described in the biological levels—differentiating the organs and the limbs, etc. within the embryo. Putting parts back into a whole corresponds to the biological integrating. As we become more complex within, the pulmonary, cardiac, intestinal systems, and so on have to be integrated. This corresponds to synthesis in the mental life.

You are probably familiar now with the research of the two hemispheres of the brain, which was actually done in the '60s but is only now being disseminated to the public and to education. The right and left hemispheres of the brain, it is now known, specialize, at least after a certain age. One half specializes in what we can call the intellectual, the verbal, the linear, the seriating part, the analytical; and the other in the intuitive, the holistic, the global, the synthesizing, the metaphoric. So this kind of double growth that characterizes the whole of human growth also characterizes the mental life very specifically, very concretely, with the two hemispheres of the brain.

Some critics of our education today in this culture say that we are emphasizing far too much one half, that we have a verbal/analytic or left-hemisphere education, a left-hemisphere culture, and this is one reason we are spinning very drastically out of balance. This is a point certainly, I think, to keep in mind. Reading is usually associated with the left half, but I think that is not the whole story. I think reading cannot get along very well, nor can any language growth, without the collaboration of the two hemispheres, of the metaphoric, holistic, spatially oriented right hemisphere, which incidentally is associated with the arts, sports, crafts.

So this dual aspect of growth is very graphically presented, if you want to think of it that way, dramatized by the physical separation of the brain into two specializing halves.

I think you can characterize the growth of thought and speech partly as a movement toward elaboration—that is, away from lumping things together globally, and toward separating things out, distinguishing, discriminating, differentiating, refining. This is a very, very general movement of growth which has been described not only by Piaget and Inhelder but very well by Heinz Werner and others. You can see it for yourself. For example, a small child will say in one word what really is a whole sentence, but he is not able yet to parcel out his thought, for one thing, to break it down into pieces and to assign to those pieces parts of speech. So this parceling-out process is precisely the direction in which he is going to grow. A very small child might say one word. He might say "coat." What he means is a sentence, but it is globally lumped together into one word. What he really means is, "I see my coat over there," or "I want my coat," or "What has happened to my coat?" But he says the one word "coat," and that *stands* for the whole sentence. So the direction of growth will be toward breaking his own thought down to fit the way in which his material and social world breaks things down.

Being incarnated on this material plane means we have to learn the laws by which the material plane is being run. Things are broken down; you have to know the difference between one thing and another, or one person and another, or else you get into trouble. You have to learn what the differences are, and in a sense this direction of growth is divisive and perhaps in some ways negative. It's a growth toward the natural, material breakdown of the physical and social world. In the beginning the child does not distinguish himself from the things around him but finally he must. In this first separation of self from world, his first breakdown, first analysis, is the model for all the breakdown analysis that is to follow. He learns that the ongoing panorama around him breaks down into pieces, and he has to know one piece from another and the names of the pieces, and so on.

Elaboration literally means, "working out," so one direction of growth is from the inside out. Since everything is already inside, latently—like genetic coding—it's just a matter of how it's going to be worked out, well or badly, and this depends on the other half of growth, the interaction of the organism and the environment.

Elaboration in language terms works out in vocabulary, in sentence structure, in composition and comprehension in very, very specific, concrete ways that teachers deal with all the time. The growth of vocabulary again is from the global to the finely differentiated. A child will at first use the word "boat" for every water-plying vessel, whether it goes on oceans or rivers, whether it is sail- or motor-powered, whether it is passenger or freight. You see what I mean. And these break down more and more finely, as sailors all know, into catamarans and schooners and all sorts of things that I don't know much about. It is a very, very fine breakdown, and the vocabulary follows the breakdown of reality, of boats into superordinate and subordinate classes, and subordinate classes ramify in turn on down into a million kinds of sailing vessels. So the process of growth is getting into these systems of superordinate/subordinate classes. But in the beginning, *boat* does for all. It's global.

The same thing happens with sentence structure. Sentences at first are called kernel sentences, and this is an evolution itself out of the single-word sentence I mentioned a moment ago with the example of "coat." Finally we get into phrases and then into whole sentences and, of course, the sentences again elaborate. But for teaching purposes what is important is how things get elaborated. I mean what teases or tempts the growing mind to elaborate? Why doesn't it stay global? You *can* stay more or less global. This is what we mean by differences in development; some kids are more advanced, and others seem retarded, verbally, or cognitively. This has to do with how much they have been teased out—this eliciting process from the environment.

Let's put it this way. You can try artificially to stimulate the growth of sentence structure by lots of drills and exercises and by trying to teach kids directly to analyze the sentence and the parts and to ticket all the parts and so on. I think this has nothing to do with really effective growth and may have a retarding effect. What makes people complicate their sentences, essentially, is questioning by other people. Assuming authentic speaking and writing situations where there is a real reason to be communicating, the elaboration of sentence structure into adverbial and adjectival modifiers depends upon the eliciting action of questions (direct or implied) of other people. *Where* did it happen? *When* did it happen?

Now the egocentric, naive speaker just blurts out things and leaves it there, as kids typically do in show-and-tell if this activity is left in the rudimentary state. We go around the class one kid after another, and each kid shows something, he blurts out something, and then stops, and that's the end of it. What needs to happen is to put show-and-tell into small groups, often without the teacher, in very small groups, three or four, and let the kids question each other about the object. This makes a tremendous difference. They can get in the habit of questioning if you model for them. The teacher models a questioning stance so that the speaker finds out that it's not obvious to the listener where this happened, or when, or how he got something—the object he has—or what you do with it, or how it was made. A million possible questions inhere in any kind of initial statement like that. But the global, subjective-minded learner has to find this out. This implies a very active social process that has not yet got going in school nearly as much as it should because, I think, it's harder to manage, or seems harder to manage, the way most of us have been trained as educators.

A movement of growth that goes along with elaboration from within and the eliciting from without is what I call going from *co-operations* to *operations.* The use of the term "operation" obviously suggests Piaget. It can be very well exemplified in, let's say, the transition between kids hanging weights on a physical pair of balance scales and their later working with equations. The whole notion of balancing from a physical operation becomes internalized as a mental operation. We speak of balancing equations. That typifies this shift from outside operations to internal ones.

But what I want to talk about is the social operations, which I'll call co-operation as it becomes internalized. It has to do with proper ways of talking together so that a process of expatiation gets going. This can occur at any age. I'm using a fancy term here, but it can happen from preschool on. This is where people listen to each other and pick up on what each other has said and take it a little bit farther, and it includes the questioning that I was mentioning a moment ago that stimulates elaboration. But it has to do with creating ideas together, with exchanging vocabulary, with building on each other's sentence structures as well as on each other's ideas, on each other's comparisons and metaphors, wit, and so on. It's social, collaborative development. If this occurs in small groups, all the time, consistently, this will become internalized and become a part of the inner mental operations of the individuals in the groups.

Now, this can go well or badly. For example, if what happens when people converse is that they all sit around and heap abuse on some outsiders, this will be internalized, and people will think that way. And when everybody simply gives instances of the same thing, for example, how awful Kate is—"Oh yeah, I remember the time she did this" and "Yeah, well, the time I was with her she did that"—it's a very simple additive process that doesn't do very much for mental development. That's what I call the and-and-and model.

There's another kind of model—the but-but-but model, which is just constant contradiction, no matter what is said or what the subject is. The topic may change, but the altercation goes on. It's for its own sake, has its own dynamic. This is often, I'm afraid, encouraged by formal debate. I used to coach debate some in prep school, but I'm not an advocate of it really. I think it's better to have more spontaneous give-and-take and not have people invested in positions they *have* to defend and maintain. That gets ego involvement going and interferes with more useful intellectual work.

You can imagine other kinds of *co*-operation—that is, verbal collaboration—that can be internalized for good or evil, but the kind I'm suggesting is the expatiation type, whereby people listen to each other, pick up on what each other has to say, and together elaborate and discover what the implications are of each other's ideas. Humor and wit come into this; people pick up on each other's remarks, their humor, and carry it a little bit further, or their metaphors, and so on, and find where things go. If this is done in groups, at all ages, it does become internalized, and individuals all alone begin to think in these very salutary, positive ways.

This is a very sketchy kind of description of growth which I think can be applied to vocabulary, to sentence structure and to compositional forms, to reading comprehension problems, and so on. It has very much to do with what, again, Piaget has called decentering and egocentricity. This in turn relates to the global thinking. That is, I think most of our problems in composing our own ideas, whether we're talking or writing, concern our difficulty in separating ourselves from our audience and from our subject, so that we assume too much; and most of our problems in comprehending what others say and write concern trouble in tuning in on an individual who is separate from ourselves.

Many, many kids, I think, have reading comprehension problems because they can't really tune in on the author, for a lot of reasons. And it takes a lot of maturity to do this, and it takes role playing. You have to put yourself in the shoes of the author. That's the best way to read. People at Stanford who were doing research in hypnosis and who weren't really particularly interested in reading have accidentally come across a correlation between reading proficiency, great interest in reading—let's say, avid reading—and susceptibility to hypnosis. Some people really are willing to go along with somebody else's line of thought, and so on. This willingness correlates very highly with reading and liking to read.

I think that tuning in or role playing is really important. From the standpoint of writing you certainly have to role-play the listener or the audience; you have to sort of guess what they are going to need. Most of the things that school teachers remark about kids' writing have to do with problems of egocentricity. I think it would be much more helpful if we could think of it this way. The problem is knowing what the reader needs or how the reader is going to respond to this or that, as to word choice, the way sentences are arranged, the things you choose to mention, the things you leave out. It's very, very hard to know what to include and what to leave out in talking or writing. You can't say everything, you want to say enough and not too much. All of this requires very close attunement with the audience and being able to role-play him, and it's a movement away from egocentricity.

Well, what breaks egocentricity? Again, it doesn't happen alone. It's a social operation. It's constant comparison, I think. Kids reading together, talking about what they read, trying to act their stories out and discovering in the process of acting them out that they didn't interpret the characters or the plot or the action in the same way. They need to find all this out; they need to compare their *incomprehension*, *talk* about their incomprehension, openly, not try to *hide* it, and *work out* problems of comprehension—to raise consciousness. You can summarize, I think, so much growth of thought and speech as consciousness raising, whether it's Piaget's decentering—that is, losing your egocentricity—or whether it's moving away from the merely global to the finely discriminated whole.

Now the final part of the growth movement is spiraling around. One comes back over points but at different levels of consciousness so that if kids learn only to break down and analyze, to separate, to divide, this is going to be a negative movement. They have at the same time to learn how to put everything back together again. Our schools, following the general drift of the culture, are somewhat trapped into the one-sidedness that goes with the overemphasis on the left hemisphere of the brain, of being overly analytic, dealing too much with the pieces. Everybody is lost among the splinters of language. It's the drills and rules approach. This has gone on for some time—this isn't new. But I think recent trends in the culture have unfortunately reinforced the worst of the past, and sometimes it wears the guise of being new.

For example, the back-to-basics movement is a double misnomer. For one thing it isn't back to anywhere; we've never been anywhere else in this country. During my childhood or during my adulthood we have followed mainly a drills and rules approach. There was an effort to get away from this in the '60s that *Newsweek* magazine and other various organs have blamed our current ills on. The other part of the misnomer is that it's not back to *basics*, it's back to some people's notion of how you teach literacy. Some people say, "I'm for basic skills," which implies that other people are not. Now I don't know anybody—parent or teacher—who is against reading and writing, do you? So it's kind of a hoax to speak of some people as being for back-to-basics and others as being against reading and writing. This unnecessarily splits us up and creates tremendous problems, and it creates an artificial skills/frills division that we certainly don't need.

The best way to teach the skills, I think, is through other things that are not verbal, that have to do with the right hemisphere functions—crafts, sports, arts. There are many connections with language that should be used. I think that there is no great mystery about how kids learn to read and write. I know we have conferences and we feel that we need them to find out more about how children learn. I think we know a lot more now than we're acting on. I consult all over the country with schools and teachers in very different situations and regions, and I get the same thing constantly, which is that they know a lot more than they're acting on. And they are doing a lot of things they do not believe in. I don't think the problem is that we lack knowledge about child development. I don't think the problem is that we lack sophisticated notions about curriculum and methods and materials. We have more than we are using. The difficulty in fitting schools to the facts of language life has to do partly with the tendency of any large institution (not just schools) to get lost in its own institutionalism. And in our case, in this culture right now, this has got caught up in some political, economic movements that have been very negative, I think, and I hope we are going to work our way out of them.

Standardized testing is really dictating the curriculum with tremendous tyranny. These national standardized tests don't even test very well the things they are supposed to test—for example, reading and writing. Writing is construed as a lot of skills like formal grammatical analysis, or making dry runs on dummy sentences or correcting dummy paragraphs. No one has ever proved these add up to writing. Do you realize that there isn't any standardized test of writing where people really write, and, therefore, there is a very little instruction in schools in real writing? There are a lot of things alleged to teach writing. They are called composition, but they are various word and sentence and paragraph drills—what I call working with the pieces. I think we are going to have to acknowledge that this is so before we start talking about why writing has gone down, or why literacy has gone down.

The curriculum that is dictated by these very narrow standardized tests comes to us through commercial corporations which, frankly, cannot be trusted. They operate, as most large commercial corporations do, on very selfish principles that make it really impossible to get a worthwhile curriculum into schools through commercial processes. Educational manufacturers, I would say, cannot offer to schools the kind of materials that the curriculum in schools really needs at this point. I think they find it too hard to produce and too hard to sell. Schools, I think, have to take cognizance of this. Teachers have to teach what they know how to teach and not what comes through to them from commercial corporations.

A good model for school learning is home learning of speech; this is very organic, very spontaneous, very interactive, and it works really well. And learning to talk is much harder than learning to read and write. Cognitively speaking, in pure learning terms, it is much easier to learn to read and write than to learn to talk. It doesn't look that way, because there seem to be so many problems with learning to read and write. These problems arise from learning to read and write *in school,* in large groups and mass institutions. I think if we look at it that way we'll make a lot more progress. The problems are not learning problems essentially. They are institutional problems that are being governed by such things as the specific objectives and the accountability movement, which is tied in with standardized testing, which is tied in with commercial programmed materials. We must do our own consciousness raising about the whole educational–industrial complex that is really determining the materials, methods, and curriculum way outside the classroom. I think that the difficulty is that the people who know most about how kids learn, the ones in the classroom, today have not nearly enough to say about what they can do in the classrooms. One of the aspects of accountability that isn't brought out enough is that you can't tell people how to do their job and then hold them accountable for the results.

If you applaud that, be sure you applaud too some active lobbying by teachers to assert this. Too often teachers go limp and passive. The forces are big. The teachers have to make known what they think the facts of language learning are and try to get their own environment to fit that and not let everything be determined by state legislators, by school boards, who are too far from the classroom to really know how children learn, or by various national movements or commercial corporations. You have to take things back in your own hands a little more or else there won't be much worth in coming to conferences to learn more about how children learn or what the latest methods are. You have to be able to do something about it, and I think this means putting emphasis back on wholes, on the fact that the parts are taught *through* the wholes. *Via* the wholes. By means of the wholes. Not the other way around. You can't teach the wholes by trying to add up all the little parts. So we needn't get into any conflict about who's for basics and who isn't. I think we're all for the literacy skills, along with everything else. It's just a question of whether the small things are going to be taught in the thrust of whole growth or whether they're going to be isolated out very ineffectually into the old drills and rules approach.

Let me stop at this point and leave a few minutes for questions. What would you like for me to elaborate a little bit more on in the few minutes that we have? This is very sketchy, I realize. As I say, more suggestive than documented.

QUESTION: Is development within the whole a hierarchical or sequential process?

ANSWER: Only in a very long-range sense. I think this is sometimes a frustration to educators and curriculum developers, who would like a sequence, let's say, for a year, that holds true for all kids. I don't think you are going to find it, and it's a frustration because we plan by the year. But the kind of growth patterns, or movements, that Piaget, Werner, Eric Erickson, and a lot of other people have been working on are very long-range and these stages are more like blocks of *several* years. Rudolf Steiner says every seven years there is a major turnover in development. Unfortunately, it doesn't fit the school year, and I don't think we can try to wrench it to fit. We have to accept the fact that the growth patterns are very long-range, and it's an argument for much greater collaboration among teachers over spans of several years. This is one of the main things

I find missing when I consult with schools. There is very little connection between one year and the next. Not a rigid lock step between grades 7, 8, 9, 10, and so on but some way of keeping track of individual students over a span of several years so the kids come to you, you know what they have been working on, what emphasis they need now, and you can continue to individualize even though somebody else has been working with the kids for the last few years. We need something like that very much. A kind of bookkeeping system spanning several years so we can keep track of individual kids and not feel that the only way to get growth sequence is to make all kids do the same this year and then next year. Also, the accountability movement has tended to make kids do the same things year after year. And the whole movement toward minimal criteria reinforces a very negative thing, which in this instance is covering—that each teacher has to cover herself or himself for the same minimal learning standards for each child, and what you tend to do is make the kids study the same thing year after year so that each teacher can cover himself, or herself. Let's make sure that doesn't happen.

QUESTION: Would you elaborate on some of the activities which expand the right hemisphere of the brain?

ANSWER: Again, it's an argument for not stripping off the so-called frills in this phony frills/skills split. For example, there is a lot less art and music in grade school than there used to be when I was a kid myself. I think some of the main points of entry into the whole verbal world, into reading and writing, are through other arts and through other media, many of them nonverbal, or through sports or crafts. Not only things to talk and write about but specific ways of getting into writing. For example, from photographs, or from working with physical things and then talking about them. For example, we had kids in the fifth grade making things with toothpicks and paste and so on, and then writing directions for these to other kids and then making how-to-do-it books. They worked out the best way to do it and then put the directions down. Sort of like a recipe book. But the thing is there has to be a reason. Young kids don't particularly like to talk much about the physical operations they are doing; they don't see that much of a need for it. You have to set up a situation where there is a need to verbalize the nonverbal. Well, if you want to relay your directions on to someone else for making what you've made, that's a very well-motivated reason for verbalizing.

QUESTION: Can you say more about reading and hypnosis?

ANSWER: Ernest Hilgard, Department of Psychology at Stanford—I think he is recently retired—has advanced what I said. He and his wife, who is an M.D., worked with hypnosis in a very serious way in the Department of Psychology, and they were working on a scale for measuring how susceptible various people were to hypnosis, not to any Svengali treat-ment. They had graduate students and others learning how to talk people into this. So it is independent of the personality of the one giving the in-struction. *Experience in Hypnosis* I think is the title of the book—of one book. The matter of reading came up very incidentally—practically acci-dentally.

I did cover a lot too fast, and when I do that I'm always aware of many, many unexplained things or many overstatements, and so on. So I would welcome a chance to elaborate some.

QUESTION: What's a writing sample?

ANSWER: Well, there was a writing sample, so-called, on college boards—which was removed in the '60s. It's too big a nuisance, you know. It's too hard processing students' writing. So expensive. So they dropped it. Now people are complaining about why kids can't write.

Now, there are many reasons that may account for this fairly drastic falling off in writing skills. But one of the main reasons is that the one thing that really tested writing by having kids write—it may have been under fairly artificial circumstances, but at least they really wrote a whole piece of something—was removed in the '60s. Now, all this influences teachers tremendously because to save their own necks teachers have to teach more or less directly to the tests—particularly in an era of account-ability. It puts everybody's job on the line more and more in conformity with test scores. But there is nothing now, no standardized test that I know of, that requires kids to do some honest writing.[1] What is supposed to test writing is correcting a dummy sentence here, tinkering with a dummy paragraph there with multiple-choice answers or vocabulary work, or questions having to do with formal grammatical analysis. None of these will tell you anything about how well a kid can write. A token twenty-minute writing sample is tentatively being restored to the CEEB composition test the Fall of 1978 in recognition, perhaps, of the exam's negative influence.

To some extent there is the same situation with standardized tests in reading. If the scores are negative, you don't know what to make of it. In other words, if kids do well on them—O.K., you can assume they read. But you're really worried about kids who don't do well on them, and about them you don't know anything because there is no oral component to standardize reading tests. And without an oral component you cannot really separate the decoding, word-attack aspect (so-called phonics or whatever) from comprehension. Many kids score very low on reading tests because they simply don't know the vocabulary, or the concepts, and if you *read* the passages to them they would do very badly. But, you

---

[1] Fortunately, some states and districts are now instituting real samples of writing as part of their standardized testing program.

see, nobody reads them to them. Because again, that's too expensive. Our standardized tests are cheap quickies. That's what they are. And we are paying the price for a cheap quicky; it's ruining the national curriculum, and it has been for years. And it's not *cheap*. It's very expensive.

Setting up shallow, standardized tests that then determine the curriculum, which shrinks to fit them—that's very expensive. You don't save money that way. If you really want to know if a kid can decode, have him read aloud to you—sight unseen—sight-read to you while you follow the text with your eyes and notice the discrepancies, if any, that he makes, the way in which he reads, and so on. If you want to know his *comprehension, you* read to *him*. And then talk with him about what he understood. This is what alternative schools did, for example, in Berkeley, where there are a lot of poor minority students with lots of low scores. They just finally dropped standardized tests and went to their own way of testing to try to find out what kids really could do and what they couldn't. These schools had to introduce an oral component. Have the kids read to you, you read to them, and without that, as far as I'm concerned, the standardized reading tests are not worth very much at all because they don't tell you what you really want to know—*why* the students do so badly on them. You don't know why.

QUESTION: I would like to raise the question of teaching the parts of speech to facilitate foreign language teaching.

ANSWER: I taught French for three years and at that time there was a big controversy among foreign language teachers. The audio-lingual approach was just coming in, with language laboratories and so on, so that when you say, "I'm teaching formal grammar to help the French and Spanish teachers," you may be taking part in a very heated controversy about whether they should use a grammar-translation approach or a more oral-aural, direct-method approach. My feeling is that if foreign language teachers feel it is important—and I can see an argument there—then let them teach it. Most of them want to do it their own way anyway—in a way they figure that fits the target language better. If you're teaching German you might want to go about it a little bit differently from French or Spanish or Russian.

Actually, my own feeling is that the teaching of formal, grammatical analysis, the ticketing of parts of speech in this country, is really a hangover from the nineteenth century, when English was in a very large measure taught as a second language in American public schools because of the waves of immigrants coming in—wave after wave in the nineteenth century. And it made more sense then; it makes more sense to teach formal, grammatical analysis if you are teaching a second language, because the person is older, they don't learn language the same way even by age ten or twelve that they did when they were three or four or one or two. It makes more sense maybe to codify and use their generalizing ability to teach them some of the truths about the language. But I think it is a hangover from the days when teaching English as a second language was very widespread in the public schools. Now we have special programs as, for example, in California, which has a large Mexican/American population, and so on. Bilingual programs. So it has no point any more in regular classes.

QUESTION: What about grades?

ANSWER: She is asking about grades. I think you can cook up a grade for a kid regardless of what curriculum you are working under. I taught at a very grade-conscious school for a while; those kids had their slide rules out come marking period and they were figuring up. But even so the English Department there finally decided to quit putting individual letter grades on all kids' themes and just to make a general assessment of the writing for a marking period and to come up with a letter grade for the whole marking period rather than for individual papers. And I found that if I did this, I understood students' writing better anyway. I could spot the traits and the trends by looking over all the writing and making a blanket judgment.

6

Bajan Bestiary

Background

For a shift of brain hemisphere and mode of discourse, I insert here a suite of poems that may serve as mid-book interlude. Having vowed that I would write no more utilitarian prose while recharging myself in Barbados from the two methods books, I began writing for fun little sketches of some of the critters I saw almost daily around the converted sugarmill house where we were living or down at the sea nearby, where I spearfished with a native.

Writing these poems was a different process for me, and the immediate pleasure was very different from the long-range satisfaction of the writing I was more used to. I tinkered. I lingered over single words and phrases, toyed over and over with lines, experimenting with sound play other than rhyme and with the juxtaposition of images. It was all a luxury. I sat on a patio surrounded by the old coral-stone boiling house and conical mill and tall cane fields. I watched and wrote, watched and wrote.

Three of the four animals comprising the bestiary had folk names, as I indicate in the poems, by which the natives call them and which gave me mythic, metaphorical departure points. I wanted to imagine what was in Bajan[1] minds when they invented these names. I tried to share their metaphors. But then images of my own came to me, and the poems took more personal turns. Obviously, the folk names were only "story starters" to get me going, but I liked the feeling of immersing myself first in external terms and surroundings. The outward focus made expressing myself easier and more creative. I suspect most literary writers employ some such indirection to tease out and flesh out their insides.

Whatever the worth of these poems, making them showed me a great deal about the underground working of intuition in writing. Searching within the constraints of a given image, rhythm, phrasing, you surprise yourself as these constraints force verbal felicities or turns of idea that you would not have arrived at by common pondering. When finished, I was astonished to find that I had created a progression from air to land to sea, corresponding to an increasing descent into unconscious material and to a deepening of several themes that I had unintentionally carried over from poem to poem. One such theme touched on writing itself.

[1] Barbadian, of Barbados

The first poem was published in the *English Journal* of May 1974. I had thought the whole suite was being printed, but the other poems somehow got detached and lost in the editorial offices.

Hummingbird

1

Barbados' "doctor bird" is making rounds,
Innoculating flowers, tapping samples,
Hemming the blossomed hedge a pause a stitch
As doctors moving room to room suture
Up the corridors (he drops who stops),
So curtly prodding tendered guts he leaves
An aftermath of open-mouthed patients,
Zips off to query the next expectant
Corolla, flight a rapid riffling fillip,
Then sticks in space and tucks his tail, upheld
By focus only, wings a thicker air,
Doomed to higher metabolic rate,
Like surgeon freezing speed, for who else
Staying steady operates so fleet?

2

Still, sip-supping belles, he's tip-tupping
A whole blooming harem by himself.
Have they been drained or plenished, healed or had?
That sheen of golden green suffusing black
Betrays a garb of greenhead flies rippling
In iridescent Baudelarian evil
Perhaps, or just a sober-coated servant,
Depending which reflection winks the mind.
A blurring-motored airship takes a station
To kill or succor—*some* exquisite coupling.
A tiny vampire drinks the liquid life
Away but, incubus, pollinates the sleep.

Lizard

1

Black-eyed chartreuse lizards blink the heat,
Tautly menace flies, or scout the court
And stop to tilt a head and roll an eye.
Called a "cock," the male's a thrusting intent,
A footed phallus arousing housewives,
Who call him cute and feed him bacon scraps
But think: The charming little carnivore
Lumbers exactly like an alligator.
(A reptile's a reptile and, warm clime or not,
They're cold-blooded and don't feel the way we do.
Or at least don't think the way we do.
Or at any rate don't know they're thinking.)
Tumid emotion balloons his throat, conveys
To males a threat to overwhelm with choler,
To mates a promise to overwhelm with lust:
   I'm about to pop
   With something that has to do with you.
   Get out of my sight
   Or deal with what you make me feel.

2

Across stone-coral walls they scroll their length
In florid arabesquing signatures:
Scrawled on chalky hall a green graffito;
Embossed on door a hieroglyph; on bell
Of clarinet a clef in bas relief;
A cursive monogram subscribes a painting.
At every turn a flourish of self, and that's
How a body writes his autograph.

Crab

The inland crab is solid, red and black;
The seaside crab is weightless, washed of color,
Or sandy rather, as though beach showed through shell.
He scuttles ghostly over tiny dunes

To sky-reflecting flats that make him pause
To contemplate the waves. A fit of folly:
He cocks his elbows, gets a running start, and
Like a maniac pianist's treble hand
Scribbling wild arpeggios down the keys
He sideways sprints the stretch and bams the sea
As if to bounce that wave right back to France.
He's lost to sight, a foamed-over beau geste
Hissed by seething surf. Then drifting with
The froth, two black knobs on stems pop up,
Fix on you, bespeak a shrug (you can't win
Them all) and make the mute schlemiel's appeal.

One night a tiny Saxon helmet thresh-
Holds between patio and parlor, gleaming,
Borne upon six clustered legs and peering
Eyeless at us, some local crab who'd found
A metal cone to play the hermit in,
Substituting navy gear for shell
(Quite logically, given the goal of each).
A teutonic opera extra missing spear,
Unsure of cue, helmet blocking eyes,
He stumbles toward the onstage light and sound
But, unprojecting, lingers near the wings.

Another night a bigger bumbler finds
Himself clutching my daughter's coral wall,
Witlessly weighing his pointless position,
A trophy lobster lacking varnished plaque.
Waving monstrous claws, it beetles the pillow
At just the ritual hour of nightly tale
When dad and daughter put the beasts to peace,
Fêting the safety of drapes and counterpane.
I knock him clacking down and we square off:
That crustacean's itching to pinch my flesh
And I expect to crunch his exoskeleton.
He readies curving pincers like a wrestler
Aping a ballerina rounding arms.
His straight-edged mandible lifts and drops
As wooden as a puppet's clopping chin.
They're funny all right, but that's one clown I killed.

Octopus

"Sea cats" have a feline grace and trace the
Ocean floor in muscular liquefaction.
Small, and prized as food, they're stalked in shallows
With crook or spear. You poke a pocket of rock
That seems too small for even a junior cat
But you hook and pull until the hole
Explodes as flailing star several times
The size of where it hid and webbed around
From stretching tendrils every way at once.
The skewered center ripples out in spasms
To tips encoiling nothing but open sea.
You grasp the pulsing terror about the head
And feel at once the slimy tight adhesion
Of eight mucoused whips astounding your arm
And sucking with ringed holes of piccolos.
A tighter embrace one could not dread or hope
(From man amok or virgin just delivered).
So you palp the hump of grafted viscera
Then stick two fingers up a slippery sheath
While underwater nimbus clouds are rolling
About your hands to roil the deed from view
(Some defense! to hide from what you hug)
And, pressing thumb to dome, turn the insides
Out. Faint like lovers sinking back, you
Both subside, it to die a-languishing
(For instant death you bite between the eyes)
And you to wonder whether any critter
That lumps its brains and guts together deserves
The rape it gets, or whether thus to kill
A mollusk—evict, eviscerate—may not
Evince demented need to twice expose,
By entering in while looking at, instead
Of alternating. To see by feel you kill.
Such disclosing confuses thought with touch
Even more than mollusks do and causes
Lunatics to disembowel women
For secrets never learned if brought to light.
Of course I don't undo an octopus
To understand the universe but just
To sport with feeling in deeps behind the ink,
Despite the lashing of a cat o' eight tails.

7

Integrity in the Teaching of Writing

Background

The most positive development in English education during the '70s—indeed, during the whole period since World War II—originated with teachers, not with government, and spread in grassroots fashion from the bottom up instead of from the top down. The Bay Area Writing Project, now the National Writing Project, set an in-service model that has swept the country and accomplished far more good than all of the U.S. Office of Education Project English curriculum centers of the '60s put together. The astonishing success of the one and the monumental failures of the other constitute a valuable object lesson. But the success and national institutionalization bring on dangers that the Project must watch out for.

Since the mid-1960s, when I still lived in the East, I have worked off and on with the handful of devoted, veteran educators who began and developed BAWP: Jim Gray, a supervisor of English teachers at the Berkeley campus of the University of California; Albert (Cap) Lavin, a high school English department head and textbook author (and fellow participant at the Dartmouth Seminar); Miles Myers, head of the Oakland High School English department and a politically astute lobbyist and vice-president of the California Federation of Teachers; and Keith Caldwell and Mary K. Healy, two very experienced in-service leaders as well as teachers of young people. These people really know schools and really know writing. They obtained support from the University, local systems, the California Department of Education, Carnegie Corporation of New York, and—their main funding source—the National Endowment for the Humanities. They said, "If teachers are ever going to teach writing more and teach it better, they will have to practice writing more themselves." Bravo! This is how I learned to teach writing myself. Surely, a major reason that many teachers ignore, slight, or mangle the teaching of writing is that they lack direct experience with the learning issues entailed in writing. The BAWP originators said also, "The best people to teach teachers are other teachers."

They set up a summer course in which teachers wrote, talked shop about writing, and worked up a presentation they could make as consultants for other teachers during the following school year. So in the BAWP model a higher institution and local districts collaborate to set up a seeding system whereby those who have benefited from extra learning can pass on that understanding. Leslie Whipp wrote in the November 1979 issue of the *Network Newsletter* (the Project organ, published at U.C. Berkeley): "One astonishing feature of the National Writing Project model, and the major source of its strength, is that it is teacher-centered, and in two chief ways: teachers are teaching teachers, and teachers are writing for other teachers and reading and discussing the writing of other teachers."

I have taught for several years at BAWP summer institutes in Berkeley, Chicago, and Long Island, and have consulted with other projects following the model in North Carolina, Michigan, Minnesota, New Mexico, and several areas of California. Every summer new projects start up. I feel that this wonderful burgeoning shows some pent-up spirit finally finding release from the repressive environment of today. Teaching teachers to write has touched me deeply. The booklets of their writings collected after a summer session always make very interesting reading matter, because of their individual reality, and show an artfulness, depth, and personal force that are surprising only because most classrooms don't reflect these assets—surprising not least to the authors, and that is part of what touches me every time.

I place the participants in groups of three or four for the whole institute (four to six weeks). Learning to write with these partners is undoubtedly the best part of the session. They help each other get and settle on ideas during prewriting activities, think out and talk out their ideas during mid-composition, and reflect usefully on their final drafts. They learn as they never could otherwise what are the most useful ways to respond to others' writing. A remarkable relationship usually develops in these groups as they go about balancing honesty with delicacy, task effectiveness with intimacy, difference with empathy. The difficulty comes when the groups have to break up. Only through these writing workshop groups have I ever succeeded in convincing teachers of the tremendous power of small-group process.

BAWP has attempted to be eclectic, but it's never really possible to embrace all ideas and practices, if only because of practical limitations, so selection and emphasis will always occur. Project staff or invitees give presentations or assign readings on certain methods or approaches they prefer, omitting others, and when participant teachers are asked to choose early in the institute a topic to present later, they naturally come up often with pet lessons, faddish exercises, or bad conventional practices. Besides unwittingly misleading itself and others, by adopting this open-arms pose BAWP appears to endorse or push certain methods in violation of its own "eclectic" policy. The more influential it becomes, the more everyone involved in the Project's inspiring national network should work to keep the movement universal in nature, to determine what is most fundamental, not merely widespread or fashionable. My own approach is never to recommend activities with sentences or paragraphs that are not part of an authentic discourse or that don't constitute an authentic discourse. What is universal are the kinds of utilitarian, literary, and scientific discourse practiced in our culture; the general processes for composing and revising alone and with others; and the elements of any language acquired through speaking and reading.

The following article grew rather directly out of experiences helping teachers write and think about how to help others write. It seemed to me that in order to focus on the actual writing processes themselves, it was necessary to clear up, if possible, some confusion in traditional thinking about what activities constitute writing. This led to a scale of various definitions of writing that I would put on the board and discuss with BAWP classes and with my similar summer course in writing for teachers given at the Bread Loaf School of English (Middlebury College, VT).

Phi Delta Kappan published this piece in its December 1979 issue. It will serve as an introduction to " Writing, Inner Speech, and Meditation ," Chapter 9 in this book, of which it was once a portion.

------------◄●►------------

A phalanx of educators from out of state recently visited the Bay Area Writing Project in Berkeley expecting to be shown how to teach handwriting. If these people work with primary school, as I suspect, they have a better excuse than the rest of us for construing "writing" overconcretely, because the age of their pupils forces them to deal with writing as drawing—and, indeed, drawing is one aspect of writing. Because it bridges between the invisible world of spirit and the visible world of matter, writing has so many aspects, covering such a broad spectrum of physical and mental activities, that it may be defined at whatever level of depth suits the profession, public, or other stakeholders such as governments, foundations, and commercial companies. And, as always, ambiguity lends itself to political, economic, and cultural biasing. At the moment, a very materialistic definition of writing pegs the teaching of it at such a low level of meaning that a dramatic expansion of the educational view of it seems in order.

At the lowest level, writing is drawing letters, but for the sake of perspective it may be worth backing down a little before going up. That is, drawing letters itself culminates a long history of using other material media, beginning with the body when used for signaling and symbolizing. But real writing began with message-leaving and mnemonic devices. One had to "say" something to someone not present, perhaps not born yet, and one had to remind oneself of something or keep track of some tally. For storing and transmitting information across time, beyond personal memory and face-to-face communication, the body will no longer serve, and external media then come into play. This kind of long-range communication or message-leaving is the essence of writing, which must have begun as one form of tool-using. Some of the first writing consisted of knots and notches for keeping score in business transactions. (A main advantage of writing still remains that the thinker can "take stock" of what he has got so far before proceeding.) But for concepts going beyond mere quantity, into the astronomical, geodetic, mathematical, historical, zoological, botanical, and metallurgical knowledge that we now know ancient civilizations possessed, a medium admitting of more complex symbolization was required.

The "prehistoric" form of writing was building. Modern archaeology tends increasingly to interpret ancient monuments such as megaliths, ziggurats, steles, obelisks, temples, and pyramids as *embodiments* of information, as repositories like today's libraries or, at least, like our time capsules. For this reason, the term "prehistoric," which means pre-writing, should strike us now as a misnomer and a prejudice, since building-in as a way of writing-in not only left records (for those who knew how to read) but evolved to very high levels of sophistication in the Nile, Indus, and Tigris–Euphrates valleys. But this sort of message-leaving was of course not the sole function of these monuments, which seem also to have served as observatories, tombs, surveying markers, initiation sites, places of worship, and other things, often all at once. One of the reasons, no doubt, why modern people have not credited ancient people with writing is that for a long time the ancients did not *single out* writing as a specialized activity but rather, in their typically syncretic way, fused multiple functions in each activity. (Millennia later, we have still not reintegrated writing into the rest of the curriculum!)[1]

The sequence from then to now probably followed a path of increasing specialization and abstractness in symbolizing. Some part of a building or monument depicted a story of past events, schematized the zodiac, or laid out steps in how to make something. Earlier, these ideas might materialize as effigies, bas-reliefs, or even key features of architectural layout, then later as pictures incised or drawn on walls or steles. Two-dimensionality is a higher abstraction than three-dimensionality, the symbols being farther removed from what they symbolize. As message-leaving specialized, it became more portable: tablets and scrolls supplanted murals and inscriptions. Then direct pictorialization yielded to ideography, wherein pictures become standardized and systematized into a consistent spatial order and lexicon and take on less concrete meanings associated with the pictures but (eventually) not themselves depictable.

---

[1]See, for example, Francis Hitching, *Earth Magic* (New York: Simon and Schuster, 1978); Peter Tompkins, *Secrets of the Great Pyramid* (New York: Harper and Row, 1971); and Louis Charpentier, *The Mysteries of Chartres Cathedral* (New York: Avon, 1975).

Petroglyphs thus become hieroglyphs. Incision and cuneiform, the hold-overs from monumental writing, give way to drawing and painting, less substantial but faster and more flexible for writing as a special activity. Cuneiform, the printing of a single wedge shape in different positions and numbers, no doubt led, however, to the acceptance of arbitrary, imageless symbols such as characterize the alphabet.

So although children today may be regarded as starting to write by drawing graphic symbols for sound symbols, this historical summary reminds us that just as early man worked his way up to the alphabet, so may the child—and for good reason. Most psychologists, even of variant schools, would probably accept the capsulized form in which Jerome Bruner once characterized stages of children's mental development as enactive, iconic, and symbolic—the respective acting out, depicting, and abstract representing of thought. Just as "prehistoric" man began to write before we give him credit for it, so children start writing some time before we think of some of their activities as writing. Learning to symbolize begins with mimicry and pantomime and the other signifying behavior that we call "body language"; accumulates the external, three-dimensional media of collaging and modeling and constructing; refines these to the two-dimensional media of stamping, imprinting, drawing, and painting; then proceeds to ordering pictures into a story and to drawing and sequencing the geometric shapes that comprise letters. All this sets the stage for the stunning moment when two independently evolving symbol systems come into conjunction—one vocal and auditory, the other manual and visual.

Rising on now through the spectrum of writing definitions, the next level above letter-drawing or *handwriting,* to use the school term, is the *transcribing* of speech sounds. Transcription comprises spelling and punctuation, which respectively render vocalization and intonation (stress, pitch, and juncture). They shift speech from an oral to a visual medium, and because they are basic to literacy are misleadingly called "basic skills."

From here on up the scale the issue is how much real authoring is occurring. We may start with direct *copying* of a text, a teaching method practiced in some times and places in Europe on grounds that it imprints spellings, punctuation, vocabulary, and sentence structures. We have only to reread Melville's story "Bartleby the Scrivener" to appreciate the practical importance of the amanuensis before the invention of the typewriter and the ensuing technology of copying. Perhaps we should place stenography a shade above copying on the writing scale, since the interpretation and translation of speech sounds requires more thought. Both result in writing, but in neither case does the "writer" create the content or necessarily even understand it. As a former French teacher I can attest to the value of the dictée, however, for second-language learning, where the literacy issue of matching written symbols with spoken words naturally looms as large for the learner of any age as it does for the small child with his native language.

Paraphrasing seems to mark the point of shifting from copying or transcribing toward some degree of authoring. It can range from barely changed quotation to significant shift in vocabulary and sentence structure that indicates much interpretation. But to the extent that a second party summarizes a text as well as rewords it, we are into précis or résumé and hence into the more extensive interpretation that selection and reduction entail. These French terms betray the origin of the same old-world pedagogy that underlies the copying method. Actually, the précis is intended to elicit comprehension, not interpretation, and reflects the frank avowal of traditional French schooling that a youngster should only take in until age eighteen because he or she is not ready before then to do original thinking. Though unavowed in this country, this attitude clearly operates powerfully throughout the entire curriculum.

It is impossible to understand the teaching of writing in America if one does not realize that, in one form or another, from first grade through graduate school, it serves mostly to test reading. In elementary school the main form of writing is the book report, which becomes dignified in high school and college as the "research paper" or "critical paper," then deified in graduate school as the "survey of the literature" in the doctoral dissertation. The real goal of writing instruction in the United States is to prepare for term papers and essay questions (although secondary and college teachers increasingly fall back today on multiple-choice "objective" tests, partly because "the kids can't write"). We have always been far more interested in reading than in writing, so much so that writing in schools has hardly existed except as a means to demonstrate either reading comprehension or the comprehensiveness of one's reading. Because writing produces an external result, it is a natural testing instrument if one wishes to regard it so, whereas the receptive activity of reading leaves no traces outside. Using writing to test reading, then, seems the perfect solution to an institution so bedeviled by managing and monitoring problems that it resists student productivity tooth and nail and regards testing as the solution to everything. Writing about reading quite effectively kills two birds with one stone.

So we have geared the teaching of writing in this country to the level of quotation and paraphrase, précis and book report. Students are to be told to, not to tell. Since even regurgitation entails some interpretation and synthesis by the reader, it is fair to accord to this level of "writing" some degree of authorship. But surely school practices of writing about the reading represent minimal authorship. In any case, wouldn't educators do well to ask constantly how much authoring their writing program honestly calls for and how much it truly aims to teach writing for the sake of writing? It is certainly very true that the degree of authorship is relative in *any* kind of writing. Even great professional writers usually incorporate into their thought and work, at some level of assimilation, the thoughts and works of others. But their kind of taking in and giving out exists for them to have more to say, not to prove to others' satisfaction that they have done their homework. Authoring ought to be construed, it seems to me, on a rather tough criterion of originality if only because the less a learner imitates or borrows, the more he has to do his own thinking, regardless of how much he may read.

The next-highest conception of writing emphasizes *craft*—how to construct good sentences, paragraphs, and overall organizations. Everyone respects craftsmanship, no less in writing, surely, than anywhere else, but if the question of genuine authorship is finessed, then such an approach results in a mere carpentry course. For the very reason that they are assuming that content will be supplied by books or lectures, schools have taken it for granted. The only problem is how to cut and fit. Naturally allied to the emphasis on reading and general student passivity, formalism dominates the teaching of writing, by which I mean forming the language only without nearly sufficient concern for developing the thought. This level of writing instruction does deserve the name of "composition" for the very reason that it features construction—selecting and arranging for maximum effect—but it fastens almost hypnotically on the surface level of language, at which thought *manifests* itself, and blandly stops short of the long internal processing that must go on to engender something to manifest.

At its best the crafting approach to writing can help a student see alternative and better ways to say what he has in mind, but without at least an equal emphasis on finding and developing subjects of his own, and the clear primacy of purpose over form, the "writer" ends by carpentering clichés to make the sentence or the paragraph or essay form come out right. At its worst, the approach loads a student with prescriptions and proscriptions that no serious writer could ever follow and still keep his mind on his business, and even degenerates into what I call decomposition—manipulating grammatical facts and labels as information, memorizing vocabulary lists, and doing exercises with isolated dummy sentences. Language parts are tools of the craft, right? But they must not, of course, be mistaken for the craft itself.

Well-meaning teachers try hard to make the crafting approach work by assigning "provocative" or "open" topics for the content and "creative" exercises in sentence-combining or in rear-loading of sentence modification. These valiant efforts can look successful within the narrow notion of authorship taken for granted in our schools today. But when writing on demand for a grade in an institution, how provocative and open really is "We have met the enemy and he is us," the topic of the 1978 College Board's English Achievement Test and a fair sample of topics that teachers of the craft tradition might assign (and might think appropriate because it comes from a comic strip, *Pogo*). Reporting as a reader for this exam, James Gray, head of the Bay Area Writing Project, found "mechanical paragraphs masquerading as organized essays" and "overgeneralizing, posturing, and earnest moralizing."[2] Since the crafting approach represents about the highest point on our spectrum that the teaching of writing would have attained in the schools from which these college-bound students derived, Gray's description seems a fair indication of the most we can expect from a concept of writing so unbalanced between language and technique, on the one hand, and thought and purpose, on the other. After all, how much does being allowed to make up your own sentence combinations or sentence modifications amount to in the bigger picture of rendering thought into writing, even though the exercises may seem like fun compared to grimmer alternatives? For a final commentary on the crafting emphasis, I invoke the greatest thinker of our century, who said in the preface to his *Relativity: The Special and General Theory* that when the intent is to get ideas across, "matters of elegance ought to be left to the tailor and the cobbler."[3] Einstein's ability to communicate clearly to the layman the most difficult ideas of our time certainly ranks high among his achievements.

The notions of "writing" so far reviewed, none of which honor full authoring, smack suspiciously not only, as I have suggested, of institutional convenience (usually beyond the control of teachers themselves) but also of a materialistic framework that inevitably biases schooling and anchors the teaching of writing at inferior levels of any scale aspiring to excellence. In fact, it is the materialism that places the institution over the individual, form over content. Specifically, it shows in a favoring of more *concrete* definitions of writing, as transcription or carpentry; in the *superficial* view that spelling and punctuating are basic skills, instead of thinking and speaking; and in the *analytic* isolation of language units as curriculum units (the phoneme, the word, the sentence, the paragraph). Generally, the materialistic bias of our culture practically forces us to prefer the visible domain of language forms, which linguistic science has so well delineated, to the invisible domain of thought, which is still a scary can of worms. But teachers have no business preferring either and have no choice but to work *in the gap* between thought and speech. Writing is a

[2]James Gray, "Twenty Minutes of Fluency—A Test," *The National Writing Project Network Newsletter*, volume 2, number 2, March 1979, p. 12.
[3]Albert Einstein, *Relativity: The Special and General Theory* (New York: Crown, 1961), Preface, p. v.

manifestation of thought, but, however tempting, we cannot deal with it only as it finally manifests itself visually in writing or even audibly as speech. Too much precedes the physical sounds or sights for teachers to take up only at these forms.

But how can we get at the writing process before it materializes in these forms? Answering this teaching question brings us to the top of the spectrum of writing definitions, where schools should be operating. Educators would do best, I submit, to conceive of writing, first of all, as full-fledged authoring, by which I mean authentic expression of an individual's own ideas, original in the sense that he or she has synthesized them for himself or herself. True authoring occurs naturally to the extent that the writer is composing with raw material, that is, source content not previously abstracted and formulated by others. Teaching aimed this way would emphasize subject matter lying easily at hand within and around the writer—firsthand content like feelings, fantasies, sensations, memories, and reflections, and secondhand content as drawn from interviews, stored information, and the writings of others to the extent that the writer truly re-abstracts these in his own synthesis. Insisting on maximum authorship should stave off the construing or treating of writing as only some sort of transcription or paraphrasing or verbal tailoring from ready-made cloth. (Behind the basic meaning of "author" as "adder" lies the assumption that a writer has something unique enough to add to the communal store of knowledge.)

Presupposing true authorship, the highest definition acknowledges that *any* writing, about whatever personal or impersonal subject, for whatever audience and purpose, can never comprise anything but some focused and edited version of inner speech. When writing, one writes down what one is thinking—but not everything one is thinking at that moment and not necessarily in the form that first comes to mind. What the writer transcribes is some ongoing *revision* of inner speech, which is itself some verbalized or at least verbalizable distillation of the continually flowing mixture of inner life that psychologist William James long ago named the "stream of consciousness." The writer intent on his subject presumably tries to narrow down drastically for the moment his total field of consciousness—shuts out most things and concentrates on one train which he has set in motion at will and tries to sustain. This means that to write one must control inner speech and not simply let it run at the behest of normally interplaying stimuli. We could say that composition begins with this attentional selectivity except that, at the time of writing down thoughts, a writer stands at the mercy of prior rumination about the subject as it will surface in the inner speech that spontaneously presents itself for further composition. We had best include as composition the whole continuum of inner processing that determines what will occur to the writer about the subject focused on. A person cannot write something he cannot say at least to himself—think—but he also keeps recasting a subject in his inner speech, perhaps long before he knows he will write about it.

The chief reason for defining writing as revision of inner speech is to ensure that writing be acknowledged as nothing less than thinking, manifested a certain way, and to make sure that it is taught accordingly. In addition to the more commonly accepted possibilities of revising what one has already written down, two less familiar teaching issues emerge— the immediate one of how best to set conditions for tapping and focusing inner speech at the moment of writing down, and the long-range one of how best to develop the highest quality of inner speech so that when one sits down to write, the thought that spontaneously presents itself offers the best wherewithal for the more visible and audible composition that will follow.

Compactly recapitulated, the ways in which writing may be defined array themselves in this way, reading upward from most material and external to most authorial. Lower definitions are lower not because false but because insufficient.

- Revising inner speech—starts with inchoate thought.
- Crafting conventional or given subject matter—starts with given topics and language forms.
- Paraphrasing, summarizing, plagiarizing—starts with other writers' material and ideas.
- Transcribing and copying—starts verbatim with others' speech and texts.
- Drawing and handwriting—starts with imagery for sensorimotor activities.

Writing consists of not just one of these activities but of all of them at once. All definitions are correct. When people write, they are simultaneously *drawing* letters, *transcribing* their inner voice, *plagiarizing* concepts and frameworks from their culture, *crafting* their thoughts into language forms, and *revising* the inchoate thought of their inner speech. None are wrong, but failing to include all is wrong. Nor is it true that the learner begins at the bottom and works his way up. From the outset, lettering needs to be connected to meaning, to the symbolizing of inner speech, as when the small child watches while a helper writes down his story for him or her as the child dictates it and then literally retraces the writing. All these definitions apply all at once at all stages of growth. Older students who say they have nothing to write have simply spent all their school days copying, paraphrasing, and fitting given content into given

forms and never have had a chance to see themselves as authors composing their inner speech toward a creation of their own. The scale does correspond to an order of increasing difficulty for both the writer and the
teacher of writing. Small wonder we're tempted to lop off the top!

Teachers with whom I have used this scale of definitions in workshops have said that they found it very useful. It should help a teacher
place his or her approach and to decide if change seems called for. In
which sense or senses am I teaching writing? Is that what I mean to do?
If not, why am I teaching this way? If not, how would I have to change
my classroom practices to teach writing as I think I should? The scale
should help also to think about that old bugaboo, evaluation. For each
definition here there correspond criteria mostly irrelevant to the other definitions. Do the standardized tests by which my students' "writing" or
"composition" ability is judged do justice to all these definitions, to writing as a whole? Am I teaching writing by one definition and assessing it
by another? Am I operating by certain definitions and my colleagues or
superiors or constituency assuming others? And—where do "basic skills"
and "minimal standards" fall on this array?

The ambiguity of the word "writing" not only creates tremendous
confusion about teaching methods but makes it possible to plug in any
meaning that suits any motive. Prevalently, most schools are teaching
something else and calling it writing, in a version of "let's don't and say
we did," which receives perfect support from tests that measure something else and call it writing. Nearly all the stakeholders in the teaching
of writing have reasons for wanting to interpret it as "mechanics" or decomposition or book-reporting or carpentry. All of us, in and out of
school, have tacitly conspired to lobotomize writing, precisely because, if
undertaken seriously, it threatens to be dangerous, unmanageable, and
untestable by current cheap instruments. Everyone senses, quite rightly,
that real authoring would require radical changes in student role, classroom management and methods, parents' and administrators' heads, evaluation, and the whole atmosphere of schooling.

And yet the public is now claiming to want improvement in the
teaching of writing. Since this interest and the ensuing funding were inspired by low test scores, college complaints, and popular reportage, we
needn't wonder long about where on the scale just sketched the notion
of writing in question falls. Never mind. Some interest and funds have
appeared, and this should be taken positively. But it is important that
educators try to hold this trend to the highest conception of writing, the
one that has the most educational value, and the one that works because
it stems from meaning and motive. Otherwise the current support could,
like most of the title money of the Great Society programs, end by locking in even more tightly the errors of the past.

The processes of writing cannot be realistically perceived and taught so long as we try to work from the outside in. The most fundamental and effective way to improve compositional "decisions" about word choice, phrasing, sentence structure, and overall organization is to clarify, enrich, and harmonize the thinking that predetermines the student's initial choices of these. We must never forget, no matter how much a technocratic mentality and an uncontrolled educational–industrial complex bully us the other way, that the heart of writing beats deep within a subjective inner life that, while neither audible nor visible at the time the most important action is occurring, governs all those choices that a composition course tries belatedly to straighten out.

What teaching methodology does this highest definition imply? As regards the immediate circumstances of actually getting something on paper, the definition indicates: the providing of audiences and of opportunities to grasp the various purposes of writing; individual choice of subject, form, and time; the arraying and illustrating of the entire range of kinds of writing in the diverse modes of discourse; the use of partners and coaches with whom to talk over and try out ideas before and during written composition, in order to aerate and revise inner speech across successive versions; the teaching of meditational techniques for knowing, focusing, and controlling inner speech;[4] and the interweaving of writing with other media, arts, and disciplines so that all these forms of knowing remain in natural relations with each other, providing warm-ups and follow-ups for writing and offering it as one among alternative ways to discover, develop, and render the mind.

As regards the long-range development of inner speech, the highest definition implies any means that will exercise thought itself. Enriching, refining, sharpening inner speech require, throughout all the school years: various and plentiful thinking activities as embodied in many games, practical problems to solve, imagining, and dialectic with others; much experience in small-group process where all sorts of good conversing can be practiced—task talk, topic talk, improvisation—that when internalized will become part of individual thinking; copious and wide-ranging reading as can occur only when students can individually select their own reading matter from a huge array of all sorts; rich physical and social experience with the things of this world, so that inner speech has much to reflect from the outside. The more that thought benefits from the cyclic turning over of outer and inner experience, outer and inner speech, the less revision will the actual writing phase of composition require. Deepening and clearing thought undercuts the familiar writing problems.

If we concentrate our forces on fostering the highest development of inner speech, we will automatically not only teach excellence in writing

---

[4]See "Writing, Inner Speech, and Meditation," pp. 89–137.

but lift other subjects along with it into a new learning integration, for the quality and qualities of inner speech determine and are determined by all mental activities. Reading or writing "across the curriculum," the "core curriculum," "teaching the humanities," and so on will all take care of themselves. We have to consider writing in relation to the rest of the curriculum. Because inner speech is the matrix of spontaneous discourse that can be composed in any direction and that reflects any externalities, it allows us to integrate all discursive learning.

8

On Essaying

Background

These are more thoughts prompted by working with teachers in writing. It happened that, at about the same time, the editor of the *National Writing Project Newsletter* and the editor of *fforum,* a newsletter of the English Composition Board at the University of Michigan, asked me to write a piece for them to publish. The occasion for the *fforum* piece was an issue devoted to the work of Jimmy Britton and myself. I wrote the short articles in such a way that they could later be joined back-to-back as a continuous essay on a subject I felt strongly about—the personal nature of all good writing even when content goes well beyond the individual. I had been rereading a lot of classic essays in English letters and appreciating again how well they spoke for us all by speaking so well for themselves.

The first half of what follows appeared as "Confessions of an Ex-College Freshman" in the *NWP Newsletter* of May 1980; the second half was printed in the October 1980 issue of *fforum.* As I hope is evident, I tried to make my own essay an example of what I was trying to say about essaying itself.

I flunked my first theme in college. My composition instructor had said to write on "your home town." O.K., fine, I could choose one of three—where I grew up till adolescence, where I went to high school, or where my parents currently resided, which I knew only in summertime. Today, I naturally see in my lethal choice of number three a fine example of how composition begins with decisions about which raw material to use. But those were pre-prewriting days.

Below the grade of flat E the instructor declared, with terrible justice, "A mass of tourist-guide-propaganda clichés, FW [fine writing], and J [jargon]. Moreover, you really have no exact subject—your title gives you away ['My Home Town']. Quite below college demands." Here was I not only an untested freshman fearful of losing a full scholarship by not attaining a B average, but I was half convinced anyway that I didn't really belong at Harvard and had only got in by way of some back door carelessly left open. Furthermore, I figured to major in English!

Brittle grad-school bachelor that he was, toiling away in one of twen-ty-odd sections of English A, my teacher really acted charitably. He knew I was on a trolley headed utterly the wrong way, toward endless suffer-ing, and that only a powerful jolt right at the start would derail me so that I could make it in that course and even perhaps in college generally. My first paragraph read:

> Los Angeles, while not exactly the city of angels as its Spanish name proclaims, has within its environs a multitude of entertainments to please natives and tourists alike. Regardless of what his individual tastes may be, deep-sea fishing or listening to a fugue by Handel, there is probably always something which will satisfy his whim.

Over this you can see already a *New Yorker* type of rubric, Themes I Never Finished Reading. But it was a perfect thesis paragraph, for it stated ex-actly what kind of bullshit the reader was expected to wallow through afterwards. We toured the beaches of Santa Monica, the Hollywood Bowl, where "an open sky of stars lends enchantment to the symphonic works," the nearby desert, where "the moonlight accentuates the unique charm of the quiet expanses," and the downtown L.A. theater district. One topic-sentenced paragraph was on sports, one on food, one on night-clubbing, and so on. No chance of the reader getting lost here. No prob-lems of transition or organization or coherence. The signposts were all there, and the sentences scanned grammatically. But it was atrocious writing. In fact, it wasn't really writing; it was a paste-and-scissors job, only collaged inside the head instead of with physical clippings and splic-ings. My teacher rejected it out of hand because it was so borrowed and so unreal that he had no way even of assessing it as composition, nothing to come to grips with. It was ghost writing of an unconscious sort, very much like the great majority of papers English teachers waste time mark-ing up.

I wrote that theme as I had written stuff all through school. An all-A student in all subjects through high school, I always did what teachers wanted. The teaching of writing, and of English generally, remains now about the same as then, in the '40s, some exceptions having occurred by dint of strenuous innovation, and many of those having been wiped out by the regressive movement that has prompted publishers to dust off and reissue the English textbooks of that time. Mostly, my classmates and I were asked to write about what we had read to make sure we *had* done the reading and to see if we had got the point. The teaching of writing in this country has for so long been harnessed to the testing of reading that few teachers I meet even today can grasp the enormity of this bias and the consequent mischief and fraudulence.

Whenever I was asked to write about something outside of books, the subject was so remote from me, such as national affairs, that I could know it mostly only secondhand and hence could hardly do anything but paraphrase the information and arguments that I got from newspapers, radio, and grown-up talk. But that's the point. *My teachers really just wanted familiar, adult-sounding prose.* This they equated with mature writing. They *wanted* phrasing they recognized, views they had heard aired around them, because this meant their students were joining the adult world. Isn't that the whole point of school? They loved and encouraged my five-dollar words, straight out of *Reader's Digest* vocabulary quizzes, because big words show learning and correlate with intelligence. They were nice people who didn't know much about composition as such at all. They too had never written anything besides the usual school and college testing stuff—book reports, term papers, and essay exams—and so they had never learned how to shape material not predigested for them by others. Anyway, a glittering travelog on a glossy town seemed O.K. to me.

After that first failure I got the point quickly. (No doubt I was also relieved to know that the institution I was going to spend the next four years at wasn't going to deal in that kind of bullshit.) My instructor advised me to do the assignment over—and knock it off this time. I did and got an A. Great, a happy ending, but what was the difference? Well, it was all the difference in the world, and yet I was pretty much the same person I had been the week before. I didn't know any more about organization or sentence structure, I didn't have a better vocabulary, and I hadn't acquired any new "writing skills." Nor was I a more logical thinker.

For my second chance I chose to tell about "My Boyhood in Jackson," a significant decision because that town really meant something to me. I told how my friends and I played out our adventure fantasies against the Mississippi background as Twain's characters had done in Missouri. In the dense foliage along the Pearl River we pretended to be buccaneers, explorers, and Stanley looking for Livingston. Or:

> I was a scientist—the sole survivor of an expedition sent up the Amazon on an important quest. After I staggered from the jungle into the clearing, my feverish body fell lifeless before those waiting for me. In my outstretched hand lay a small vial containing the juice of a rare plant—the cure for cancer.

I told how we dug niches for thrones in the steep white clay banks of the railroad cut, using tie spikes for tools, and lit discarded flares to stake out our thrones with. Then the train roared through the cut.

> The surging power of the locomotive was mine, for I felt it pass through me as the earth rumbled under the passing train. Besides, the engineer gave it to me by the friendly waving of his hand.

I concluded unpretentiously that although I might well have play-acted some of the same things had I lived somewhere else, the fact is that "I played and grew in Jackson, and that is what endears it to me."

In a way I was being myself in the first theme too: the glamor of Los Angeles and the emptiness masquerading as impersonality were true for me to the degree that I was attracted to the one and had learned to put on the other. So the difference between the themes was really in the level of the self. I just suddenly changed my whole orientation toward writing. My teacher had said, in effect, "No one wants to read what he knows already or could come out with himself. We read for something new. Write what only *you* know, or what you have put together for yourself. *Make* something, don't just *take* something." I had no problem with that. We all live on all planes of shallowness and depth all the time and so can shift planes at any moment if someone or something sets us straight. I thought, "Oh, I see. *That*'s how it is. Writing isn't what I've been led to believe. It's saying what you really think and feel or what you really want to put over." But, of course, I had known that before from reading great writers and from trying to write extracurricular stories. It was *curricular* writing I had a false notion of. And this dissociation of writing from reality afflicts most students in this country.

The main reasons for this are two. Traditional schooling has shown no respect for writing, exploiting composition instruction as a way to service its testing system and as a way to spawn the pencil-pushers required to stock all those clerical jobs in industry and government, where you do not want thinkers. You just want people who have passed minimal standards—can read just well enough to follow directions and write just well enough to take dictation. But I'm not talking about some conspiracy by *them*. All of us share through our culture and bear within us a deader, less evolved aspect of being that calcifies because it is still mineral or vegetates because it is still plant-like or preys because it is still animal, all while the human aspect of the self works toward its partly divined divinity. This sludgier element of individuals settles out in society as sedimentary attitudes and institutions that mire down efforts to better ourselves.

The other reason for the shallow tradition that has neutered the teaching of writing is that teachers themselves have practiced writing so little that they fall back on hopelessly irrelevant procedures. Many simply don't know how real writing takes place. It is patent to anyone who has worked much with teachers that the less practice they have had, the more they rationalize book reports, formal grammatical analysis, paragraph formulas, sentence exercises, vocabulary quizzes, and a prescriptive/proscriptive methodology. "You have to *teach* them," they say, never having learned how themselves. Compelled once to coach a sport I had never played, lacrosse, I too gravitated toward a simplistic rules–results approach that was an effort to distill experience I had never had.

The National Writing Project has succeeded and gained support precisely because it makes teachers practitioners instead of mere preachers.

When I am teaching teachers to write in summer institutes, I see the same thing happen to them that happened to me with that first freshman theme. They discover that if they write from the heart they not only have something to say, something that interests others, but that they can better order their thoughts and can actualize their latent talent. It is more than ordinarily moving to see *teachers* discover how writing really occurs, often after many years of frustrating themselves and their students. Maybe I identify with late bloomers, but I'm especially touched by the delicate transition from recalcitrance to confidence that takes place as they find out just how well they and their partners can, after all, write.

Before they have made this discovery, many teachers will call every kind of writing that is not term-paper or essay-question stuff "personal" or "creative" writing (the two terms being interchangeable) and hence put it in a big bag that goes up on the shelf. Priority goes, of course, to "exposition," which is equated with "essay," which is equated in turn with forced writing on given topics from books, lectures, or "current issues." In these institutes with teachers I break a class into trios in which members help each other for several weeks to develop subjects and techniques by hearing or reading partners' writing ideas at various stages of working up the material. Some of this material is gleaned from memory, some is information obtained fresh by interviewing or observing, and some is feeling, thought, or imagination elicited suddenly by a stimulus such as a tune or other in-class presentation. The material may take the form of stories, dialogues, essays, or songs and poems. It soon becomes obvious that ideas stem from all kinds of material and take all kinds of forms and that the very limited sort of exposition used for testing enjoys no monopoly on intellectual activity; participants can see, often with astonishment, how loaded with ideas is this rich variety of writing they have produced.

When schools narrow the notion of *essay* to fit it to testing, they are violating the whole tradition of the genre from its very inception to the present. College composition instructors and anthologists of essays have doted for years on George Orwell's "Shooting an Elephant," which they hold up to students as a model of essay or "expository writing." Please look closely at it even if you think you know it well; if a student had written it, it would be called "personal writing," that is, soft and nonintellectual. Orwell narrated in first person how as a British civil servant in Burma he was intimidated by villagers into shooting an elephant against his will. But so effectively does he say *what happens* by telling *what happened* that the force of his theme—about the individual's moral choice whether or not to conform to the group—leaves us with the *impression* that the memoir is "expository," that is, chiefly cast in the present tense of generalization and in third person. What we really want to help youngsters learn is how to express ideas of universal value in a personal voice. Fables, parables, poems and songs, fiction, and memoir may convey ideas as well

as or better than editorials and critiques. Orwell does indeed provide a
fine model, but teachers should not let prejudice fool them into misunderstanding the actual kind of discourse in which he wrote that and other
excellent essays, for this leads to a terribly confusing double standard
whereby we ask students to emulate a great writer but to do it in another
form.

Orwell wrote deep in a tradition of English letters honoring the essay
as a candid blend of personal and universal. It was resurrected if not invented during the Renaissance by Montaigne, who coined the term *essai*
from *essayer,* to attempt. From his position of philosophical skepticism
("What do I know?") he saw his writing as personal attempts to discover
truth, what he thought and what could be thought, in exactly the same
sense that Donald Murray or Janet Emig or I might speak of writing as
discovery. From Burton's *Anatomy of Melancholy* and Browne's *Urn Burial;*
Addison's and Steele's *Spectator* articles; through the essays of Swift, Lamb,
Hazlitt, and De Quincey to those of Orwell, Virginia Woolf, Joan Didion,
and Norman Mailer, English literature has maintained a marvelous tradition, fusing personal experience, private vision, and downright eccentric-
ity with intellectual vigor and verbal objectification. In color, depth, and
stylistic orginality it rivals some of our best poetry. Look again at Hazlitt's
"The Fight" (and compare it with Mailer's reportage of the Ali-Frazier
fight in *King of the Hill*) or "On the Feeling of Immortality in Youth" or
"On Familiar Style"; De Quincey's "Confessions of an English Opium-
Eater" or "On the Knocking at the Gate in Macbeth," which begins,
"From my boyish days I had always felt a great perplexity on one point
in *Macbeth*"; or Lamb's "The Two Races of Men," "Poor Relations," "San-
ity of True Genius." Consider, too, a book like Henry Adams's *The Education of Henry Adams* for its simultaneous treatment of personal and national or historical.

Some essayists, like Montaigne and Emerson, tend toward generality,
as reflected in titles like "Friendship" or "Self-Reliance," but tone and
source are personal, and we cannot doubt the clear kinship between essays featuring memoir or eyewitness reportage and those of generality,
for the same writers do both, sometimes in a single essay, sometimes in
separate pieces; and Lamb and Thoreau stand in the same relation to
Montaigne and Emerson as fable to moral or parable to proverb. The difference lies not in the fundamental approach, which is in any case personal, but in the degree of explicitness of the theme. "I bear within me
the exemplar of the human condition," said Montaigne. Descending deep
enough within, the essayist links up personal with universal, self with
Self.

These essayists frequently write about their reading, and they love
reading. They set, in fact, a model for writing about reading that is very
different from writing-as-testing, because *they* have selected what to read

according to their own ongoing pursuits, and, second, they cite ideas and instances from books *in mixture with* ideas and instances drawn from everyday experience, thus fusing life with literature. Many openly framed assignments that I have long advocated will elicit from students exactly the kinds of essays that constitute our fine heritage in this flexible form. They call for the writer to crystallize memories, capture places, "write a narrative of any sort that makes a general point applying beyond the particular material," "put together three or four incidents drawn from life or reading that all seem to show the same thing, that are connected in your mind by some idea," or "make a general statement about something you have observed to be true, illustrating by referring to events and situations you know of or have read of." The point is to *leave subject matter to the writer, including reading selections.* Any student who has done such assignments will be better able, strictly as a bonus, to cough up some prose to show he has done his homework than if he has been especially trained to write about reading.[1]

Schools mistreat writing because the society suffers at the moment from drastic misunderstandings about the nature of knowledge. Applying "scientific" criteria that would be unacceptable to most real scientists making the breakthroughs out there on the frontier, many people have come to think that subtracting the self makes for objectivity and validity. But depersonalization is not impartiality. It is, quite literally, madness. Einstein said, "The observer is the essence of the situation." It is not by abandoning the self but by developing it that we achieve impartiality and validity. The deeper we go *consciously* into ourselves, the better chance we have of reaching universality, as Montaigne knew so well. Transpersonal, not impersonal. It is an undeterred faith in this that makes a great writer cultivate his individuality until we feel he utters us better than we do ourselves. Teachers should be the first to understand this misunderstanding and to start undoing it, so that schooling in general and writing in particular can offset rather than reinforce the problem.

Here are two examples of what we're up against—one from a famous current encyclopedia and one from a leading publisher, typical and telling symptoms. Most English majors probably have sampled or at least heard of Sir Thomas Browne, a very individualistic seventeenth-century master of an original prose style, a writer's writer much admired by successors. Of his *Pseudodoxia Epidemica* Funk and Wagnalls's *Standard Reference Encyclopedia* says, "Its unscientific approach and odd assemblage of obscure facts typify his haphazard erudition," and then concludes the entry: "Despite Browne's deficiencies as a thinker, his style entitles him to high rank among the masters of English prose." What this verdict tells me is that

---

[1]For these and other recommended writing assignments, see James Moffett, *Active Voice: A Writing Program Across the Curriculum*, Boynton/Cook Publishers, 1981.

the scholar who wrote that entry felt overwhelmed by all the books Browne had read that he had not and that our scholar knew far less than he should have about the enormously important and complex networks of thought and knowledge, called esoteric, that after several millenia of evolution still had great influence on Newton, Bacon, and Descartes (who displayed at times equally "irrational" intellectual behavior). Such a judgment on such a writer is nothing but smart-ass chauvinism; permitted to poison basic information sources, it makes "science" as deadly a censor as ever the Church was during its Inquisition.

We can avoid producing Brownes from our school system by having all youngsters read and write the same things—a goal we have closely approximated—and then their approach will not be unscientific, their assemblage odd, their facts obscure, or their erudition haphazard. And we will have ensured that no one will be able to emulate the great essayists we hold up as models (or even read them with any comprehension). Real essaying cannot thrive without cultivation of the individual. Who would have any reason to read anyone else? (And I want to know how Browne's style could be worth so much if he was not a good thinker.)

The second example is personal. When I received back from the publisher the edited manuscript of the original edition of *Student-Centered Language Arts and Reading, K–13*, I was aghast. "My" editor had rewritten sentences throughout the whole book to eliminate first-person references and other elements of the author's presence and voice. This included altering diction and sentence structure at times to get a more anonymous or distanced effect. Faced with the appalling labor of restoring all those sentences, I called up the editor, furious. She said righteously, "But we always do that—it's policy." It never occurred to her to exempt, or even to warn, an author who wouldn't be publishing the book in the first place if he weren't regarded as some kind of expert in writing.

You can't trust your encyclopedia, your publisher, your school administration. And you can't trust yourself until you learn to spot how you too may be spreading the plague, as Camus calls it. The double standard about "Look at the greats, but don't do what they did" naturally goes along with our era of Scientific Inquisition, which is really technocratic plague. Teachers stand in a fine position to spread infection. If you let yourself be convinced that "personal" or "creative" writing is merely narcissistic, self-indulgent, and weak-minded, then you have just removed your own first person.

9

Writing, Inner Speech, and Meditation

Background

I first became interested in inner speech while studying literature as an undergraduate. A natural tendency to introspection and a strong interest in fictional technique combined. Innovations toward interior monologue or stream-of-consciousness by Joyce, Woolf, Faulkner, and Eliot fascinated me. I ended by writing a senior honors thesis called "The Relation of the Inner and Outer Lives in the Works of Virginia Woolf," which won the Bowdoin essay prize, mostly, I suspect, because of boosting by Albert Guerard, Jr., a professor of comparative literature, now at Stanford but then at Harvard, who is a novelist himself and an unusually perceptive critic. In his lectures and articles he opened new doors for me to fictional process. Like most literature professors in the heyday of Hemingway, he preferred masculine action novels and wondered if Virginia Woolf was really readable, but his support of my weird preoccupation with her valiant and artful efforts to make inner events as dramatic as outer testified to the ability he had, which made him a real teacher, to subordinate his own attitudes to the education of his student.

As a teacher myself later, learning through trials and errors at Exeter, I gradually worked out a spectrum of fictional techniques scaled according to the point of view of the narrator, whether avowed ("first person") or anonymous ("third person"). With the help of colleague Kenneth McElheny, I embodied this spectrum in an anthology of short stories (*Points of View,* a Mentor book, New American Library). The matrix was interior monologue, the fictionalization of inner speech, the initial "narrative" point of view from which others are departures to varying removes in inner and outer space/time. An important concept from Guerard, which I've never properly acknowledged, is that of the "imperceptive narrator," who tells a different story from what he thinks he is telling, because he is not on top of the experience recounted. Guerard pointed out examples in Gide and Dostoevski and other modern novelists. Eudora Welty's "Why I Live at the P.O." is a fine instance, and, descending to burlesque, so also is the popular song of some twenty years ago, "I Saw Mommy Kissing Santa Claus underneath the Mistletoe Last Night." Such a narrator stands somewhere between raw (unabstracted) inner speech and "objective" discourse.

Then matters got out of hand. I began to see such a scale not only in narration but in all discourse. Carried away, across the whole hierarchy of levels of abstraction, I tried to get rid of my obsession by writing it up, or out, as key chapters of *Teaching the Universe of Discourse.* Always it was from the amorphous, undifferentiated crucible of inner speech that these gradations of discourse were generated. (*Matrix, mother,* and *matter* all come from the same root.) By then I was reading scientific descriptions of what I had first known from my own introspection and from literature, and these helped me to formulate and support my theories.

Just as my old preoccupation was becoming perhaps too much of a head trip, and stagnating there, I began to practice meditation and then to undergo the inner disciplining of Swami Sivalingam.[o] Then I saw inner speech very differently from the way I had through either psychology or literature, though perhaps I was only going back in a new way to where I had begun, in introspection. This career-long trip spiraled over into another dimension, and I had to start re-viewing and re-casting most of what I had ever thought about language and literature, as I am still doing. Some of us just seem to take a long time getting to the point—late bloomers I guess we're supposed to call us in education.

This essay went through three lecture versions in 1979—one delivered from detailed notes at the convention of the California Association of Teachers of English in San Diego, a much longer one read over three evening sessions from a written text at the Bread Loaf Summer School of English in Vermont, and a reduced form of that to the first annual conference on writing of the Independent School Association of Massachusetts in Cambridge. In 1980 I spoke on this subject at the Third International Conference on the Teaching of English at Sydney, Australia. The article is published here for the first time.

<hr />

Writing and meditating are naturally allied activities. Both are important for their own sake, and through each people can practice the other. Relating the two by means of a bridging concept, that of inner speech, brings out aspects of all three that can illuminate old educational goals and identify new ones. To work with this three-way interrelationship, we must construe writing in its highest sense—beyond copying and transcribing, paraphrasing and plagiarizing—as authentic *authoring,* because inner speech and meditation concern forms of thought, the composing of mind that constitutes the real art and worth of writing. Authoring is working up a final revision, for an audience and a purpose, of those thought forms that have surfaced to the realm of inner speech.

[o]Now Swami Vignanananda, a yogi from south India with whom my wife and I worked closely for several years in Berkeley as both students and teachers of yoga.

Inner and Outer Speech

Whatever eventuates as a piece of writing can begin only as some fo-cusing on, narrowing of, tapping off of, and editing of that great ongoing inner panorama that William James dubbed the "stream of conscious-ness." What I will call here "inner speech" is a version of that stream which has been more verbally distilled and which can hence more directly serve as the wellspring of writing. We might ask someone suddenly to say what he is thinking and thereby learn the subject matter, the order or dis-order of the thoughts and images, and perhaps some aura or vein char-acterizing this material, but until asked to tell us, the person may not even have been aware of his stream and, even if aware, may not have put it into words. And the selection, wording, and emphasis with which he ver-balizes the material to us may not be the same as he did verbalize or would have verbalized it to himself. So we must understand "inner speech" as referring to an uncertain level of consciousness where material may not be so much verbalized as verbalizable, that is, at least potentially available to consciousness if some stimulus directs attention there, and potentially capable of being put into words because it is language-con-genial thought (discursive).

When James Joyce and other fiction writers have simulated stream of consciousness, verbalization often shifts or wavers between that of the persona and that of the author, between the literal realism of speech that is "in character" and the poetic realism of language that cleaves to a truth beneath words. The two samples here from *Ulysses* may illustrate how the literary technique of "interior monologue" plays in between stream of consciousness as distilled for oneself into inner speech and stream of con-sciousness that might, without an author's intervention, remain as sub-verbal imagery and feeling. Strolling near Trinity in Dublin, Leopold Bloom watches the great Parnell pass by talking to a woman at his side:

> Her stockings are loose over her ankles. I detest that: so tasteless. Those literary ethereal people they are all. Dreamy, cloudy, symbol-istic Esthetes they are. I wouldn't be surprised if it was that kind of food you see produces the like waves of the brain the poetical. For example one of those policemen sweating Irish stew into their shirts; you couldn't squeeze a line of poetry out of him. Don't know what poetry is even. Must be in a certain mood.
>
> The dreamy cloudy gull
> Waves o'er the waters dull.[1]

Now Stephen Dedalus, alone suddenly in the library:

> Coffined thoughts around me, in mummycases, embalmed in spice of

[1]James Joyce, *Ulysses* (New York: Random House, 1934), p. 163.

words. Thoth, god of libraries, a birdgod, moonycrowned. And I heard the voice of that Egyptian highpriest. *In painted chambers loaded with tilebooks.*

They are still. Once quick in the brains of men. Still: but an itch of death is in them, to tell me in my ear a maudlin tale, urge me to wreak their will.[2]

Inner speech distills not just *the* stream but a confluence of streams issuing from sensory receptors, memory, and a variety of more or less emotional or logical kinds of reflection. All the elements of this rich mixture trigger, interrupt, and reinforce each other. Sometimes they interplay rapidly, indicating perhaps that attention is free to skip more "randomly" or "spontaneously." Sometimes strong external influence or strong inner will sustains attention so steadily on one current that a clear continuity develops. Sword fighting, for example, holds consciousness to sensory information. An old person finished with striving may "dwell in the past," shutting out environmental stimulation and letting the memory current flow with little interruption—chronically, in some cases. Another person well into maturity may constantly see in everyday occurrences or news instances of generalizations that he is given to forging, so that reflection stands in high ratio to memories and sensations. A teenager may spend much time worrying about what will befall him in the future or making scenarios to help meet trying situations he is busy foreseeing. At any moment this heady stuff can be tapped off and converted to ink.

Clearly, numberless circumstances, inner and outer, determine what sort of mixture the stream consists of and hence what kind and qualities of discourse might ultimately be further distilled from the inner speech. Some of these circumstances are immediate, like what the person is doing at the moment, what his surroundings are, his mood, the state of his mind and organism, and so on. Other circumstances span a long time—personal traits, conditioning, habits, relations. Stephen's and Bloom's interior monologues are meant to contrast in this way, partly by holding time and place constant to some extent so that both react to the same external circumstances and thus differentiate character. Influences on the qualities of inner speech range then, in time, from immediate to long-term and, in space, from the most indwelling nature to the farthest-flung cultural and material environments.

If talking to oneself and hearing voices indicate insanity, then the whole culture is crazy. True, for most of us this does not happen "out loud," for we learned some time befor entering school that some things that come to the tongue you had jolly well better keep to yourself and let "come to mind" only. But the main reason the child splits off his ex-

[2]Ibid., p. 191.

ternal speech and shunts some of it inward to subvocalization or silent thought concerns not merely social disapproval but social irrelevance. What Piaget has called the "egocentric speech" of the small child comprises play prattle (often to objects), "task mediation" or guiding and planning talk accompanying an activity, self-reminders, and just a kind of rehearsing of verbal powers in the form of running observations cued by ongoing or surrounding stimuli. Speech that is egocentric does not distinguish speaker from listener or speaker from subject, in keeping with the general trend of cognitive development to begin in syncretism and move toward discrimination. As the child realizes that some speech is really for himself, he deflects it inward. Momentous indeed is this shift from thinking out loud to thinking silently, for the inner life that was constantly manifesting itself in external speech as well as action now becomes inaudible and invisible (expressive body action becoming more subdued also), so that henceforward we cannot regard the child as an open book but must expect him to manifest his mind by excerpting and editing his inner speech.

As fluency is confluency, so interior monologue is really interior dialogue. We can gain tremendous perception and perspective from regarding inner speech as colloquy among the individual's many personas—the roles, factions, viewpoints, and other divisions within himself and the culture he has incorporated. George Herbert Mead described some time ago with great justice this process of introjecting the "other" into one's inner life.[3] When the child shunts some of his outer speech inward, he is necessarily internalizing the voices of others whose language he or she learned.

The idea that most thinking, the discursive part, derives from internalized speech seems rather universally agreed on by specialists in cognition today, as shown by the enthusiasm of Piaget and Americans for the work of Lev Vygotsky and A. R. Luria, whose school has for decades insisted that the sociohistorical origins of thought have not been adequately emphasized.[4] Society peoples the head of the individual via speech, which is learned from and for others but in shifting inward merges with universal inborn logical faculties, biologically given, and with idiosyncratic penchants of mind to result in thinking that is at once personal and cultural. As Hans Furth reminds us from his work with the education of the deaf, not all thinking is verbal, and conceptual maturation may occur

---

[3]George Herbert Mead, "Self" in *On Social Psychology: Selected Papers,* ed. Anselm Strauss (Chicago: University of Chicago Press, 1964).

[4]First see Lev Vygotsky, *Thought and Language* (Cambridge, Mass.: The M.I.T. Press, 1962). Included in this volume is an insert, "Comments" by Jean Piaget, that gives Piaget's main views of inner speech, especially as related to Vygotsky's. Then see his *Mind and Society* (Cambridge, Mass.: Harvard University Press, 1978) and A. R. Luria, *Cognitive Development: Its Cultural and Social Foundations* (Cambridge, Mass.: Harvard University Press, 1976).

among people who cannot speak.[5] The Russian psycholinguists accept that thought and speech originate separately, but they play down the independence of innate mentation because they believe that human psychosocial evolution ("historical dialectic") determines individual thinking more than the biological givens.

Surely, we have here a serpent with its tail in its mouth: mind and society feed in and out of each other. Such biological givens as the faculties of analyzing and synthesizing can be neither given nor taken away by society, and idiosyncrasy asserts itself very powerfully not only among citizens sharing the same sociohistorical conditions but also among siblings sharing the same familial determinants.

Individuals influence history and language and are influenced by them. But the Russian emphasis does restore our balance and receives support not only from the too evident truth of McLuhan's (very Marxist) insight about technological shifts altering consciousness but also from recent findings about specialization of the brain hemispheres. This specialization into analytic and holistic does not occur in other mammals and occurs in humans only after around age seven, after inner speech has become established, that is, after the pristine thinking of the innate equipment has become thoroughly imbued with the culture's ways of perceiving and conceiving, embodied in the language and in the social relations in which it is learned. Joseph Chilton Pearce and others, including myself, believe that specialization of the hemispheres may occur to salvage holistic, nonverbal, metaphorical thinking from the heavy acculturation that makes the analytic dominate, even after the split, and that hits children at just about the time hemispheric specialization occurs (and when the notorious slump in school performance and attitude begins, toward the end of third grade).[6]

On the biological foundation, culture builds its own psychological structure, different from one epoch to another. Individuals are in a sense "bugged" by institutions, implanted with an invisible transmitter in the form of a discursive system that structures their own nervous system so that they are in some degree participating in group thinking whether they know it or not or like it or not. Language works by resonance, between sender and receiver, and this requires tuning all circuits to the same frequency. An insane person can no longer resonate with the society, but we note that the auditory hallucination so common to classic schizophrenia usually consists of hearing the voices of parents, God or the devil, or other authoritative voices from the near and far culture. Or to vary the comparison, it is as if acculturation hypnotizes us at the outset, when we are

[5]Hans Furth, *Thinking without Language: Phychological Implications of Deafness* (New York: Free Press, 1966).
[6]Joseph Chilton Pearce, *Exploring the Crack in the Cosmic Egg* (New York: Julian, 1974) and *The Magical Child* (New York: E. P. Dutton, 1977).

utterly open and undefensive, "suggests" by voice but by nonverbal means also that the world is so and so and not such and such, and thenceforward that is how we see and think about it. This is group hypnosis and, once built in, self-hypnosis—except to the extent that idiosyncrasy does indeed assert itself even to the point sometimes of affecting the very language and history that will in the future hypnotize subsequent generations.

Probably nothing is so important to education as this circularity of inner and outer speech, mind and society. By external speech, individuals communicate to each other, and by inner speech each informs himself. Aside from the broad matter of consonance or dissonance among individuals and between individuals and their shared institutions, this circularity of internal and external applies to other school activities such as listening, viewing, and reading, all of which entail wholesale introjection into one's stream of consciousness of someone else's stream. That is, in varying degree the auditor, viewer, or reader allows some interlocutor, performer, screen, or book to supplant his inner continuity with their or its own. Unless "entranced" or "spellbound" we probably never permit another to take over our consciousness completely, but pre-adolescent children are especially suggestible, and even much older people "lose themselves" in a book (if their ego is strong enough not to doubt regaining themselves). The effects of films and television may become clearer if we regard such programs as supplanting inner programs.

It may be helpful for teachers to regard listening or reading, say, as assimilating someone else's outer speech into one's ongoing inner speech, the effect being something like a garbled script or heavily annotated and superscribed text. Evidences of this hearing or reading may evince themselves minutes or years later when our receiver becomes sender in turn and synthesizes his own continuity for others to introject, naturally drawing on what he has heard and read along with other experience and his unique creativity. The circles keep turning over. People learn to talk and write by listening and reading as much as by anything else.

Educators need not feel that in staying especially mindful of the cultural inculcation of the individual, via such routes as the internalization of outer speech, they are subscribing to any school of psychology or political view. Growth means change, and educators have to concern themselves with the changeable aspects of people, which are not usually the biological givens but the cultural forces and, the individual willing, his idiosyncratic traits. Even to know if or how he wants to change, the individual has to be at least partly awakened from the hypnosis of acculturation. And education, finally, should foster human evolution. I am not interested in helping to teach young people to read just well enough to follow directions or write just well enough to take dictation.

Writing as Revised Inner Speech

However personal or impersonal the subject matter, *all* writing as authoring must be some revision of inner speech for a purpose and an audience. To say this is not at all to say that writing is solipsistic thinking about narcissistic content or even that it favors "personal experience." Because of the circularity just discussed, one's revised inner speech may reflect convention so much as to hardly bear a personal mark. "Off the top of the head," as we say. In Samuel Beckett's play *Waiting for Godot* a slavish character called Lucky gives a remarkable soliloquy that starts as a surface verbal stream full of stock stuff and familiar phrases straight out of ads and folk talk and official promulgations, then moves downward to poetic and original verbalization of the deeper self, à la Molly Bloom or Anna Livia Plurabelle. (Beckett was not Joyce's secretary for nothing.) I saw the Trinidad dancer, Geoffrey Holder, perform this soliloquy by dancing out this descent into the self at the same time he vocalized the deepening verbal stream, creating an unforgettable audio-visual emblem as he bucked and spluttered his way down through tensions into the grace of unconflicted fluency.

Egocentricity is merely a localization within the larger circles of ethnocentricity, biocentricity, and geocentricity that are concentric to it. This is why "subjectivity" is not so personal as it is usually made out to be and why it is not the only issue to consider in adapting inner speech to public communication. So much of the dullness, awkwardness, shallowness, and opacity that teachers object to in student writing owes to skimming along in the froth instead of plunging into the current, where intuition lines up with intelligence and particularities of experience correct for cliché. Seldom has anyone shown them how to work their way down, like Lucky. Most discourse in society today follows the now notorious circuit of the computer, "garbage in, garbage out." Something really significant has to happen inside—mediation by mind. If "output" differs from "input" mainly in being more amateurishly put together, then subjectivity has little meaning, and objectivity cannot be an authentic enough issue to be dealt with.

What really teaches composition—"putting together"—is disorder. Clarity and objectivity become learning challenges only when content and form are *not* given to the learner but when he must find and forge his own from his inchoate thought. Now, *that's* hard, not the glorified book-reporting or the filling in of instances to fit someone else's generalization (topic). All this traditional school and college writing only *looks* mature because it is laced with generalizations of a high abstraction level—quotations from the greats, current formulations of issues, and other ideas received from books or teachers. Such haste to score, to make a quick intellectual killing, merely retards learning, because those kids have not worked up those generalizations themselves. This short-circuits the natural circularity between thought and society, bypasses any true mediation by mind, and results in a simply more insidious form of inculcation, less honest than straight formula feeding because book criticism, research papers, and essay exams make students *appear* to be more the authors of the ideas than they really are. Consider too what a deceptive view this conveys to youngsters of both writing and themselves.

I invite the reader to think of writing not only as Lucky's descent into self but also as the ascent from chaos to cosmos. I certainly don't mean to equate the self with chaos, but the inner speech that boils off the self represents some sort of confused concoction of self and society, whereas through writing we may use composition to achieve composure.

A human being is literally *made to order* and will *make* sense of everything that comes into his ken, weird as his cosmology may look to another individual or another culture. The typifying trait of humankind is to "get his head together" even if his only symbolic medium for doing so is iconographic, and no matter how chaotic his environment. Once tool-using includes symbol-making, then people are naturally and necessarily creative in the practical if not esthetic sense. Writing throws out to society samples of the cosmology that any individual has to be making for himself all the time as an ongoing orientation to this world and an unceasingly updated guide for behavior. Writing is a further abstraction, via inner speech, of an involuntary abstracting that the individual engages in constantly for survival anyway. As micro-cosmos he reflects to some degree the cosmos of culture and the macro-cosmos of nature, but he is always in the process of converting chaos to cosmos—or perhaps of discovering the order concealed in apparent disorder—and the particular instance of this composition that we call writing partakes of this general ordering. Writing is an opportunity to find out who I am and what I am to do with my life.

Lest all this sound entirely *too* cosmic to the teacher mired in the pseudo-pragmatic routines of the conventional classroom, the movement from inner speech to the written product gets us into all those familiar alternatives of thought and language that writing teachers call organization, transition, sentence structure, and word choice, or thesis, illustration, and conclusion, but this approach from inner speech shifts the perspective of written composition back downward to where classification and generalization are being spontaneously, even involuntarily, generated and where instances are original; where theses, transitions, and conclusions to thinking chains are all occurring thick and fast (without being assigned) but remain *implicit*, perhaps still in mythic or metaphoric form. Making the implicit appropriately explicit may well be the chief task of writing. Teaching writing is teaching how to *manifest* thought into language, and this requires raising consciousness of all this spontaneous

and often unconscious cosmologizing to the point that it passes from verbalizable to verbalized. At the same time, the writer has to become conscious of how the verbalization now manifesting to himself needs to
evolve to that degree of explicitness that will make his ideas emerge
sharply for others. Also, working deeper in the sources leaves open alternatives about *mode* of discourse that teachers too often foreclose on because of the prejudice about "expository writing." Mythic, imagistic,
metaphorical writing does not say *less,* as the highest literary creations
show.

Private ways of verbalizing often reflected in rapid note-taking may
omit some parts of speech and much punctuation and let a few key words
or ideas stand for other unverbalized material that clusters around these
saliencies. This inchoate departure point for language use, far from encouraging muddy or solipsistic expression, serves as foil to bring out the
real utility of all the parts of speech, the kinds of punctuation, complete
sentences, and elaborated sentences, and all the resources of wide-ranging
word choice and careful phrasing. Taking-for-granted is the enemy in
this regard. Language usually comes across to youngsters as very arbitrary
indeed or as picayune "rules." Only when they have to keep adjusting
the language of their inner speech to accommodate actual audiences and
purposes do the real reasons for language being as it is become clear to
novice writers and the full resources of the language become available to
them.

People learn to write by practice in conceptualizing and practice in
conversing. If these are practiced copiously, realistically, and intelligently,
writing itself becomes mere writing down on paper, self-dictation. How
much a person actually has to practice with pen and paper depends on
how much prior work has gone on with conceptualizing and oral verbalizing. Speaking and writing differ considerably, not least in the opportunity that writing affords to look back over what one has put down, react
to it, and revise it. But revision starts much farther back in the inner life
as one recapitulates and reformulates experience, reviews and re-states it
in his own mind. *The inner speech that presents itself for revision into writing has
been much determined in advance by this continual rumination.* Teaching methodology has to be based on this continuity of thought into speech and
speech into writing. Progressive revisions at all stages mark this continuity; only *one* kind of revision occurs when someone revises his inner
speech as he dictates it to himself. Opportunities for good teaching exist
all along this continuity.

True, we learn to write by writing, by realistic practice of the target
activity itself, but writing must be construed to begin with self-convers-
ing and the outer conversing that feeds into it not only ideas and attitudes
but also vocabulary, sentence structure, and even organization too (consider, for example, the differences in structure between gossip, scolding,

interrogation, how-to-do-it directions, etc.). Writing must have continual holistic interplay of many activities over a span of years—of observing and data-gathering, individualized reading, discussion, composition in other media than verbal, and opportunities at any time to practice the whole range of forms of writing practiced in the world beyond school. The subject matter of student writing needs to be material not previously interpreted or abstracted by others—his or her own eyewitnessing, memories, interviews, experiments, feelings, reflections, and reactions to reading. But central is the process of *expatiation* that takes the interplay of inner voices back out into the social world, where the give-and-take of minds and voices can lift each member beyond where he or she started. This requires enormously more small-group interaction than schools now foster—task talk, improvisation, and topic discussion. This global, long-range, and in-depth approach to writing I have already dealt with extensively—as theory in *Teaching the Universe of Discourse*, as teaching methodology in *Student-Centered Language Arts and Reading, K–12*, and *Active Voice: A Writing Program Across the Curriculum*, and as school materials for students in *Interaction.*[7] To the extent that some teachers emphasize "oral-language development" and "pre-writing" and "integrated language arts," they are moving in this direction, but a rationale for teaching writing based on revision of inner speech would support such efforts at a time when schooling trends work against them.

Although I'm not one who believes that improved curriculum waits on further research findings, and in fact see this stand as often really a dodge or a stall, still certain especially germane research with learners may help teachers, I think. Encouraging, I find, are recent trends to look directly at what people do when they try to write—from elementary children (Donald Graves[8] and David Dirlam[9]) to secondary students (Janet Emig[10]) through college (Mina Shaughnessy,[11] Sondra Perl,[12] and Adela Karliner[13]) even to famous professional writers (as, for example, they talk

[7]James Moffett, *Teaching the Universe of Discourse* (Boston: Houghton Mifflin, 1968); James Moffett and Betty Jane Wagner, *Student-Centered Language Arts and Reading, K–12* (Boston: Houghton Mifflin, revised 1976); James Moffett, *Active Voice: A Writing Program Across the Curriculum*, Boynton/Cook Publishers, 1981; and James Moffett, senior author, *Interaction: A Student-Centered Language Arts and Reading Program* (Boston: Houghton Mifflin, 1973).
[8]Donald Graves, "An Examination of the Writing Process of Seven-Year-Old Children," *Research in the Teaching of English,* 9 (1975).
[9]David Dirlam, "The Changing Wisdoms in Children's Writing," unpublished talk delivered May 22, 1980, to the New York State Education Department Conference on Writing Education.
[10]Janet Emig, *The Composing Processes of Twelfth-Graders* (Urbana, Ill.: National Council of Teachers of English, 1971).
[11]Mina Shaughnessy, *Errors and Expectations: A Guide for Teachers of Basic Writing* (New York: Oxford University Press, 1977). She sets a good example of trying to account for the "errors" of student writing by getting into their minds and points of view as much as possible.
[12]Sondra Perl, "The Composing Processes of Unskilled College Writers," *Research in the Teaching of English,* December 1979.
[13]Suzanne E. Jacobs and Adela B. Karliner, "Helping Writers to Think: The Effect of Speech Roles in Individual Conferences on the Quality of Thought in Student Writing," *College English,* January 1977.

about their methods and habits to interviewers in the *Paris Review*). The research of James Britton and colleagues in Britain (now being replicated in Australia) complements this American research.[14] The work of Graves and Karliner may illustrate also a felicitous teaching method which, quite independently of each other, they call "conferencing" and which consists of mid-composition dialogue between a writer and a coach about what the writer is trying to say. Comparisons between transcripts of this supportively groping dialogue with final versions of the compositions demonstrate improvement over first efforts and show again the value of socializing inner speech during writing.

The concept of inner speech will both support and benefit from another relevant research trend called the "psychobiology of writing," because the very nature of inner speech brings together neurophysiological functioning, linguistic structuring of thought, and transitions between personal and social expression. This includes much brain research, most outside the field of education, like the classic work of Wilder Penfield[15] and successors, and some that has moved from outside into education, like that with the hemispherical specialization of the brain[16] as well as the kind of psycholinguistic research that Courtney Cazden[17] summarizes for educators. For too long we have ransacked linguistic, rhetorical, and literary theory for paradigms or even just clues to the teaching of writing, but foremost we should look to the functioning of the human organism. To view writing as revision of inner speech is to see more clearly the way to go in both teaching methods and research procedures and to make this way reciprocal.

Some other advantages of teaching writing from inner speech regard therapy, art, and general self-development. The processes of psychotherapy and of writing both require maximum availability of information from all internal and external sources and maximum synthesizing of this firsthand and secondhand knowledge into a full, harmonious expression of individual experience. This calls for the removal of spells to which the person has not agreed and of which he is unconscious. Freud asked the patient to start talking about anything and just keep uttering as fluently, fully, and spontaneously as possible everything that came into his head— in other words, to attempt to verbalize aloud his stream of consciousness or externalize his inner speech. This technique presupposes that from the apparent chaos of all this disjointed rambling will emerge for analyst and patient an order, eventually "betrayed" by motifs, by sequencing, by

[14]J. Britton, T. Burgess, N. Martin, A. McLeod, and H. Rosen, *The Development of Writing Abilities, 11–18* (New York: Macmillan, 1975).
[15]Wilder Penfield, *The Mystery of the Mind: A Critical Study of Consciousness and the Human Brain* (Princeton, N.J.: Princeton University Press, 1975).
[16]A good account for the layman of hemispherical specialization is Howard Gardner, *The Shattered Mind* (New York: Alfred Knopf, 1975).
[17]Courtney Cazden, *Child Language and Education* (New York: Holt, Rinehart and Winston, 1972).

gradual filling in of the personal cosmology. Thus, if successful, the subject's cosmologizing processes, the idiosyncratic ways of structuring and symbolizing experience, stand more clearly revealed and presumably more amenable to deliberate change, if desired. The most important thing a writer needs to know is how he himself does think and verbalize and how he might.

Both writing and psychoanalytic procedure work with discourse to mediate between mind and society, considering society as introjected into the mind of a self that must in turn accommodate itself to that society while keeping its own integrity. More specifically, both tap inner speech to further the individual's dual goals of knowing himself and communicating with others. Regarding method, the critical parallel is that set and setting make enormous practical difference in the effectiveness with which the subject succeeds in getting command over inner speech. Just as the analyst's approach influences strongly what and how the patient will think when he free-associates (they say Jungian patients even start obediently dreaming mandalas), so the way a teacher "sets up the assignment" will influence crucially the focus, level, and selectivity of the student's inner speech. In fact, since writing will be some revision of inner speech, however the teacher conceives composition, it is wiser to create a set and setting that will acknowledge this at the outset and make it work best.

Not for a moment do I suggest that the teacher play psychiatrist. The therapeutic benefits from writing are natural fallout and nothing for a school teacher to strive for. They inhere in the very parallelism described here. Good therapy and composition aim at clear thinking, effective relating, and satisfying self-expression. Precisely because it is not thought of as therapy and works toward another goal, writing can effect fine therapy sometimes. At any rate, self-awareness is the means in both cases, and this requires focusing attention on one's inner speech.

Artful simulation of inner speech occurs much more in literature than merely as a rare technique of modern fiction. In fact, prose interior monologue comes as a late representation of it. As stage soliloquy, it was a mainstay of Greek and Elizabethan drama. Classical Greek theater arrayed beautifully, as a matter of fact, the whole range of vocalization—from inner and outer monologue to staccato dialogue to the chorus, thus uttering individual inner life, exposition, interplay of personality types, and communal attitudes, the whole cycle of personal and social minds. The soliloquy endures today in the one stage convention of modern times that permits anything so "unrealistic" as voicing thoughts aloud to an audience—the musical, where song is the medium for self-verbalization ("If I Were a Rich Man," for example, from *Fiddler on the Roof*).

Song connects drama to the other great literary tradition of artful inner speech, which we find in much lyric poetry of both yesterday and to day, such as Keats's "Ode to a Nightingale" and T. S. Eliot's "The Love Song of J. Alfred Prufrock." (Note the titles, incidentally.) Although not so specific as to time, place, and character as Robert Browning's "Soliloquy of a Spanish Cloister," a considerable amount of lyric poetry sustains the outpouring of some soul whose setting and persona simply remain unstated and may or may not be those of the poet. The soul sings itself. This is why the more directly that literature gives it voice, the more lyrical—poetic and musical—becomes the language. Even prose writers like Joyce, Faulkner, and Virginia Woolf moved their language more into poetry the more they simulated inner speech. Joyce's final work, *Finnegan's Wake*, became one long polyglot poem as he attempted to give voice not merely to one person's stream of consciousness but to the race's collective unconscious. Perhaps the use of the aria for soliloquy in opera epitomizes this artful soul vocalization, bringing together as it does drama, poetry, and music.

The literature of inner speech can provide a powerful connection between what students read and what they write. I don't advocate "model writing" if that means fairly close imitation. This connection can, for the most part, operate implicitly. Let's say that, in a general way, as students are learning to capture their inner speech either by jotting down or by speaking spontaneously with partners (perhaps taping), and learning to work this material up for different audiences and purposes, they are also experiencing prose, poetry, drama, and song that simulate inner speech and make an art form of it. Much of this literature, interestingly enough, either was written for performance or readily lends itself to performance. This is so because inner speech moves, like the performing arts, moment by moment in time, so that, if "transcribed," it naturally becomes a script. So students can come to know this literature via a variety of means and media—silent reading, sight reading aloud with partners, giving a rehearsed reading, witnessing a performance live, listening to a recording of the text, or viewing a film or television performance. Thus a literature that might seem less accessible, because inner, turns out, in fact, to be very accessible indeed because inherently dramatic, performable.

This literature of inner speech will accomplish several very valuable services for students. In the first place, it validates this approach to writing at the same time it shows what to do with it. Through the literature closest to the chaos of "random subjectivity," it triumphs as public communication. Partly, it turns to advantage its apparent drawbacks—subjectivity and the moment-to-moment randomness. If the writer grasps the patterns of his own inner life well enough, chances are he will strike responsive chords in others, because patterns abstract experiences to a point where others can share. As shared medium, language makes this easier. And the moment-to-moment movement in time gives drama, vitality, freshness, and novelty of detail. This literature, then, demonstrates for students in a lively way just what teachers would like to help their students learn—to revise inner speech into successful communication. The key is the artfulness, just what the undeveloped or naive learner lacks most, the knacks and skills, the profound tricks of the trade. This literature virtually *enacts* for students, before their very eyes, the process the teacher engages them in. It is unnecessary and unwise to point to strokes of genius and say, "That's what I want you to do too!" Immersion works best. Let them steep in this literature, and they will intuit technique. We are not trying to make little literati—in this respect the chips can fall where they may—but we are, rather, putting to work for us the best teacher in these matters, art. Trust it. Art is, after all, another version of composition, because both are cosmologizing, ordering.

Reciprocally, working at the art of converting one's own inner speech sensitizes students to literary techniques and textures as direct efforts to induce "literary appreciation" (postmortems and vivisections) never can do. For students unused to acknowledging and thinking about inner speech I recommend dealing with it first by improvising a skit in which a made-up character imagined in a definite setting and activity says aloud what he or she is thinking. Since this reverts to familiar play prattle, no one ever finds this activity strange.To get from vocal speech to paper, students can then either tape and transcribe their own improvised soliloquies or make up new ones on paper in the first place, that is, write down as a kind of script what their character is thinking. A further step at some point is to shift from an imaginary character to oneself and simply write down everything that comes into one's head for a certain length of time.

In revising their self-dictations, students should be reminded that these revisions may take any direction, not only toward drama, poetry, song, or prose but more specific directions within any of these toward lyricism, narrative, or reflection. Seeing these options becomes a real possibility when students start with the matrix itself from which stem all the adult examples they encounter. To see options as a writer facilitates enormously the appreciating of options made by the writers of the works one reads. Role playing the professional is the best way to understand what the professional is doing . . . and to learn his art. The proper relation between literature and composition is not for students to write about the reading but for them to make their own literature and read that of others as a fellow practitioner, however humble the state of their own art at the moment. Such a writing reader more readily attunes to tone, makes out the main point, differentiates voices and styles, follows threads of story or argument, and perceives motifs and patterns.

Most of all, keeping inner speech as the matrix of all writing keeps teaching of writing centered on authentic authorship, so that all these other benefits of writing accrue to the novice as well as to the professional. The novice needs, after all, not fewer but more kinds of motivation.

The student needs to enjoy and value the benefits of self-expression, communication, therapy, and art. The more evident are all these benefits the more easily can learners muster the strength it takes to stick at practice. Writing can be hard work, and until someone does enough of it to find for himself how well it pays off, he needs every enriching connection possible. Too specialized and isolated, writing becomes deadly indeed. Teachers would do well to situate it in those multiple contexts it deserves—of other arts and media, of related investigative disciplines, and of practical self-healing and self-development. The very complexity of writing invites and facilitates the exploitation of these numerous organic connections. Although not easy, this is easier than trying to teach writing within self-defeating conventions not derived from actual learning processes.

Finally, let me crystallize what I may merely have implied so far, that writing does not merely convey what one thinks, it shows what one *is* thinking and even helps to discover what, further, one *might be* thinking. That is, *if* practiced as real authoring, not disguised playback, writing *discovers* as much as it communicates, and this basic benefit must ever be held out and made clear to students. Writing is hauling in a long line from the depths to find out what things are strung on it. Sustained attention to inner speech reveals ideas one did not know one thought, unsuspected connections that illuminate both oneself and the outside objects of one's thought. No better motivation exists, because young people do want to find out what they and the world are like. But only if we construe writing at its maximum meaning will the discovery aspect of it become real for students. Instead of using writing to test other subjects, we can elevate it to where it will *teach* other subjects, for in *making sense* the writer is *making knowledge.* Certainly I'm not alone in arguing that writing should appear to students as a serious learning method itself to discover things about external subjects as well as oneself. Paradoxically, writing does not become an instrument of investigation and discovery of external things until it is acknowledged to be grounded in inner speech, because only when the individual brings some consciousness to the monitoring of the stream of experience does he start to become the master instead of the dupe of that awesome symbolic apparatus that, ill or well, creates his cosmos.

I want now to go beyond *discovery* of one's own mind to *control* of one's own mind, a much less familiar kind of learning that bears special affinity to writing but that will take us into another mental dimension.

Meditation as Control of Inner Speech

It's best to head off at the outset the common notion that meditation comes from another culture, that it is a practice only of strange and dangerous cults, or that it inculcates a particular religious doctrine. Meditation has always been and never ceased to be practiced in Western culture.

All cultures of all times, in fact, have included some forms of it. Though often connected with religions, meditation presupposes such serious intention and self-discipline that it has tended to thrive more outside the church than in, or, if in the church, in special groups well advanced beyond the mass membership. That is, spiritual discipline intended to alter consciousness was too much for most people, even in the ancient world, well before the rise of materialism. Thus each religion spun off an outrider group that became the custodian of the purest spiritual discipline—for Vedanta and Hinduism, yoga; for Mohammedanism, Sufism; for Buddhism, Zen; for Amerindians, shamanism; and for Christianity, the Gnostics, certain early Church Fathers, whose tradition survived in Eastern Orthodox Christianity, and some medieval mystics. When Christ went into the wilderness to fast and meditate, as the Gospel relates, he was following ancient spiritual traditions that from all evidence seem to reach back to the Indus, Tigris/Euphrates, and Nile valleys, "pooling" in the Mediterranean/Balkan basins, and maybe even to stem from an earlier common source.

The modern meaning of meditate—"to turn over in the mind, reflect on"—represents a much more cerebral version of former practices, an idea of which we can gain from the etymology of the word. The Latin *meditari* crosses the words "to heal" in *medicari* and *mederi* via the Indo-European root *med-*, "measure, consider, reflect," and perhaps also in the Avestan (ancient Persian) word *vi-mad*, healer. The shaman and medicine man are one and the same. The association of meditation with healing is truly universal, however, and no doubt expressed what we call today psychosomatic medicine or holistic healing.

It seems clear that the meaning of meditation has changed as our culture has shifted to an emphasis on the new-brain, left-hemisphere, literate, technical, abstract modes of knowing. Consider this reference in Psalm XIX, 14: "Let the words of my mouth and the meditation of my heart be acceptable in Thy sight." This idea that the heart, not the head, is the chief organ of knowledge has been cheapened in modern romanticism but is another serious cross-cultural belief from ancient times, ruling as strongly in yogic emphasis on waking the heart chakra (cardiac plexus or energy center) as in the Christian tradition of the "sacred heart." The Tibetan Rinpoche Thartang Tulkhu once said at a meditation workshop that "Meditation is non-conceptualization," that is, a bypassing of the whole cultural system for filtering reality based on logic and language.[18] My own yoga teacher, Swami Sivalingam, once said it was relaxation, by which he meant a total release of both muscles and thoughts right down practically to the cellular level of functioning.[19]

[18]Founder and head lhama of the Nyingma Tibetan Meditation Center in Berkeley, Ca., and author of many books published there.
[19]See fn. p. 90.

Surely, central to any definition of meditation as a spiritual practice would be some notion of transcending intellectual knowledge, which by itself will indeed proceed on the basis, as John Locke stated for the modern age, that "nothing is in the mind that was not in the senses." Sensory experience and hence memory provide grist for the intellectual mill to recombine by ratiocination into inferences. If intellect is the only source of knowledge, then Locke is right, as our epoch of culture tends to assume, although it somehow allows for, without understanding it, the role of intuition, usually chalked off (unscientifically!) to some swifter intellectual shortcutting. But the "higher knowledge" at which meditation aims, although no doubt related to our notion of intuition, cannot be merely relegated to the right hemisphere as just the way the (currently) nondominant half of our head works. It may well depend on unusual collaboration and harmonization of the two hemispheres, as scientific research with the electroencephalograms of meditators today is indicating,[20] but other universal traditions associate higher knowledge with the pineal gland, recently also become an object of serious scientific study,[21] taking us back to Descartes's belief that the pineal gland was the seat of the soul, but far before him to his own source in both the West and the East, according to which advanced meditation awakens dormant power in the pineal gland and opens connections between it, the pituitary gland, and cosmic energy or intelligence. All this suggests that deep meditation causes some "re-wiring" of the neurophysiological circuits and not merely loading up more heavily the existing circuits as conventional education tends to do.

The variety we are confronted with today represents not only alternative techniques preferred by individuals or cultures but also a gradation in depth owing to historical changes. Accordingly, meditation varies all the way from highly focused discursive reflection, close to the current meaning of the word, to rare mystic experiences of ecstasy ("being outside" oneself), but at this upper reach, meditation crosses over into what is called "contemplation." The meaning of *contemplari* was to gaze attentively, to observe (in both senses), but the literal meaning underlying this was, astonishingly, "to mark out an inaugural temple, "to set aside a place for religious observance or initiation, and, of course, the word "temple" for the sides of the head derives from the same source as the temple of contemplation!

But all these allusions to etymology and anatomy, useful as a suggestive framework for definition, cannot make clear the central notions of meditation so well as an account of some of the practices themselves,

---

[20]The *Brain/Mind Bulletin* of January 16, 1978, summarized such research by a team in Switzerland led by David Orme-Johnson and reported at the Ninth Annual Conference of Electroencephalography and Clinical Neurophysiology at Amsterdam.
[21]*The Pineal*, a research annual, Eden Medical Research, Inc., St. Albans, Vermont.

which will also move us closer to the reconsideration of writing method-ology. My own practical definition of meditation states it as some control of inner speech ranging from merely *watching* it to *focusing* it to *suspending* it altogether. This range of meditative techniques suggests a rough devel-opmental sequence of teaching methods relevant to writing. It starts in the pre-verbal and ends in the post-verbal and runs from uncontrolled to controlled mind.

Researchers at Harvard's Preschool Project reported that the children they observed whom adults described later, in school, as the "brightest, happiest, and most charming" had spent as much as 20 percent of their preschool time "staring" with absorption at some object or another, the largest amount of time the children had allotted to any single activity.[22] "Staring" is the small child's meditation and a chief way he or she learns. This affords direct knowledge, not yet mediated by discourse, and should be encouraged in school. Many bright thinkers and writers don't talk much in the early years but pay such rapt attention that when they do start talking they have a lot to say and know how to say it well. (Recall the etymological connection between gazing and contemplation.) Al-though it is wise, as we have claimed, to gain awareness of inner speech once it flourishes in oneself, it is unwise to push verbalization the way commercial greenhouses force growth in plants they are readying for the market: you can get a lot of blossoms fast for a short while, but the plant itself weakens and seldom if ever blooms again. The spontaneous gazing of the preschool years can easily continue as a pleasant school activity if children are furnished with engaging materials and encouraged to get deep into them individually, as some Montessori schools do. Besides coming to know things deeply this way, children may also want to gaze at simple positive images such as a star or candle flame.

For this and the following techniques a quiet location and a comfort-able sitting position are essential. Although some Christian meditations stipulate kneeling, standing, or even walking, and the Tibetan Buddhist Chogyam Trungpa speaks of "meditation in action,"[23] most techniques require, certainly for the beginner, maximum quiet in the environment and stillness of the meditator. Sitting cross-legged on the floor or sitting on a chair (preferably without touching the back of the chair), one keeps the spine erect but not stiff, releases muscles, and slows and deepens breathing. The key to meditation is a *relaxed body* and an *alert awareness*.

A variation of gazing is visualization. The meditator closes his eyes and transfers the image inward to the middle of the forehead. Alternately gazing outward and visualizing inward teaches one to develop inner at-tention and imagination without forcing verbalization. Other pure visu-alization meditations can follow. Staying focused either in or out frees the

[22]Reported in Burton White, *The First Three Years of Life* (Englewood Cliffs, N.J.: Prentice Hall, 1975).
[23]Chogyam Trungpa, *Meditation in Action* (Berkeley, Ca.: Shambala Publications, 1969).

meditator a while from the excitations of the environment and lets him or her feel the strength of the self, the deeper self that abides at least somewhat independently of the outside. Writing presupposes just such inner strength. A writer of whatever age has to feel full of himself and have a degree of confidence, belief that he has something to say, faith in his will, and control of his attention. Gazing and visualizing, finally, develop *vision*—seeing and perceiving in both outer and inner ways prerequisite for writing. These first meditation techniques should help develop selfhood, control, and perception. From here on the techniques run from most discursive to least discursive.

The next simplest and easiest meditation technique consists of letting inner speech flow spontaneously but of *witnessing* it. Instead of floating along on this stream and being borne away from the center of the self, one sits on the bank, so to speak, and watches it flow by, staying separate from it, not trying to influence it, but above all not being "carried away" by it. The meditator centers within his inner sanctum, and focuses attention on the meditation object—in this case, his trains of thoughts. He watches and notes what flows by, as if he were a spectator at someone else's presentation, at a movie, and thus gains new knowledge of his thoughts and detachment from them.

Most of us most of the time do not know what is going on in our minds. The ancient dictum "know thyself" surely meant "know your own mind and the evanescent fluctuations of your temporal existence" as well as "know that thou art divine, despite these evanescent fluctuations." "Know your unconscious," says the psychoanalyst, eliciting the patient's inner speech until this speaker begins truly to hear himself—until both become aware of this incessant inner haranguing and dialoguing and detect the patterns and meaning of it. Swami Sivalingam constantly reminds his students to "watch your mind," in or out of meditation, and says "writing teaches you to watch your thoughts." This is in line with both Eastern traditions of "mindfulness" in keeping constant disciplined attention on the moment and Western traditions of "raising consciousness."

The "summoning" of thoughts about a subject that comes while writing depends on much prior awareness of thoughts that occur in inner speech when one is not writing. To appreciate the value of this mind-witnessing technique, you have to realize how much people normally think without knowing it and consequently how much of their thought they do not have access to at other times for writing or for any other purpose, although these thoughts are unconsciously influencing their behavior. It's important to distinguish the self-consciousness that this technique induces from the awkward self-entanglement associated with young people growing into and through adolescence. The latter sort of self-consciousness comes from unevenness of growth, unsureness of identity and role, and acute concern about how *others* view oneself. Such confusion, in fact, naturally makes clear thinking harder, and posturing is a common resort, on or off paper. Witnessing will actually heal this sort of self-consciousness the homeopathic way, by redirecting it so that another form of the symptom cures the symptom. Periodically settling down and collecting oneself helps to center and balance the inner life while the insights gained from witnessing clarify problems and suggest how best to handle them.

The following techniques require and also develop increasing control of inner speech. Once able to still himself, turn inward, and witness his thoughts, the meditator may deliberately attempt to narrow down and focus his inner speech, to exert some control over it. Will comes more into play. Now, even to observe is to alter, so maintaining the witness distance and not getting "lost in thought" already assert some influence no doubt on the direction and content of inner speech. The present step consists, however, of setting a subject, holding the mind to it without distraction, focusing on it with special intensity, and developing it to an understanding not achievable by ordinary, relatively wayward reflection.

But this focusing differs from just intellectual concentration by a factor that only the most sensitive and original school teachers would ever allow for—the *state of consciousness* in which the meditator beams the topic. Passion, memory, imagination converge with intellect and intuition like rays of different colors coming together to create white light. Drawing on every faculty at once in a kind of all-out effort to penetrate the topic permits reinforcement effects like radiations from variant sources fitting their wave lengths and amplitudes together to make a super ray. Success owes much to set (mental and circumstantial) and setting (physical body and surroundings), to what we might call the assignment conditions. And success evinces itself not just as new ideas but as a more pervasive alteration of the meditator's inner and outer life, this global effect being the real goal rather than an intellectual breakthrough for its own sake.

Orthodox Buddhism and Christianity both have set forth in texts and teachings their methods for this very discursive sort of meditation and the themes they deem appropriate to focus on. Buddhist texts list, for example, such prescribed subjects as the four elements of earth, fire, air, and water; virtues or "stations of Brahma" such as compassion, friendliness, and evenmindedness; "repulsive things" such as skeletons and corpses in various states; and "formless states" of endless space, unlimited consciousness, and nothingness.[24] The death's head or "memento mori" has of course been a widespread Christian meditation object, the reminder of death or mortality, as sometimes depicted in medieval and Renaissance art. In both traditions the purpose may be to break attachment to the body, counter our belief in physical reality, and induce a deeper perspec-

---

[24]These themes are drawn from Edward Conze, *Buddhist Meditation* (London: George Allen and Unwin, 1956).

tive in which the invisible nature and purpose of human existence can be grasped. Meditating on one's greatest temptation—sex or wealth or power—has the goal of thinking it to death. The meditator may follow specific directions to break down the temptation into parts or aspects, break these down in turn, and thus proceed literally to "analyze the subject to pieces." If successful, the meditator should release himself from this temptation.

In contrast to this use of the destructive potentialities of discourse, some topical meditation is devotional and uses thought trains to lead into a beatific or compassionate state transcending the usual egoistic viewpoint with its limited personal feelings. Christians draw their subjects mostly from the life or sayings of Christ and meditate on one until it reaches its fullest meaning or until this focal intensity elevates feeling to finer levels. Church sermons often try to set a meditation example in how to discourse on a "text." Holding the mind to positive or transcendental topics or objects becomes a way of regulating state of mind and mood, or, as we say today, of altering the state of consciousness, in a beneficial way. Inasmuch as discursive meditation consists of a given subject and a stipulated procedure for focusing inner speech on that subject, it offers a remarkable analogy to school composition assignments, which we call, significantly, "themes," the same term by which church manuals commonly referred to meditation subjects.

Providing a splendid historical parallel between meditation and composition, Louis Martz developed during the 1950s the thesis that the traits our century came to recognize and admire in the so-called "metaphysical poets" of the seventeenth century derived rather directly from very popular meditation practices initiated by Saint Ignatius Loyola, spread by the Jesuits as part of the Counter-Reformation, and taken to heart by these poets. This Jesuitical meditation may best represent what I am calling discursive meditation, the sort most obviously related to writing as a finished product.

At the start of his exposition of this thesis in *The Poetry of Meditation*, Martz quotes Yeats and then summarizes his argument:

> Such thought—such thought have I that hold it tight
> Till meditation master all its parts,
> Nothing can stay my glance
> Until that glance run in the world's despite
>
> To where the damned have howled away their hearts,
> And where the blessed dance;
> Such thought, that in it bound
> I need no other thing,
> Wound in mind's wandering
> As mummies in the mummy-cloth are wound.

> —William Butler Yeats, "Oxford, Autumn 1920"

"Day after day I have sat in my chair turning a symbol over in my mind, exploring all its details, defining and again defining its elements, testing my convictions and those of others by its unity, attempting to substitute particulars for an abstraction like that of algebra."

Such meditation is the subject of this study: intense, imaginative meditation that brings together the senses, the emotions, and the intellectual faculties of man; brings them together in a moment of dramatic, creative experience. One period when such meditation flourished coincides exactly with the flourishing of English religious poetry in the seventeenth century. There is, I believe, much more than mere coincidence here, for the qualities developed by the "art of meditation" (as Joseph Hall described it) are essentially the qualities that the twentieth century has admired in Donne, or Herbert, or Marvell. Those qualities, some thirty years ago, received their classic definition in the introduction to Grierson's anthology, *Metaphysical Lyrics and Poems,* and in Eliot's essay inspired by that volume. Developed in a series of influential books issued during the 1930s, the definition views Donne as the master and father of a new kind of English poetry, with these distinguishing marks: an acute self-consciousness that shows itself in minute analysis of moods and motives; a conversational tone and accent, expressed in language that is "as a rule simple and pure"; highly unconventional imagery, including the whole range of human experience, from theology to the commonest details of bed and board; an "intellectual, argumentative evolution" within each poem, a "strain of passionate paradoxical reasoning which knits the first line to the last" and which often results in "the elaboration of a figure of speech to the farthest stage to which ingenuity can carry it"; above all, including all, that "unification of sensibility" which could achieve "a direct sensuous apprehension of thought, or a recreation of thought into feeling," and made it possible for Donne to feel his thought "as immediately as the odour of a rose. . . ."

The "metaphysical poets" may be seen, not as Donne and his school, but as a group of writers, widely different in temper and outlook, drawn together by resemblances that result, basically, from the common practice of certain methods of religious meditation. (W. B. Yeats, *A Vision* [New York, Macmillan, 1938], p. 301; T. S. Eliot, "The Metaphysical Poets," *Selected Essays, 1917–1932* [New York, Harcourt Brace, 1932], pp. 242, 245–248. *Metaphysical Lyrics and Poems of the Seventeenth Century,* ed. Herbert J. C. Grierson [Oxford, Clarendon Press, 1921], p. xxxiv.)[25]

The Jesuitical meditation structure that Martz says accounts for these traits of the poetry comprised (1) a prelude called the "composition of

[25]Louis Martz, *The Poetry of Meditation* (New Haven: Yale University Press, 1954), pp. 1–2.

place," (2) a point-by-point analysis of the subject, and (3) a concluding "colloquy." Sometimes more preliminaries were recommended, and sometimes the number of analytic points or colloquies might be five, say, instead of three, but the main format was this trinity.[26] During the famous "composition of place" or "seeing the spot" the meditator tried to create as vividly as possible in his mind some scene or situation such as an incident from the life of Christ, the Judgment Day, the agonies of Hell, the miseries of his own life, the hour of death, or the glory and felicity of the kingdom of heaven. On this spot he brought to bear all the powers of his memory, imagination, and intelligence, to fill out the scene in fullest sensory detail and make it as real as if he were either there or it existed in him. An important specific suggestion of the manuals was to employ "similitudes" of various sorts to enable the meditator to feel the reality of the conjured moment and to relate it to his familiar world. Within this mental stage setting, virtually a controlled hallucination, the intellect made several distinct points by analyzing the scene or situation into components, aspects, causes, effects, and so on. Such points, stimulated by the dramatic and graphic intensity of "seeing the spot," not only deepened the meditator's spiritual understanding but brought on in turn a swelling of "affections" or feeling, a shift from head to heart, that the "colloquies" expressed. These seem to have been not so much dialogue as direct address or petition from the meditator to God, some other spirit or figure, other earthly creatures such as animals, or his own soul or self. In poetic rhetoric the equivalent, I assume, would be called "apostrophe." It was "familiar talke," as St. François de Sales called it, "colloquial," as we would say today.

Preliminaries included "premeditation," often the night before morning meditation, and prayers or petitions between the composition of place and the analysis. Like the Buddhist texts, the manuals enumerated appropriate topics, gave examples of meditations on these topics, and set forth the sequence of steps forming the structure of the whole meditation, frequently encouraging the meditator, however, to depart when spontaneity seemed right. No clear distinction was made between prayer and meditation, and the whole procedure was called "mental prayer" as well as "meditation." Finally, each of the three main steps corresponds to a human faculty and to a person of the Holy Trinity. "The minde is the image of God, in which are these three things, Memory, Understanding, and Will or Love. . . . By Memory, wee are like to the Father, by Understanding to the Sonne, by Will to the Holy Ghost."[27]

Martz relates both the general structure and specific traits of Jesuitical meditation to those of metaphysical poetry. He does not claim, however,

---

[26]Martz included as an appendix to his *The Meditative Poem: An Anthology of 17th Century Verse,* a typical manual of the time, Edward Dawson's "The Practical Methode of Meditation," 1614.

[27]*The Poetry of Meditation,* p. 36.

that the triune structure as an entirety informs more than a few of the poems, but rather that parts of the structure occur in many of the poems and that the typical traits singled out by Grierson and Eliot can be recognized as features of one or another of the three stages. The dramatic scenic openings, for example, for which metaphysical poetry is famous, the sudden, graphic beginnings, were generated, he says, from the poet's experience with the "composition of place, seeing the spot." The imagery drawn from commonplaces of everyday life as well as the daring comparisons, sometimes attenuated into "conceits," arose from this composition when accomplished by "similitude." The wit, the "passionate paradoxical reasoning," the "intellectual, argumentative evolution" derive from the middle, analytic section of the meditation *as set in motion by the graphic opening focus and the similitudes.* And the "colloquy" inspired the characteristic lapses into familiar address, simple and colloquial lines, conversational tone. One has simply to recall well-known poems of Donne or Herbert not only to see the more obvious thematic connections between the meditation and the poetry of the period but also to feel the truth of the thesis that as a mode of discourse the composition of Jesuitical meditations strongly influenced the composition of "metaphysical" poetry. The opening sestet of a holy sonnet by Donne:

> What if this present were the world's last night?
> Mark in my heart, O soul, where thou dost dwell,
> The picture of Christ crucified, and tell
> Whether his countenance can thee affright:
> Tears in his eyes quench the amazing light,
> Blood fills his frowns, which from his pierced head fell.

The "theme" here is both Judgment Day and the Crucifixion. The scene-setting for this meditation is graphically fixed before the mind. Then the argumentative octet, addressed to the soul in a kind of colloquy:

> And can that tongue adjudge thee unto hell,
> Which prayed forgiveness for his foes' fierce spite?
> No, no; but as in my idolatry
> I said to all my profane mistresses,
> Beauty, of pity, foulness only is
> A sign of rigor; so I say to thee:
> To wicked spirits are horrid shapes assigned;
> This beauteous form assumes a piteous mind.

The argument is that as beauty signifies only pity, and foulness only rigor, so the beauteous form of Christ can mean only that the poet-meditator will be forgiven.

Donne's "Good Friday, 1613, Riding Westward" opens with a developed "similitude" that makes concrete the rather abstract subject, in accordance with meditation procedure when the focus is not on a clear scene or incident. Then Donne does settle on the image of himself journeying away from the scene of the crucifixion:

> Let man's soul be a sphere, and then in this
> The intelligence that moves, devotion is;
> And as the other spheres, by being grown
> Subject to foreign motion, lose their own,
> And being by others hurried every day
> Scarce in a year their natural form obey,
> Pleasure or business, so, our souls admit
> For their first mover, and are whirled by it.
> Hence is't that I am carried towards the west
> This day, when my soul's form bends towards the east.

Herbert's "Discipline" opens with a colloquy, which often was shifted around even in the meditations themselves:

> Throw away thy rod,
> Throw away thy wrath.
>   Oh my God,
> Take the gentle path.

He opens "The Collar" abruptly and dramatically with a moment of rebellion from his own life:

> I struck the board and cried, No more!
>   I will abroad.
> What? Shall I ever sigh and pine?
> My lines and life are free, free as the road. . . .

And closes, also in conversational style, but in colloquy with God, not himself:

> But as I raved and grew more fierce and wild
>   At every word,
> Me thoughts I heard one calling, Child!
>   And I replied, My Lord.

Martz's argument may be most true for the example he cites who is both Jesuit and poet, Robert Southey, but who also wrote the least poetically. And Martz acknowledges that Renaissance meditation itself derived in turn at least partly from classical logic and rhetoric. Still, even all these ins and outs of inner and outer speech turning over into each other—treatises of classical rhetoric and logic, oral public sermons, manuals of meditation procedures influencing the inner speech of individuals at private devotionals, and these private thought practices returning outward as they influence the ways of writing poetry—all this relates germanely to teaching writing. We have here in Martz's demonstration a relatively clear instance from history of efforts to control inner speech affecting writing. The fact that meditation had another goal than improving writing need not detract from the utility of applying meditation techniques to teaching it. And indeed, is the goal of writing so different from that of meditation?

The metaphysical poets had, like all serious writers, given themselves their own kind of composition course, drawing on those discursive paradigms from society that meant most to them. It was natural. Their utilization of current meditation practices to direct and organize their personal thoughts shows but another way that the individual may internalize outer speech into inner, society into mind. (Part of *Ulysses* is narrated in the question-and-answer form of catechism.) What did writers of other cultures utilize as paradigms for controlling inner speech? Did, for example, the initiation rites and teachings of the Eleusinian, Orphic, Brahmanic, and Odinic "mysteries" exert a comparable influence on the thinking and writing of their time? Manly Hall says that world mythologies are allegories of steps in these rites.[28] What rites and routines today are influencing how writers compose?

I can look upon this historical example as both negative and positive for the teaching of writing. For Donnes, Herberts, Vaughns, and Crashaws, it's all well and good to spell out what to think about and how to think about it. Like the others who made these manuals so popular, they chose freely to follow the meditation procedures. And, as original and creative minds, they knew how to utilize the contents and form for their own growth and self-expression. But *assign* such procedures? And to *school children?* Could it be possible that the American composition tradition of the five-paragraph "theme" preserves some residue of this very historical connection between church teaching and writing? Oh, not of course directly, because this country instituted at the outset the vaunted separation of church and state. But suppose the tradition lingers as a general exploitation of composition for moral inculcation. Look again at the 1978 CEEB topic, "We have met the enemy and he is us." (Confess, you sinner!) The composition is called a "theme" because subjects are essentially given, some allowance, of course, being necessary for individual variation in *which* prelisted topic to write on and in *which* points to make about this familiar topic. A theme is really variations on a theme. Then the tradition prescribes a structure, a sequence, for dealing with this topic, allowance again made for some leeway. Like the meditation structure, the five-paragraph organization calls for an introduction that conveys the theme in some arresting way, makes its three points analytically in the middle (one point per each of three paragraphs, though more of each are

[28]Manly Hall, *The Secret Teachings of All Ages: An Encyclopedic Outline of Masonic, Hermetic, Qabbalistic, and Rosicrucian Symbolical Philosophy* (Los Angeles: The Philosophical Research Society, 1978).

allowed if you want extra credit), then concludes with the uplifting per-oration, the emotional dessert after the feast of reason. Some caricature helps us play devil's advocate here so that the dangers may emerge of ap-plying such meditational techniques to the teaching of writing. And sure-ly, at their worst, Renaissance meditation manuals must have locked onto the tendency any of us may have toward sterile exercises and petty piety. And all too easily can we imagine how the church and the society may by this means have reinserted into private minds its authoritative bugging device. The institution always parodies the individual—church, school system, or whatever.

These suggestive glimpses of discursive meditation cannot, of course, do justice to all of its possibilities either as variations of inner speech or as teaching measures. It can run a wide gamut from ordinary concentra-tion or Wordsworthian experience "recollected in tranquillity" through many degrees of the Jesuitical "interior oratory and debate," as Martz once called it, to the edge of silence, into trance. Interestingly, to continue along the meditation scale I am delineating, we have to move backward in history, farther still away from the contemporaneous sense of medi-tation as merely turning things over in the rational mind. The extraordi-nary twentieth-century spiritual scholar and philosopher, Rudolf Steiner, has described the Christian mystics of the Middle Ages and early Renaissance—Eckhart, Boehme, Paracelsus, Buso, Silesius, and others—in a way that makes clear that, despite a scientific bent or a scholastic train-ing among some of them, their spiritual thinking began nearer, and car-ried them farther toward, esctatic transcendence of thought and language, the merging of the personal mind into cosmic "mind," or God, as they thought of it.[29] But these mystics themselves grew from an earlier tradi-tion that affords an even sharper contrast with the meditation of the Counter-Reformation.

During the first few centuries of Christianity certain of the so-called "Desert Fathers" and "Church Fathers," especially in the Eastern or By-zantine church, practiced nondiscursive meditations, as they described and prescribed in writings collected in the Middle Ages and called *Philo-kalia.*[30] The central meditation of this Christian strain—called Hesychast and focused on the so-called "Jesus prayer of the heart"—will exemplify nondiscursive meditation. It still survives in certain Greek and Russian traditions, has been revived recently in the United States as part of the Charismatic Movement, and was attempted by Frannie in Salinger's story

[29]Rudolf Steiner, *Mystics of the Renaissance* (New York: G. P. Putnam, 1911).
[30]*Writings from the Philokalia on Prayer of the Heart,* trans. E. Kadloubovsky and G. E. H. Palmer (London: Faber & Faber, 1951). For current material see George Maloney, *The Jesus Prayer* and Father David Geraets, *Jesus Beads* (Pecos, N.M.: Dove Publications, 1974 and 1969 respectively). These two books are published by the Benedictine Abbey at Pecos, which also publishes on the Charismatic Move-ment, in which the Abbey is active.

Frannie and Zooey.[31] The fact is that the meditation of silence has disappeared from view the more our culture has "advanced" into technological and discursive intricacies. Even in the church the mystic has seldom been long welcome. Far from enjoying papal blessing, practitioners of truly mystical meditation either inhibited their ultimate reaches to avoid breaking with the church, as Rudolf Steiner says, became so recluse as to make the whole matter academic, or did, in effect, break away. When his thought moves too far away from society (and the church is always part of society), the individual becomes either mystic or insane, depending on whether he yields his mind or simply loses it. From outside, the distinction blurs to the degree that for practical purposes it's all the same to the society, because the individual has got beyond its control. The individual may say he's now under God's control, but the church is not so sure. Once the agent in the ranks—internalized inner speech—has been silenced, church and society have been bypassed.

The Jesus prayer of the heart typifies the meditation method that consists of repeating over and over to oneself a *single* idea put in a *single* piece of speech until the focus of that idea and the incantation of that verbal sound induce trance. Consciousness is then altered beyond thought and speech. The "prayer" is, "Lord Jesus Christ, have mercy upon me!" This is too simple—and too *religious.* But the holy fathers say, "Sit in your cell and this prayer will teach you everything." This quotation is from St. Simeon The New Theologian, who describes the meditation this way:

> Keep your mind there (in the heart), trying by every possible means to find the place where the heart is, in order that, having found it, your mind should constantly abide there. Wrestling thus, the mind will find the place of the heart. This happens when grace produces sweetness and warmth in prayer. From that moment onwards, from whatever side a thought may appear, the mind immediately chases it away, before it has had time to enter, and become a thought or an image, destroying it by Jesus' name, that is, Lord Jesus Christ, have mercy upon me![32]

But how can just saying something over and over reveal the highest truths about life? And what if you don't happen to believe in Jesus, or even God?

To answer that I will ask a third question: How does meditation differ from prayer? The astonishing healer, Edgar Cayce, answered that

[31]Salinger's Glass family had been reading *The Way of a Pilgrim* and *The Pilgrim Continues His Way,* trans. Helen Bacovcin (Garden City, N.Y.: Doubleday, Image, 1978).

[32]Quoted on p. 79 of *The Spiritual Instructions of Saint Seraphim of Sarov,* ed. Franklin Jones (San Francisco: Dawn Horse, 1973), which puts this tradition in relation to yoga and Oriental thought.

prayer is talking to God; meditation is listening to God.[33] Discourse versus silence. Among other things, people are transmitter/receiver sets, which means they are made both to transmit and to receive but not *at the same time.* If you want to listen, you have to switch the channel over to receiving and keep still. If God or Nature or Cosmic Intelligence is transmitting at the other end, and the individual is holding the line muttering and squawking and debating and petitioning, he is missing a lot! Missing perhaps what he most wants to know, for lack of which he must mutter, squawk, debate, and petition. But as everyone knows who has ever tried to stop thinking, it is very difficult indeed. The mind is a drunken monkey, say the yogis. But one way to cure the habit of ceaselessly speaking to ourselves is—homeopathically—to go ahead and speak to ourselves but to say the same thing over and over.

What Christians often call a prayer the Hindus call a *mantra,* a word or phrase intoned repeatedly in exactly the spirit the Christian Fathers did the Jesus prayer of the heart. When the priest tells the parishioner in need of strength to go say so many Hail Marys or Our Fathers, he is doing the same thing the guru does when he tells the disciple to "go say the mantra." Also like the Jesus prayer, a mantra usually refers to some aspect of divinity. Yogis call the repetition of a mantra *japa;* Westerners unfamiliar with their own spiritual traditions and not realizing the universality of meditation have associated it with the particular form of japa that the Maharishi Mahesh Yogi learned from his guru and introduced into the United States under the name of Transcendental Meditation. Hanging near me as I write is a sandalwood rosary that Swami Sivalingam brought me from India—called a *mala*—which is used to count the number of repetitions of a mantra without having to voice or subvocalize the counting, exactly as the nun "tells the beads" as she "prays." *Om,* sometimes spelled *aum,* the master mantra of Hinduism, has the same origin as the Christian *amen,* which evolved from an earlier word *aumen* and which was a mantra, not merely, as now, an affirmation of what preceded it.[34] Just as monks take vows of silence, the yogis practice *mauna,* the withholding of speech. Controlling outer speech aids the controlling of inner speech. It helps fulfill the aim of mantric meditation, to suspend ordinary thinking. Also parallel in both Eastern and Western spiritual traditions is the widespread practice of chanting or singing mantras aloud, alone or in groups. Much chanting or singing of hymns and prayers is really group recitation of mantras. The *kyrie eleison,* for example, which is Greek for "Lord, have mercy . . . ," fairly represents Christian choral literature as exemplary mantra. In fact, it would be proper to view virtually all West-

---

[33] *A Dictionary: Definitions and Comments from the Edgar Cayce Readings,* compiled by Gerald J. Cataldo (Virginia Beach, Va.: A.R.E. Press, 1973), p. 52.
[34] H. Spencer Lewis, "The Mystical Meaning of Amen," *The Rosicrucian Digest,* February 1976.

ern church services as modeling for the congregation the kinds of meditation—discursive in the sermon, mantric in the liturgy—that they may
practice at home.

The adage "You become what you think" summarizes much spiritual
lore. Christian, Caballistic, Buddhist, or Sufi, a true mantra must always
symbolize the highest spiritual concepts, even though meaning may dissolve during repetition. The repeated word or phrase most often refers to
an aspect of divinity by name or epithet. Thus in arguing that the teaching of Transcendental Meditation in American schools violated the principle separating church from state, the American Civil Liberties Union
technically argued a sound case in those states where some teachers or
schools had introduced TM into the classroom, because the TM mantras
are usually Sanskrit names for different aspects of divinity. This presents
no problem except legally; permitting one church's language and not
those of other churches does violate the law. But in such cases the interpretation of the law should not make *any* practicing of meditation in
schools illegal. The intent of the founding fathers, a very spiritual group,
was not to hinder the growth of the soul! At any rate, the unbelievable
power of the one-pointed meditation resulting from the mantric repetition makes it critical to keep mantras positive and elevated. But mantras
need have no connection whatsoever with a church or religion. What
makes them work fundamentally is *the suspension of inner speech* that they
effect. Any mantra may accomplish this if the meditator succeeds in
holding focus well enough, but in the meantime this tremendous concentration on a negative emblem could have the same bad effects that institutional, commercial, political, or other brainwashing can have.

Through hymns and chants the church attempts to use the internalization of social speech as a way of planting in the individual's mind both
certain uplifting symbols and the internal speech habits that will, through
repetition, remind him of the symbols. Unfortunately, less benevolent
agencies of the society work the same way. Propaganda and advertising
rely on repetition of group chants and rhythmic tunes to set revolving in
the individual the shibboleths, slogans, and brand names they want per-
petuated. Precisely because outer speech converts to inner speech, all
spiritual traditions have come down hard on idle or loose speech, on giving voice to evil things, or, in modern idiom, "talking negatively." The
reason is not superstition but good mental hygiene. The question arises,
however, of what speech shall be repeated to suspend speech so the meditator can pay attention to the transpersonal or divine part of himself for
a change. If a mantra is wrong, the cure could be worse than the disease.
On the other hand, if children are picking up bad mantras from mass media and hate litanies around them, then perhaps school should try to help
them take over more control of their inner speech.

To understand nondiscursive meditation we have to consider both what the mind is aimed at and what it is aimed from. The root meaning of "discourse" is "running to and fro." The meaning of "mystic" derives from *mystos,* "keeping silence," derived in turn from the Greek *myein,* "to keep closed" (of eyes and lips). The mantra substitutes for inner speech, which "runs to and fro," in usual discursive fashion and relatively so even in the focused devotional. During mantra repetition, inner speech continues, in a sense, but changes profoundly from *serial* thoughts, a *train* of thoughts, to a *point* of thought. The voice moves on in time, repeating the same words, but the mind becomes, as yogis say, "one-pointed." Repeating the mantra suspends or at least mitigates inner speech so that nonconceptual intuition can take over in an altered state of consciousness both more receptive and more perceptive. Not only does the idea or object contemplated reveal itself more deeply, but it is as if a whole new and finer attunement occurs, enabling the individual to detect signals from within and from the environment that the ordinary mind drowns out or filters out. Although some people may regard this as a kind of self-hypnosis, which would wrongly put meditation in some category of unconscious vulnerability to others, meditation succeeds actually to the extent that it *de*-hypnotizes the individual from the prior environmental conditioning and acculturation. (Hypnosis has no single brainwave pattern to define it, whereas meditation, like other definite states recognized by science, such as sleeping, dreaming, and waking, yields a distinctive electroencephalographic reading.)[35] This is why spiritual masters refer to the aim of meditation as "awakening" or "liberation."

Many modern people tend to be put off by talk of "higher knowledge" or "awakening" or "direct perception of reality." Let me put the matter this way. Pure light cannot itself really be seen, although it enables grosser things to be seen by illuminating them. Broken down into colors, however, light does manifest itself to normal human vision (although even then, of course, we are not seeing the color in the same sense that we see the object reflecting the color). Just as a prism breaks down light into colors, which we can perceive, so the ordinary verbal/conceptual mind breaks down reality in ways which it can manage, in the terms of its own medium. It translates reality, and because the ordinary mind undergoes such powerful influences from culture and language, it translates reality according to sociohistorical biases. The deepest nondiscursive meditation temporarily turns off that whole information system. Veils fall. Zen masters constantly compare this liberated consciousness to a perfectly still body of water that directly reflects reality, no longer distorting it with ruffles of egoistic feeling or ripplings of the social mind. Or, to use another comparison, the meditator attunes directly to nature

[35]Robert Keith Wallace, Herbert Benson, and Archie Wilson, "A Wakeful Hypometabolic Physiologic State," *American Journal of Physiology,* September 1971.

instead of just to human frequencies. But he may at any time switch back on the old information system, which is necessary, and he may tune at will either to the more limited, interpreted world of humankind or to the unrefracted sources themselves. I think that the religious trinity was a practical breakdown of primal unity, to facilitate understanding of what otherwise would be incomprehensible. Trinities like Father, Son, and Holy Ghost or Vishnu, Brahma, and Shiva (or I, you, and it) make a concession to the limitations of conceptualized understanding, which must have parts, categories, and divisions and can do nothing with unity. This is why mystical means silent. But reintegration is essential, and this is why all cultures, as we will see, have developed some way of shifting attunement periodically from the social mediating of nature to nature itself. The breakdown is the process of becoming aware of all the possible divisions within unity. When the mind returns to unity without losing this awareness, this is direct knowledge, higher knowledge, or awakening.

All these meditation techniques may be summarized in the form of a scale progressing from nonverbal to verbal and then, within the verbal, from babble to silence. Put another way, it goes from external focus to internal focus and then, within the internal focus, from uncontrolled to controlled inner speech.

Non-verbal		GAZING—Rapt absorption in outer object, eyes open.
		VISUALIZING—Imagining of inner object, eyes closed.
	Uncontrolled	WITNESSING INNER SPEECH—Watching as bystander the inner stream.
Verbal		FOCUSING INNER SPEECH—Narrowing down to and developing a subject intensively with all faculties of mind and heart together.
	Controlled	SUSPENDING INNER SPEECH—Holding the mind on one point until it transcends discourse and culture and merges with cosmos, in trance.

If we think of gazing as the small child's "staring," then this progression comes full circle in the sense that it begins and ends in silence and rapture, but the circling rises rather than closes—spirals—because the child's gazing is spontaneous and unaware, whereas the meditator who has succeeded in suspending inner speech goes into conscious voluntary trance. Willed gazing or visualizing can be one means of suspending inner speech, since anything that holds the mind one-pointed will do. Also, we must imagine some gradations on this scale between any two adjacent methods, as some witnessing when one is trying to visualize or trying to focus inner speech, or some focusing when one is trying to suspend inner speech. Likewise, success in intensive focusing of inner speech moves the meditator already into the state of altered consciousness that ultimately becomes ecstatic after inner speech yields completely to silence.[36]

The Grand Paradox

Much scientific experimentation has demonstrated that how people perceive the world even on the sensory level is governed by conceptualization and verbalization. People wearing upside-down glasses will start seeing rightside-up after a while because they *know* that's "the way it s'pozed to be." "Concept dominates percept," as the psychologists say, and the concept is verbal and social. Most thinking is mass thinking carried on in an illusion of privacy. We have so thoroughly learned our lessons, internalized the local cosmology, that because we think alone, the thought seems ours. Most of our "original" thoughts resemble the minute variations, imperceptible to outsiders, that Balinese dancers "improvise" within traditional dances. We live in a verbal-conceptual cage and think we live in the world, which reaches us ordinarily only by some dim translation relayed in changing versions through all the offices of our sensorial, memorial, emotional, and rational bureaucracy. God only knows *what* the truth is. The reason that such rumor-mongering passes for an efficient information system rests on our social dependency: The main thing is to fit in with how everyone else is thinking; we'll get around to the rest of reality when we have a free moment.

According to the extraordinary thesis of psychologist Julian Jaynes, however, until about 3,000 years ago people had no individual consciousness at all, certainly not inner speech as personal as we have described.[37] Rather, members of a culture heard and followed authoritative voices of "gods" of that culture that they hallucinated exactly as today's schizophrenics "hear" the voice of a parent, god or devil, or other introjected authority figure. It was not, he said, until cultures conflicted and the need for individual decision-making arose that consciousness replaced this earlier, "bicameral" or gods-attuned mind, which had "told" one what to do in novel situations not governed by hard and fast custom. Though I believe the date is much too recent, Jaynes's remarkable idea fits a number of reasonable assumptions such as the role of inner speech in guiding behavior, the social origin of inner speech, and the evolution of human be-

[36]For perhaps the best Western book on meditation see Claudio Naranjo and Robert Ornstein, *The Psychology of Meditation* (New York: Viking, 1971). This book benefits from the psychiatric, psychological, and neurophysiological background of the authors and from Naranjo's unusual understanding of Eastern teachings and his personal training in spiritual disciplines. See also Robert Keith Wallace and Herbert Benson, "The Physiology of Meditation," *Scientific American,* February 1972, but this and much other relevant research can be followed currently in *Brain/Mind Bulletin,* P.O. Box 42211, Los Angeles, Ca., 90042.

[37]Julian Jaynes, *The Origin of Consciousness in the Breakdown of the Bicameral Mind* (Boston: Houghton Mifflin, 1976).

ings toward higher consciousness. Jaynes's brilliant and controversial work lends corroboration and perspective to the notion I have advanced of inner speech as social hypnosis and to my contention that the original and fundamental role of the arts was and is to counter the negative effects of inner speech.

Is, then, our rich inner life a lie? Are our "beautiful thoughts" only an illusion? No, these are real, but what mostly gives us the feeling of richness, beauty, and originality, I submit, owes, precisely, to our managing to escape a while from the cage. We would best regard fresh perception and original thinking as *un*thinking prior thoughts that were not so or were too partial, as *removing limitations that we previously "took for granted."* Most scientific breakthroughs push a dent out in the battered sphere of truth by undoing an epoch's "current abstractions," to use Alfred North Whitehead's phrase for the local cosmology.

Modern scientists, artists, and mathematicians have well recognized the limitations of ordinary language and have devised purer symbols to transcend them. But even in common parlance we all acknowledge the inadequacies of verbal-conceptual symbolism to do justice to those extremities of experience lying off the range of the workaday world. We are "struck speechless." "Words cannot express . . ." "I cannot tell you how . . ." The best and worst are "beyond words." Horror is "unspeakable," and bliss is "ineffable." Again, conceptual thought and speech serve the mid-range, socialized experience, and the modern intellectual who might regard as mere superstition the taboo on naming God would overlook the sagacity of this constant reminder that there is more in heaven and earth, as Hamlet says, than dreamt of in our "philosophy," that is, in discourse. The General Semanticist says, "The map is not the territory." Montaigne says, "What do I know?" like a true and, originally, positive skeptic. And nobody appreciates this caution better than today's theoretical physicist contemplating subatomic "particles" that are really processes, not objects, and black holes that tease him out of thought. The reminder is to stay as a small child, who keeps his antennae out and still feels awe and wonder because he hasn't yet put a grid over reality. To the charges against language that it limits, biases, and stereotypes perception according to cultural imperatives, we have to add a second charge, that in reducing reality to the terms of its own symbolism—and all symbols will do this—it devitalizes and negativises experience itself.

Discourse is divisive. Concepts are based on the analogies that the right hemisphere of the brain creates with its metaphorizing capacity. Naming is classifying, and classifying parcels reality into ticketed piles of "like" things (different for different cultures). These named things are then linked via the predicative and conjunctive logics of language to form chains of thought. The left, temporal hemisphere specializes in this chaining or logical sequencing. This entire collaboration of the two halves of the brain—one an analog computer and the other a digital computer—requires and thrives on division. Although the right hemisphere, the analog computer, specializes in synthesizing wholes out of disparate items, these categories or constellations depend of course on selection and exclusion and therefore on dividing. It feeds these categories and constellations to the left hemisphere, which is divisive not only by the very nature of its chief function, to analyze or break down, but also by the fact of sequencing. The discrete items that the right hemisphere brings together as a class of similar things or a figure of interrelated things become available or "discrete" in the first place by virtue of some analytic breakdown instigated by the left hemisphere. And what are wholes as synthesized by the right become parts again when sequenced or serialized by the left into its logical enchainments. This circular processing by the new brain as an entirety generates and depends on division. This is why merely "teaching for the right hemisphere" does not go far enough. These brain functions account for the very nature of discourse—lexicon and syntax and "rules" of operation.

Hindu philosophy distinguishes two kinds of "mind," a lower called *manas,* which probably corresponds to the functions of the cerebrum just described, and a higher mind called *buddhi,* for which Western science or philosophy has no clear equivalent. Outside of mystical literature itself, the closest parallel to *manas* and *buddhi* in the West may be the distinction between *phenomena* and *noumena,* knowledge derived à la Locke from some logical permutation of the evidence of the senses versus knowledge perceived directly, without sensory data, by "intellectual intuition," a dictionary definition[38] of noumena that, significantly, has to collapse a major Western dichotomy to render the concept. This dichotomy between intellect and intuition invokes, in fact, a difference commonly used to distinguish the functions of the left and right brain hemispheres.

Noumenal knowledge may no doubt seem vague or vapid because instead of corresponding to a definite physiological site, like the cerebrum, it cannot be so located. Being unlocatable may indicate, precisely, the nature of being "higher": that is, noumen or buddhi may represent a superorganization of old and new brains, or a whole cerebro-spinal system, with the whole endocrine or glandular system, including activation of dormant functions in the pituitary and pineal glands. Past physiological research loses relevance at this point. The West's three leading brain researchers—Sherrington, Eccles, and Penfield—all concluded at the end of their careers that it is impossible to explain the mind by the brain. Meditation perhaps does not simply switch off the discursive and phenomenal system but switches on a larger system that subsumes and subjugates it.

From a different quarter comes one of the best statements of the negativity of inner speech. Across the tetralogy of his "conversations with

[38] *Webster's New Twentieth Century Dictionary* (New York: Collins World, 1977), p. 1225.

Don Juan," Carlos Castaneda keeps reconceiving the nature and the terms of the spiritual discipline through which the Yaqui shaman is pulling him and which he periodically reports. Never does he refer to meditation, and indeed Don Juan seems not to have taught it in any form, at least as we have discussed it here, but he teaches Castaneda a variety of techniques, mostly attentional, that result in *seeing*, supervision, by "stopping the world," as Castaneda earlier called the effect of these techniques. By the fourth book he has recast the terms of his cumulative experience and changed his summary of these techniques to "stopping the inner dialogue."

"You think and talk too much. You must stop talking to yourself."

"What do you mean?"

"You talk to yourself too much. You're not unique at that. Every one of us does that. We carry on an internal talk. Think about it. Whenever you are alone, what do you do?"

"I talk to myself."

"What do you talk to yourself about?"

"I don't know; anything, I suppose."

"I'll tell you what we talk to ourselves about. We talk about our world. In fact we maintain our world with our internal talk."

"How do we do that?"

"Whenever we finish talking to ourselves the world is always as it should be. We renew it, we kindle it with life, we uphold it with our internal talk. Not only that, but we also choose our paths as we talk to ourselves. Thus we repeat the same choices over and over until the day we die, because we keep on repeating the same internal talk over and over until the day we die.

"A warrior is aware of this and strives to stop his talking. . . ."[39]

Recapitulating all the techniques he has taught him over the years, Don Juan says, "Stopping the internal dialogue is, however, the key. . . . The rest of the activities are only props; all they do is accelerate the effect of stopping the internal dialogue."[40]

In astonishing accord with Don Juan, the classic yoga text, the *Yoga Sutras* (aphorisms) of Patanjali, written probably two or three centuries after Christ but codifying yogic practices and principles transmitted through two or three millennia before, states in a sutra at the very outset:

Yoga is the restriction of the fluctuations of mind-stuff.

—James Woods, the Harvard Oriental Series

[39]Carlos Castaneda, *A Separate Reality: Further Conversations with Don Juan* (New York: Simon and Schuster), p. 263.
[40]Carlos Castaneda, *Tales of Power* (New York: Simon and Schuster, 1974), p. 233.

Yoga is the suppression of the modifications of mind.

—Swami Hariharananda Aranya

Yoga is the control of thought waves in the mind.

—Swami Prabhavananda and Christopher Isherwood[41]

I have quoted three translations of the same sutra to help the reader distill more surely for himself this key point. Also in common, Don Juan and Patanjali both say the mastery of stopping inner dialogue enables the successful practitioner to assume extraordinary physical and psychical powers (*siddhis*).

The reader can see already the paradox that we have been engaging with. If discourse is "running to and fro," why encourage it—especially if people desire composure? If the deepest and most desirable "meditation" is silence, "nonconceptualization," then why think? If suspending inner speech opens the gate to higher knowledge, who wants to *develop* inner speech? If language just distorts reality through a social lens, what good will it do to learn to write well? Doesn't successful verbal expression conflict with the very goal of expression—to speak the truth? Or is writing just a parlor game, to entertain and blandish, not to symbolize reality?

Certainly we have to face the negative aspects of speech, and even of conceptual thought itself. To do so, however, seems to undermine the main aims of schooling. If we are not trying to teach kids to think and to express themselves, then, hell's bells, what are we up to anyway? How can we old poetry-loving English teachers with our rich inner life and our great investments in language turn around and talk it down? Because, precisely, we have to say the truth, and the truth is that speech is double-edged, a curse and a blessing. (The root of *sacred* means both holy and cursed.)

The teaching of writing must rise to a new sophistication consonant with a new stage in human evolution. A paradox is literally a "double teaching," and that's exactly what we must do—teach two apparently contradictory things at once. Youngsters need to develop inner speech as fully as possible and at the same time learn to suspend it. They must talk through to silence. Of course, I can hear now the teacher who says, "Well, you don't know *my* kids. They come to me so inarticulate they can hardly talk at all—couldn't care less about language—are so brainwashed by TV they hardly have an inner life of their own—and here you talk of making them nonverbal and stopping their inner speech." But this state of affairs is all part of the paradox. Articulation is essential, and silence is golden indeed. Melville's male *ingénu* Billy Budd kills Claggett in a moment of

[41]These translations come from the three following sources, respectively: James Haughton Woods, *The Yoga-System of Patanjali,* the Harvard Oriental Series (Delhi, India: Motilal Barnarsidass, 1966); Swami Hariharananda Aranya, *Yoga Philosophy of Patanjali* (Calcutta, India: Calcutta University Press, 1963); and Swami Prabhavananda and Christopher Isherwood, *How to Know God: The Yoga Aphorisms of Patanjali* (Hollywood: Vedanta Press, 1953).

helpless *stuttering* anger. He struck out because he could not speak out. The real goal is control and choice—exercise of will—so that people can avail themselves of discourse and still transcend it.

We can no longer regard schooling as only learning to verbalize. This is naive and irresponsible. It ignores the dangerous side of discourse, which if not balanced can be put into the service, like atomic energy, of the worst motives and phobias. Furthermore, it attunes us to humankind only, not to the whole of nature, leaving us with less than a half truth and therefore not even understanding humankind. ("Human voices wake us, and we drown.") Finally, the best way to teach how to fill out job applications is not to pound away at this as a "minimal criterion" but to help kids connect writing to the whole range of personal and social usage of discourse. Isolating a skill merely deprives it of the context and connections that would teach it. This is true of filling out job applications and of discourse itself. A paradox is not a real but an apparent contradiction. To develop and undo discourse at the same time would not be working against ourselves. Teaching both ways at once, double teaching, has its reason. People are at once both human and what we call divine, that is, they participate in the social subsystem which in turn participates in the total cosmic system. The new stage of evolution at which we are arriving demands education for conscious attunement to both. This means the ability to switch deliberately back and forth and know where one's mind is all the time.

Even if one rejects this dual aim and dual method, it is a practical fact that people who can suspend discourse think and speak better when they turn it back on. Thought straightens and deepens during the hiatus in accordance perhaps with William James's idea that we learn to swim in winter and ice skate in summer, that is, by lying fallow during the off season. Swami Sivalingam can switch with great ease from inner silence to very energetic speech. Given to long meditation all his life, still he thinks and verbalizes with tremendous speed and fluency, although seldom does he have the opportunity today to speak in his native Tamil. It is difficult to keep up with his thoughts and words even though he may be using a lately learned language. When Swami Sivalingam puts pen to paper he writes virtually without pause in a smooth transcription of inner flow. His own guru was the renowned Swami Sivananda, a Western-trained medical doctor turned yogi who wrote over 300 books, most on subtle and difficult subjects. Because their will is lined up behind their mind, and their thought is resolved, advanced meditators talk and write with a combination of depth and fluency that writing teachers should pay attention to and that demonstrates very convincingly how suspending inner speech benefits it.

Harder to believe perhaps is that this truth holds for so-called non-verbal or inarticulate people. Such people do in fact have a busy inner life, but (1) they are less conscious of it, and (2) they are talking to themselves in far more restricted, compulsive ways, telling themselves the same few things over and over, or rerunning in a mental twilight things others have said or shown them. Such people desperately need release from this narrow and uncontrolled repetition, which limits in turn what they can see, say, and do about things outside. So even for the "speechless" person the mind works better if it can be turned down or off from time to time.

Counterspell

It should be clear at this point, in the view developed here, that learning to write well is nothing less than learning to discourse well, and that, educationally, speaking up and shutting up have to be considered together. This means that we would do well not only to take a very broad view of what teaches writing but also to recognize that many of the best ways of teaching writing may be themselves ends as much as means. In any sensible set of humanistic values, meditation deserves a place in schools for its own sake, regardless of its value to writing, and writing might well be regarded as adjunct to meditation rather than the reverse. Aside from clerical maintenance that may be done by computers, what is writing for, anyway, if not to develop understanding? Let's keep this perspective in mind as we approach the question of what methodology may best act as counterspell to teach paradoxically.

First of all, *language* may be used as a counterspell to itself. The incantatory use of language, which is nondiscursive or only half discursive, resolves most directly the paradox of teaching and unteaching discourse at the same time. Rhythm, rhyme, repetition, nonsense, imagery, sheer sound and beat and vocal play—these take a minimum of meaning and charge it with a mental energy that works below the level of symbols and communication (and best appeals to the "nonverbal" or "inarticulate" person). Incantation makes words operate like music or dance or graphic arts. The tense emphasis school usually places on communication alone not only misses the proper entrance point into writing for less verbal people but also misses a key solution to the limitations of discourse, for the incantatory uses of language to undo language cast a counterspell.

Why does poetry always precede prose in the history of literature? Why is it considered the highest form of composition? Because in addition to, or beyond, any symbolization or conveying of meaning, it *summons power.* Vocal potency we no longer think of or think we believe in, although it works its effects on people today as much as ever, on writer as well as reader. Perhaps for the very reason that language is learned in an early state of susceptibility and internalizes the world, it evokes, invokes, conduces, induces, vibrates, and resonates. Yogis associate the energy center of the throat with those just above and below it along the cerebro-spinal chain, at the brain and heart, and regard this place of speech not just as expressing thought and feeling but as a vibrational power source of great influence on what falls within its range. The allegory in Genesis of God *saying* things into existence means likewise that vocalization commands, exerts force like other energy but is directed by intelligence. Magic formulas of the "Open Sesame" sort popularize this ancient and universal conviction about language. "Logos" is translated as "word" in "In the beginning was the word," but an earlier meaning of "logos" than thought (logic) is "energy source of the solar system." In short, teachers will gain enormously from reinstating in school the primal and not merely primitive view of language as not just knowledge but also *power*, a vibratory force that acts on world as well as mind.

Schools need to emphasize, in parity with the symbolic uses of language to express ideas, the forms of language that transcend ideas and alter consciousness, induce trance. This means far more time devoted to song and poetry and to drama and fiction as rhythmic influences, not merely as thematic vehicles. And students should write more in these forms and *perform* such writings of others, not always read them silently. By organizing specialties like "creative drama" and "creative writing," schools have effectively placed them out of bounds for most students most of the time, whereas writing and performing of these art forms of language should occur constantly at all ages as a daily staple. Again, other educators and I have written much about this elsewhere—to no great avail so far because of state doctrines favoring lower goals falsely regarded as utilitarian.

Communicative discourse itself, however, can become a major way of teaching the paradox, in conjunction with silence. We have to think of "developing discourse" as not just throwing open the sluice gates, but of *channeling* discourse and especially *raising the quality* of it. The internalization process itself will accomplish this if well arranged in the classroom. Where can rich variety come from into the inner life? And how can the individual become aware of how he does think and talk and how he might think and talk? From hearing out the world. From listening to and reading or viewing a far broader spectrum of discourse than schools and parents have so far facilitated. Inner speech must be elaborated, refined, and enriched, and this takes a school revolution, for now both student activities and the type and timing of materials are so overcontrolled as to caricature the growth of inner speech. The model of inculcation, dearer perhaps to the public even than to the profession, must go for good. Far from working toward a counterspell, it merely deepens the original social hypnosis, which parents still asleep think they want for their children.

At any rate, in addition to quieting the mind as one method of awakening, we should employ what only appears to be the opposite—namely shaking up the mind, stimulating and activating it so that it *moves*. If the mind *either* holds still enough *or* moves enough it will shake off conditioning, for either liberates, and that is the key. Running to and fro, which is compulsive, must change to running straight on and on along the individual's proper path. If inner speech keeps evolving, people eventually work through the world of words and on out the other side. The more we consciously employ language, the more detached we become from it and know what it can do and what it cannot do. Only after we have spoken up can we shut up. I suspect that when Shakespeare announced his early retirement through Prospero, the magus of his last play, *The Tempest,* he had talked his way into silence and made composition coincide with composure. Teachers don't aim to make little Shakespeares, but we should not miss the lesson that the best way to improve writing is to keep refining inner speech till it evaporates. (A playwright shows most clearly how to set up colloquies in which different aspects of oneself talk toward inner resolution.) A main effect of writing, anyway, is personal growth, which is the best guarantee of effective communication, whether in a job application or a poem. Writing should be taught unabashedly as a spiritual discipline.

But, of course, I'm suggesting that forms of meditation are the main counterspells. To connect meditation more directly with schooling, let's look again at the scale of meditation techniques sketched earlier. This array can serve to find the best meditation for a given writer and topic. The point on the scale closest to the finished composition lies near the middle, where we found the structured discourse of the Jesuits. But if fluency comes hard, maybe one should babble first, just witness the spontaneous production of ideas, words, and images. If depth is needed, perhaps one should aim for silence, try to get beyond what one has already heard and said and read about something and just focus on the subject nondiscursively—that is, just hold, centered in consciousness, some idea, emblem, or phrasing of the subject, sink deep in without trying to have thoughts about it; *then* the meditator could back up on the scale toward discourse and begin to permit trains of thoughts to build up about his subject. More generally, where on this scale, a teacher might ask, can a certain student find himself at the moment, given his verbal and nonverbal development so far?

Gazing, contemplating, may be done at any age as a way to know most fully some object of the material world. The famous biology professor Louis Agassiz, at Harvard, would send a student back repeatedly to look at a fish and describe it until the observer began to see *internal* features of it that he would normally not perceive. Let a learner visually lock into some object he or she has chosen either out of curiosity or deep involvement or as part of a project requiring further knowledge of the object. As a meditation, gazing slips the limits of conceptualization and enables one to see more and hence have more to say when back in the discursive mode.

Students can practice visualizing in connection with many imaginative activities in school, including the already popular "guided fantasy" technique some teachers have adopted. Alone, the meditator imagines, with eyes closed, an inner picture at the "third eye" (Cyclopean) position in the middle of the forehead. Though common to probably all cultures, including Christian, the conjuring and holding of an image before the inner vision has been especially developed in Tibetan meditation, which draws on Buddhism and yoga, especially tantric yoga.[42] Tantra emphasizes transcending rather than shunning the senses as a means to spiritual development. This means that the aspirant subtilizes his sensory vision right onto a higher plane, partly by gazing at "art objects" especially made for this (as indeed was much Christian art) and then by introjecting these, eyes closed, and continuing to see the object. Sometimes one uses a visual construction, called a *yantra,* that is especially designed to be contemplated for its effect on consciousness, being a schema of cosmos as both unity and multiplicity. Carl Jung's mandalas, some Persian rug patterns, and Navajo sand paintings are yantras. Found or student-made yantras can serve to establish visualization as a general practice for imagining anything at will. Through visualization, incidentally, the old link between meditation and healing, buried, as I pointed out, in the etymology of the word, has come alive again in recent years: After Dr. Carl Simonton showed at a military hospital that some "terminal" cancer patients could reverse the disease by meditating and visualizing their cure in some graphic way of their own, Dr. Irving Oyle and many other physicians and therapists have begun incorporating this combination of techniques into general medical practice and into the current holistic health movement.[43]

Since television may well cause some atrophying of the visualizing faculty, as some of us educators have conjectured in regard, usually, to reading problems, visualization practice may improve both comprehension and composition at once. It played an important role in the "composition of place" and no doubt also in the production of "similitudes," which entail *seeing* similarities between points in one's subject and comparable concrete items.

The way in which the Jesuitical sort of discursive meditation might be applied to writing found a spokesman in Gordon Rohman over a decade ago.[44] Rohman lifted out of the ecclesiastical context the essential process that worked for meditators and writers of the seventeenth century and offered it to teachers as one pre-writing technique, leaving subject matter open and capturing the spirit rather than the letter of the

[42]Phillip Rawson, *The Art of Tantra* (Greenwich, Conn.: New York Graphic Society, 1973).

[43]Carl Simonton et al., *Getting Well Again* (New York: J. P. Tarcher, 1978), and Irving Oyle, *The Healing Mind* (New York: Pocket Books, 1976).

[44]Gordon Rohman, "Pre-Writing: The Stage of Discovery in the Writing Process," *College Composition and Communication,* May 1965.

procedure. Doing the same thing in my own way, I would recommend that teachers coach students on how to get themselves into a meditative state of unusual absorption in a subject that interests them and then to visualize, imagine, feel, and think everything they can about that subject without at first concerning themselves about writing something down. After students have brought to bear on a subject all their faculties and thus focused intensively for a time their inner speech, then they would write down some version of these thoughts and proceed from there to work up a composition, presumably with mid-writing response from others and as much repetition of these inner and outer processes as is appropriate for student and subject. So the aim of discursive meditation is to channel and intensify inner speech in a state of heightened consciousness and self-communication that enables the writer to summon all he is capable of saying about the subject. Previous or concurrent practice in visualization will aid this much.

The yogic or Hesychast type of nondiscursive meditation does not have to be done with a mantra. Virtually any focal point that is powerful and positive for the meditator can serve well. When using mantras, students should make or choose their own. Making and discussing mantras should, in fact, become an important classroom activity. What is a good thing to keep saying to yourself? Are we already repeating, consciously or unconsciously to ourselves, certain key words or magic phrases? Are they good or bad for us? What ideas are "elevated" or spiritual? What aspects of language form make for good mantras? Word? Phrase? Sentence? Stanza? Work with mantras can become part of writing and performing song and poetry.

Alternatives to mantras are yantras and other tantra, that is, all arts and sensory avenues. Repetitive external sound may work well to help some individuals to stay one-pointed. Verbal or nonverbal, visual or auditory, physical or imaginary—these are good choices to have for individualizing. A phrase may be sung aloud or intoned within. A verbal person may start to still his inner chatter *only* by vocalizing something. A nonverbal person may achieve good focus best on an image. An unimaginative person may do well to transfer an image by alternately gazing and visualizing. A lonely person may release some anxious "running to and fro" by chanting with others.

Zen Buddhist practitioners of the meditation technique called za-zen focus on their normal breathing, which moves in time but stays the same in the sense that in even respiration one breath is like another. In this respect breath is like a mantra, and in some meditation practices, like the Hesychast, breathing and repetition of the mantra are coordinated. Za-zen emphasizes the here-and-now in contrast with conceptualization, which by its abstract nature necessarily refers out of the present. Holding attention on regular breathing is perfectly safe and may be an easy, fitting focus for many students, offering an alternative to senses.

Breath has a very close connection to thought, almost entirely unsuspected in our era, that I think science will soon begin to rediscover. Though za-zen is simply attending to breathing without altering it, some of the most powerful consciousness-altering exercises entail slowing, holding, or patterning the breath. *Pranayama,* or breath control, has for thousands of years been associated by yogis with mind control, in keeping with the etymological connection in all languages I have heard of between breath and spirit. Pranayama is the specialty of my own teacher, Swami Sivalingam, who has said that it is a "short-cut meditation." So powerful is breath control, in fact, that it can be dangerous without a teacher when carried beyond the more elementary exercises. Some day soon, educators should work out with wise specialists like Swami Sivalingam just which exercises can be safely done at which ages and with how much or how little monitoring by others.

Yogic texts say, "Quiet the breath, quiet the mind."[45] We can notice for ourselves how breath alters as certain emotion-laden thoughts or events occur to us. When the yogi says, "I am in your breath," he means he is following your thoughts and feelings in his concentration. But again, this insight about breath exists in our own heritage as well as in the East. The Christian mystics and fathers refer often enough to control of the breath to show that they too understood very well its connection with the mind and spirit. And it was undoubtedly part of pre-Christian spiritual discipline in the West. Any serious consideration of meditation must in one way or another deal with breathing, since it is likely that thought and breath each can be controlled from either end. I have myself experienced, in common with many others I have talked with, a natural slowing and even stopping of the breath during meditation, but as soon as I become aware of cessation, it starts again, responding directly to the thought. This accompanies a general slowing of metabolic processes, probably related biologically to hibernation processes, that scientific monitoring of meditation corroborates. This is very good for health and might well ease many school problems concerning excitation, emotion, attention, and energy. Aside from its indirect value to writing as an adjunct to meditation, breath control affects clear thinking and expression quite directly by steadying the mind. "Alternate breathing," through one nostril at a time, will, I think, soon be shown to stimulate the respective brain hemispheres through crossed-over neural connections between nostrils and hemispheres. It is nothing less than naive to continue to regard writing as only "mental," and if the trend toward the psychobiology of it succeeds in helping the teaching of writing, it will do so by treating discourse within the total functioning of the organism.

[45]For specific references both to connections between thought and breath and to general doctrines of Tibetan yogic techniques of enlightenment see W. Y. Evans-Wentz, *The Tibetan Book of the Great Liberation or the Method of Realizing Nirvana through Knowing the Mind,* Commentary by C. G. Jung (New York: Oxford University Press, 1954).

Because meditation techniques are the closest to writing, I have featured them, but suspending inner speech as a means to greater knowledge and power underlies a prodigious array of activities of all cultures of all times that may suggest how teachers might go about finding and devising counterspells in lieu of or in league with meditation. The "techniques of ecstasy," as the scholar Mircea Eliade has called them,[46] may be physiological as well as psychological. Physical activity calling for totally external focus of attention or total bodily involvement can make inner speech virtually impossible. In writing about "sports highs" that athletes report, Michael Murphy has recently made this connection.[47] This explains why martial arts like judo and aikido are considered spiritual disciplines. (As my younger daughter said of her high school fencing class, "Your mind doesn't wander!") Think now of the real meaning of Shakers, Quakers, and Holy Rollers, who attempt to bring on this state by dancing of a sort, as do the Sufi Whirling Dervishes, whom I have seen do authentically their gradually accelerating revolving movement with eyes closed and to the accompaniment of chanting. All of the arts originally aimed at trance induction for purposes of enlightenment, as typified by some of the Greek Mysteries, the main source of Western drama, music, art, and dance to the extent that these did not derive more directly from the mysteries of earlier civilizations.

Chemical means were sometimes used in combination with sensorimotor activities. A distinguished scientist/scholar trio has recently asserted, for example, that the mysteries of Eleusis included ingestion of a psychotropic drug from a fungus similar to the peyote mushroom employed since ancient times in Meso-America for shedding the veil of ordinary reality.[48] Aldous Huxley's classic account of the effects of a similar psychotropic drug, "Opening the Doors of Perception," accords remarkably with this ancient chemical approach.[49] But fasting and breath control can also produce liberation from the ordinary mind or "highs" by affecting the chemistry of the brain without the need of ingesting drugs.

There are electrical as well as chemical means for suspending inner speech. Natural sleep produces slow brainwaves of long amplitude that cancel out the higher frequency crackling of thoughts, and electroshock therapy "works" in the brutal fashion it does by shooting through the nervous system a charge so strong that it likewise overwhelms the finer

[46]See Mircea Eliade, *Shamanism: Archaic Techniques of Ecstasy*, Bollingen Series LXXVI (Princeton, N.J.: Princeton University Press, 1964). Eliade's remarkable scholarship combines with rare personal understanding to make him one of the most valuable contemporary explainers and presenters of spiritual disciplines. See also his *Yoga: Immortality and Freedom*, Bollingen Series LVI (Princeton, N.J.: Princeton University Press, 1958).

[47]Michael Murphy and Rhea White, *The Psychic Side of Sports* (Reading, Mass.: Addison Wesley, 1978).

[48]R. Gordon Wasson, Carl A. P. Ruok, Albert Hoffmann, *The Road to Eleusis: Unveiling the Secret of the Mysteries* (New York: Harcourt Brace Jovanovich, 1978).

[49]Aldous Huxley, *The Doors of Perception* (New York: Harper & Row, 1970).

neural activities like thinking and literally shocks the patient right out of his mind. Epileptic attacks have been described by brain researcher Wilder Penfield as a kind of electrical storm, which, although they may end in a coma that parodies meditation trance, do seem to occur in people gifted with unusual insight, if not clairvoyance, like Dostoevski. Scientists have found that when psychics are performing their feats while wired to an electroencephalograph they yield unusual brain-wave patterns characterized by the very low frequencies called theta and delta associated with creativity and trance states. (The way most true psychics describe their concentration for a task indicates pretty clearly that they shut off inner speech.) In the case of one famous psychic, Matthew Manning, the electrical activity, which formed a pattern unrecognizable to twenty of the twenty-one scientists present, was traced to the old brain. Also, a common experience reported unexpectedly by some psychics polled for a survey was that they had received a severe electric shock before the age of ten.[50] Although teachers will not want to employ chemical or electrical means, of course, I think knowledge of these means helps teachers to gain insight into such behavior of students as attraction to drugs and into conditions of the body and the environment that in good and bad ways can suspend or reduce students' inner speech.

Other bodily activities are more directly relevant to teaching methods. Pleasantly monotonous craft movements like knitting and weaving or work activities like hauling a rope or wielding a pickaxe or shovel or thrusting seedlings into mud tend to "entrance" the ordinary mind and constitute a natural kind of meditation. Crafts, arts, sports, and many practical self-help activities hold inner speech in abeyance or mute it and thus help attune us beyond discursive thought. Since these possible counterspells should be curriculum candidates anyway, in keeping with the principle that worthy means are also worthy ends, they will offer opportunities to integrate writing with many other kinds of learning to which it is organically related by way of regulating and balancing one's own mind and body.

Let me summarize the value of regarding writing as revised inner speech and of applying meditation techniques to the teaching of writing. We may compare this approach to prevention in medicine as opposed to curing. If health is neglected for years, then at a certain point it appears there is nothing for it but to undergo surgery, consume drugs, or take some other drastic treatment. Good schooling would never let reading or writing get to the point that they are now, where most teaching is remedying, that is, resorting to very artificial "cures" for "weak vocabulary," "ineffective sentence structure," "poor organization," and "short, shallow papers." In effect, schools teach one year of beginning reading and writ-

[50]Matthew Manning, *The Link* (Holt, Rinehart and Winston: 1974), pp. 20–26, part of an introduction by Peter Bander.

ing and eleven years of remedial reading and writing, because the approach is based on the mechanistic functioning of inorganic matter instead of on the realistic way that human beings learn to conceptualize and verbalize. Then severe problems of thinking and language arise which it seems only specialized drills will remedy. The causes of this colossal misdirection go well back into the whole culture, beyond the education profession itself, and form another story unto itself. The point here is that we can head off a myriad of learning problems by making the rise, growth, and self-control of inner speech a central focus in curriculum.

Some teachers teach meditation under other names or have initiated related activities. *The Centering Book* and its successor *The Second Centering Book,* pioneering works by education professors, contain many verbatim directions for leading youngsters in exercises of relaxation, concentration, breathing, visualizing, centering, and inner attention.[51] Other books are coming out all the time on the teaching of meditation to young people, usually based on experience in school or community settings. The most educational experimentation with meditation has occurred outside of school, however, in workshops for adults. In his *Intensive Journal* workshops Ira Progoff, a psychotherapist, teaches people how to use writing to discover what they really feel and think and want and are.[52] I have been greatly struck, as have some others, by the similarities between the kinds of writing and the climate for writing of my own approach for school teaching of language arts and Progoff's approach for adult therapy, both developed independently at about the same time. I am struck too that Progoff has also come to use meditation as a method of engaging people in writing.

But to teach meditation one must practice meditation. Though always surprised at how many teachers "come out of the closet" when I talk about meditation, the profession needs far more practitioners. Any interested person can start to meditate without joining an organization, paying money, or necessarily having a teacher, by practicing one of the techniques described in this article. To the extent that schools have the money, projects for changing teachers and the "facilitative behaviors" movement in staff development have tried to improve curriculum by arranging experiences in self-awareness and personal growth for the teachers. Since meditation naturally fulfills this aim, if staff development included it, then schools would simultaneously prepare teachers to improve writing while fostering their general adult growth.

[51]Gay Hendriks and Russel Wills, *The Centering Book* (Englewood Cliffs, N.J.: Prentice-Hall, 1975). Also, Gay Hendriks and T. Roberts, *The Second Centering Book: More Advanced Awareness Activities for Children, Parents, and Teachers* (Englewood Cliffs, N.J.: Prentice-Hall, 1977). For early rationale for introducing meditation into schools see *Phi Delta Kappan,* December 1972, which featured articles on Transcendental Meditation and education.

[52]Ira Progoff, *At a Journal Workshop: The Basic Text and Guide for Using the Intensive Journal* (New York: Dialogue House, 1975). For a useful incorporation of some of Progoff's practices into schools see Mark Hanson, *Sources* (Box 262, Lakeside, Ca. 92040: Interact).

Meditation techniques show how to witness one's own mind, direct one's own mind, and silence one's own mind. Teachers can give no greater gift to their students than to help them expand and master inner speech. Good writing will ensue, whereas fiddling with form alone will teach, if anything, only how to carpenter better the craziness of themselves and their world. Let's direct discourse toward its own self-transformation and self-transcendence. In doing so we will also accomplish better the traditional curriculum goals.

> Meanwhile the mind from pleasure less
> Withdraws into its happiness;
> The mind, that ocean where each kind
> Does straight its own resemblance find,
> Yet it creates, transcending these,
> Far other worlds and other seas,
> Annihilating all that's made
> To a green thought in a green shade.
>
> From "The Garden," Andrew Marvell

10

Excerpts from an Educator's Notebook

Background

Soon after the Third International Conference on the Teaching of English was held in Sydney (1980), the director of the conference, Roslyn Arnold, a lecturer at the University of Sydney, began compiling a collection of articles to supplement the official publication of the conference papers by the Australian Association for the Teaching of English. Most people that she invited to contribute had been, like myself, participants at the conference. Titled *Timely Voices: English Teaching in the Eighties* (Melbourne: Oxford University Press, 1983) it was meant to continue the international forum on English education.

My contribution bore its own headnote explaining the mixture of topics. The portion titled "The Terrible Twos of Junior High" is excerpted from a position paper, "ETV for Grades Seven and Eight," which I wrote in 1978 for the Agency for Instructional Technology (AIT), known before 1984 as the Agency for Instructional Television, to whom I am grateful for permission to use this piece.

————— ◄●► —————

I keep notebooks on ideas that occur to me about language, learning, and other matters that to me seem related. Some notes may end as a talk or article; some may remain isolated and undeveloped, for now. Topics vary as much as the three here. The first came off the wall, the second in response to an assignment commissioned me, the third as part of long-range ruminations about a subject I constantly refer to. These are not unedited inner speech but elaborations to be shared with other educators, who may keep and value similar notebooks.

Tally Me a Story

Have you ever noticed a connection between telling stories and counting? The root of the word *tell* means to calculate or reckon, based on the idea of number, series, and list. In "The Eve of St. Agnes" Keats writes, "Numb were the beadsman's fingers, while he told/His rosary . . .," that is, while he counted the beads to tally the repetitions of his prayer. A tale is a kind of tally. A raconteur recounts stories. Corresponding to the idea of counting *over* again in the French verb *raconter*, the German *zahlen* means to count and *erzahlen* to recount or narrate. The Spanish *contar* means both to count and to tell.

The chief connection seems to be the idea of a series. Like numbers, events have a fixed order, chronology. Thus in telling a story we enumerate events. But since reckoning or calculating goes beyond mere seriating to the idea of permuting or recombining numbers, does telling imply more than listing over the sequence of actions? In addition to "keeping track," does a narrator perform other arithmetical operations? Is he a manipulator or creator?

We also *relate* stories. Perhaps the most fundamental comparison makes of counting and narrating two ways to make sense, to relate elements (quantities and events). At any rate, the parallel between counting and narrating becomes amplified on a grand scale when we look at the roots of such words as *reason, ratio, rite, arithmetic, read, art,* and *rhythm,* which all derive ultimately, it seems, from the Greek *arariskein,* to fit or measure, and they share the idea of proportion and number.

Consider accounting as the practice of relating sets of figures so that they mesh, match, and mean something. We give an account of what happened when we relate events. Thus, "rendering an account" could result in a fiscal balance sheet or a narrative report. Both relate elements to make meaning and to explain.

The idea of repetition in *recount* may stem from the preliterate practice of telling a story over and over from memory—*reciting* tales in lieu of reading books—as well as from the idea that the counting of events corresponds to the original noting of their sequence as one experienced or heard about it and that, therefore, any narrating of events has to be a *re*-counting.

Then, of course, some of the very first writing was simply symbolizing quantities of goods that had been tallied or was the tallying itself, as in the Sumerian cuneiform tablets or ledgers recording business transactions. The ultimate connection between counting and telling may lie in gematria, the ancient practice, so central to caballistic traditions, of identifying letters with numerals so that the spelling of words corresponded to the summing of numbers. Hence numbers meant not just quantities as applied to objects, but constituted a kind of code for a subterranean message underriding that of the letters.

The terrible twos of junior high

Grades seven and eight make up a unique and strongly characterized stage of children's growth and hence of curriculum development.

Whenever in talking with teachers I compare this stage to the "terrible twos" of pre-school life, I get smiles and nods of recognition. Around age two children are feeling their oats because they are experiencing a surge of power from learning to walk and talk and gain other control over their body and their environment. They declare their independence, say no to adults as a matter of principle, and yet still depend desperately on adults. At age 12–14 children get another huge surge of power from discovering through the change of puberty that they can now do what seems to make adults adults. And yet they don't feel nearly ready to take on the world alone, and are in fact bewildered and intimidated about both it and their own feelings. So again they go through an independence/dependence syndrome, spiralling at a higher level over a place they went through about ten or twelve years before. One moment they will be barking off adults, or defying them outright, but the next they may be all child again, asking for help and stroking. This erratic and turbulent behavior drives many adults wild. Teachers tend to abhor or adore this age, reacting extremely to the extremity of the age itself.

Junior high youngsters turn toward peers more than do any other age group. Primary children still orient very much to adults. Upper elementary children begin creating and obeying a peer code and behavior system, but split their allegiance because they need adults very much, are still undergoing massive inculcation and acculturation in and out of school, and devote much energy to building individual skills and competencies in a variety of areas. Whereas pre-school children are naturally non-conformist, and primary children not yet thoroughly acculturated, children of grades three or four to six tend to conform considerably to the adult world, at least in their conscious thought and voluntary behavior. Senior high students, on the other hand, identify increasingly with the adult world. They take their sexual power more for granted, start to look for jobs and mates, and enter the stage of more abstract and formal logical operations. They too orient very much to their peer group, but this peer group more nearly resembles the general older membership of the society. Comparatively, then, junior high youngsters represent the peak of peer orientation when peers still constitute a non-adult sub-culture. They represent also the resurgence of non-conformist experimentation. To some extent, this exploratory spirit arises from a state of being at sixes and sevens—unsure of identity, role, and ability; half child, half adult; thoroughly acculturated by adults but impelled to use peers as a bridge toward independence from adults.

A third development for practical consideration may actually be more induced by school and society than programmed by nature. The fact is, as many parents and teachers know very well, around third and fourth grades a great slump occurs in school children that often lasts through upper elementary and affects junior high considerably. Children lose enthusiasm and seem not to know any longer things they knew before, even including how to read. Many get on a negative track, building up a deficit of school defeats that leads to dropping out. Entering junior high, these students are so shaky academically (as well as otherwise too perhaps) that they become superficially sensitive and capable of freaking out at any moment. The heavy conformist acculturation of the elementary years, the formalization of schooling into specialized "subjects" that occurs during upper elementary, and the further specializing, during junior high, into separate classes, rooms, and teachers generates considerable anxiety and feelings of remoteness and conflict. So several negative potentialities of growing up in our society may culminate in junior high, compared with which senior high represents a land of survivors, of self-selected students who made it through the worst of these negative possibilities.

In my experience consulting with schools and putting together curricula, I find that Grades 7 and 8 are the hottest spot in the whole school curriculum, the area educators feel they know least what to do about. Primary goes all out for initial literacy, elementary fills in introductory knowledge of content areas, and senior high prepares for college or vocations. These teachers at least *feel* they know what they are doing and that their mission is clear, even if results often do not fit what they have in mind. Consequently, I find, the greatest exertion toward curricular innovation occurs in junior high, where, closer to desperation, teachers reach out and try out more readily than anywhere else. They *know* they need help, and they feel they have little to lose in making changes. It follows that media producers can expect the kind of receptivity that goes with a feeling that conventional stuff doesn't really work, and special measures have to be taken.

What about thought and language itself at this age? Although Piaget's theory that formal logical operations become possible only after puberty has been recently questioned as underestimating younger children, still it is safe to say at least that the fullest maturation of logical powers will occur only after puberty. The best policy is to assume the best and offer *opportunities* for higher thinking by proposing a choice of projects for students that entail, or *can* entail, such thinking, and by organizing them into working parties that facilitate pooling of their resources and cross-stimulation of minds.

In accordance with the general transitional unevenness of this stage, thinking capacity may run a wide gamut among individuals of Grades 7 and 8 and across the same individual on different occasions and for different subjects and situations. Group projects calling for mixed sorts of thinking—categorizing, serializing, assigning causes, analyzing, synthesizing, summarizing, syllogizing—will allow students to try out different thinking roles, witness peers' thinking, and eventually exercise or explore whatever kinds they are capable of. Serious introspection begins after puberty as the complexity of inner-outer relations requires more self-knowledge, and as drastic physical and psychological changes within call attention to themselves. So inner life becomes more the subject itself of inner speech or thought.

In language, students of this age will want very much to follow peer codes and fashions in what they talk about and which words and structures they express themselves in. So they could do collaborative projects about topics they consider important but that force them, in effect, to enlarge their language expression beyond the peer group. Uncertainty, the tentative quality of feelings and ideas, inchoate identity, conflicts with tradition—all of these make thought and language less distinct and coherent, more groping and inconsistent. For such a strongly transitional stage of growth, it makes sense to afford much practice in thinking, talking, and writing that is *dilatory* and *exploratory*, not always neatly definitive, and to afford working-up phases before a final closure or polished product. Junior high students need a lot of scope and time to find out what they think, and to formulate what they perceive.

Their thought and language derive strongly from models they identify with, from heroes and heroines or other significant figures in their immediate environment or media-relayed worlds. Seventh- and eighth-graders are constantly *acting*, consciously or not, as they try out different roles and relationships, and this "casting" about or seeking identities influences much of their thought and language. In reading, they look for figures representing a kind of person, they think tentatively, they might like to become. Many still use animals and fantasy actions as symbols through which to look on feelings or issues they are not ready to treat explicitly.

In summary, the learning needs of seventh- and eighth-graders center around peer interaction balanced by adult direction; exploratory thought and language permitting much trying out of roles and ideas; exercise of the new capacity for introspection; new kinds of activities different from grade school; personal and integrative approaches offsetting the traditional impersonality and fragmentation of secondary school; and the learning of ways to deal independently with their own problems and those of the environment.

The Wordless World

Language is not entirely a good thing. However useful and beautiful it may seem at times, it is also very dangerous. It is divisive and dualistic, stereotyped, partial, and far too crude to be any match for reality itself. As the general semanticists say, it is only a map to the terrritory, not the territory itself, which remains forever unspeakable. Now, we can recite that semantic credo to ourselves as much as we wish, but mostly we limit ourselves and our world because we seldom really believe it. Most of the time we go on assuming that statements can be made about the world that are true. But statements are never true; they are only useful or beautiful. The reason that we persist in believing our maps, and having faith, is that we learned language as infants and were hypnotized by it at our most susceptible moment without knowing what happened. So we have never in our maturity known reality directly, unabstracted by language. We don't even know what it is we don't know. The thoughts, feelings, perceptions, and behavior of our maturity are essentially post-hypnotic suggestions, verbal/conceptual commands absorbed during the trance of early childhood and carried out somnambulistically in adulthood. This is no doubt why mystical literature refers to the ultimate enlightenment as an awakening.

So we share a great linguistic dream, much as the original Balinese are said to have hallucinated together. This sharing enables us to communicate, because communication is based on convention and agreement, but *what* we can say is limited to those consensuses we have agreed on, that is, that others agreed on before we were born. So strongly does concept dominate percept, in symbolically-organized creatures, that we end by being limited in what we can see to what we can say. To gain a management of reality through symbols we trade off some of reality itself. It is a law of the abstracting process that the more abstract the map the less it resembles the territory, and the more it resembles some inner structure of our own, the neural networks of our nervous system, our webs of intent, and so on.

But it would not be nearly enough anyway to understand the general semanticists' dictum that map and territory are different, that utility is one thing, truth another. To grasp our situation as symbol-making animal we would have to realize that normally we never know the territory *any other way* than through some map. We cannot even compare map with territory to check for distortion and omission. We can only compare map with map. We can put aside the realtor's description and go look at the land parcel described, but what we see will only be a less abstract construction that our visual perception makes as it peers through the mesh of our verbal/conceptual cage. Ironically, the cage itself is invisible, because we have been seeing *through* it too long to be able to *see* it. Our so-called facts are social artifacts. Language fixes and transmits these illusions.

By its very nature language is divisive. The Biblical story of the tower of Babel probably refers not just to the nationalistic divisions within a polyglot world but to the fundamentally fragmenting effect of any lexicon. To name things is to cut up the indivisible unity of the world into man-made "objects," to segment the continuous movement of the world into man-made entities like time and space, and, falsest of all, to reify, to make *things* out of vibrations, to convert energy to matter. Thus broken down, these named objects must be related to each other with other words that make statements—certain verbs of mental action, including *to be*, adverbs and prepositions of time, place, manner, etc., and conjunctions of time, space, causality, conditionality, etc. Behind language lies the man-made analysis and classification of a god-made world. Mathematician Norbert Wiener said, "Scientific discovery consists in the interpretation for our own convenience of a system of existence which has been made with no eye to our convenience at all." By means of grammar and connector words we try to put back together our own pieces of this world we never made but feel compelled to dissect and re-make to suit ourselves. God composes and man decomposes.

It was Adam, not God, who gave names to the creatures of the earth, according to Genesis; and when Adam and Eve ate of the tree of knowledge of good and evil what they partook of was conceptualization with all its mortal dualities and breakdowns and assumptions. That the knowledge of this tree is very limited and social is shown both by the necessity of the fig-leaf and by the very strong contrast the Bible draws between the tree of knowledge and the tree of life, which is also located in the center of the garden. It is very clear that Adam was not expelled merely as punishment, but to bar him from the tree of life, "lest he put forth his hand and take also of the tree of life, and eat, and live forever." (This was not unkind of God; expulsion insured they would develop spiritually.) After the expulsion, God placed cherubim at the east of Eden "and a flaming sword which turned every way, to keep the way of the tree of life." Very ambiguous indeed. A flaming sword is both a defense and a beacon, and "keep the way" means both to guard the gate and to maintain the roadway. The home fires are burning, but expect an ordeal regaining paradise. The way of life is not the way of mundane knowledge, the kind embodied in language.

Language not only divides the indivisible, it stereotypes the unique. Existentially, nothing ever recurs, and nothing belongs to a class. These are fancies. But language can operate only by rough-shod generalizing and by suppressing particularity, constantly forcing us to favor similarity over difference. This sameness may make the world more manageable but it also makes it seem more boring and remote. To begin to match its territory less grossly, language would have to forsake common nouns for proper nouns and even to date the proper nouns, since things change. Or, like the characters in a novel of Jean Giraudoux, make up new words for "indescribable" moments of experience—let's say, glimpsing a shiny frog at the same time as hearing a train whistle while mulling over a business problem in a wooded Montana valley. What's the word for *that* experience? But how can I complain one moment about language being divisive, then complain the next about its not being particular enough? Neither is a complaint. Both, rather, define language for what it really is—a kind of bourgeois compromise between the unity and the uniqueness of things of this world, what seems like a contradiction when put into language. Blake had to say it as a paradox, the universe in a grain of sand. A compromise that touches neither the truth of wholeness nor of particularity is all right . . . so long as we know every minute what this can and cannot do. But can we really know this in our normal state? Can a spellbound person dispel the spell from within?

Verbal stereotyping fulfils itself: we perceive in the way language habits structure perception, then our consequently gross and standard-ized perception seems to corroborate the structure of language. Benja-min Lee Whorf's hypothesis about thought and speech has been dis-puted, resulting in a strong version that language *determines* thought and a weak version that language only *influences* thought. One example from his cultural comparisons is a Hopi word that stands for any object having a *Gestalt* or silhouette like that of a mushroom, including disparate things, or what seem from our functional point of view to be disparate things, such as a hammer, a mushroom itself, and presumably an atomic explosion. Classifying by shape rather than by purpose is certainly a different way of cutting up the pie of reality and indeed could hardly fail to influence thought.

An example from our own culture will illustrate not just how lan-guages may vary in their influence on thought but how language locks in outright mistakes and prevents their exposure. In Western medicine the concept "involuntary" has been used to designate body functions thought to be beyond the control of the conscious self—heart beat, respiration, electrical brain activity, skin temperature, glandular secretion, etc.—but which yogis and swamis have been learning to control for centuries, as Western monitoring devices are now proving, and as Westerners them-selves are learning to do. We will never know how much this miseduca-tion of generations of doctors has set back man's development in our culture. It is a truism in science that half of making a discovery is knowing that it can be done at all. If the scientific community says certain functions cannot be controlled, this creates a mental set few colleagues or laymen are likely ever to break. The basic problem here, of course, was the dual-ity, built into the language, about voluntary and involuntary, one term implying the other.

Why tolerate such blinders? Well, doesn't language just as often remove blinders by allowing us to think new thoughts? Yes, but if you examine closely a case of a new concept "liberating" our minds, you will almost certainly find that the "new" concept would not have been neces-sary had we not previously believed some other concept that was false or limited. In other words, most so-called breakthroughs in thinking are really cases of *un*thinking something that was not so. Language never appears so effective as when undoing its own mischief—naturally—for it speaks truest about itself, which is precisely its basic limitation . . . and the limitation actually of any symbols.

But in a sense none of us really wants an open mind: the economy would burst overnight. Ours is a society that *needs* all its problems, in order to generate jobs, markets, and votes, so we all have an investment in believing that the solutions to grave problems of commerce, govern-ment, law, medicine and education, require perpetual conceptualizing and verbalizing—more research, more negotiation, more legislation, more administration. The more our problems are man-made—and which of them isn't?—the more they involve replacing old concepts with new concepts, that is, one mental limit with a perhaps less narrow one, but one almost certain to spawn other problems that will sustain jobs, markets, and votes. The art of living in our society is the art of converting worthless states of nature into valuable problems calling for expensive treatment—but I for one am tired of brilliant solutions to stupid problems.

So far I've said that language does not tell "the truth" because symbols constitute only a facsimile of the reality they point to. It does not give us "nothing but the truth" because it speaks as much about itself as medium as it does about its message. Now, last, it does not tell the "whole truth" because the editing that goes on as a medium simulates reality omits much of the reality it tries to capture. Language is partial, partial in two senses: it's not the "whole truth," and it's biased. But a biased truth is a half-truth. The underlying difficulty of all verbal concepts is that, by their very analytical and categorical nature, they cannot ever get beyond the relative knowledge of which Adam and Eve partook with the apple to the total, instantaneous knowledge that constitutes the "whole truth," the tree of life. Part of the difficulty with language is that it is linear, not simultaneous, and no amount of stringing language can build up a whole, because the linearity is only a surface reflection of the analytic nature of language. The partiality comes not just from the analytic breakdown, however, but from the impossibility of putting the pieces back together again, which requires an instantaneous fusion, not merely an additive or linear linking. Humpty Dumpty's egg reappears in some oriental philosophy, as indeed in other Western lore, as a symbol of original unity. Once you've shattered that unity by conceptualizing, you can never put the pieces back together, even if you're a king, and you stand, like Adam and Eve, barred from the tree of life.

The original sin is not anything as frivolous as sex, which was enjoyed before the fall, but the sin of objectivication, of losing primal oneness with the world. This oneness carries with it the insider's truth, which is the whole truth. Once you're outside, you can spend all your life rattling different gates trying to get back in. There is another meaning of objectivity, however, that does fit unity. They come together in the word "impartiality," which means freed of local or relative viewpoints by virtue of being integral, whole. So the hunger for a transcendent perspective seems better fulfilled by oneness of human with world than by analysis by human of world. And if language is only a worldly tool for getting the day's work done—the tree of knowledge, not the tree of life—then we are caught in the big metaphysical catch, namely, that our worldly problems require, precisely, a holistic and holy understanding well beyond anything we will ever get from verbal concepts.

The purpose of all the arts—music, dance, drama, painting—was originally to offset the strictures imposed by verbal thought and to restore attunement to inner and outer forces of nature, unmediated by local culture. The arts are among the techniques developed to suspend inner speech.

But isn't literature art, and isn't it also verbal? Yes. In fact, it may well be the highest function of literature to undo language with language. Poetry represents this function in purest form, and that is the real meaning of "poetic licence." It has the culture's blessing to go counter-cultural in the sense of presenting, through imagination, alternative realities that expand consciousness beyond those very limits set by ordinary verbalizing. Although readers expand their minds from the best literature, the writer benefits more. It follows that students should create as well as consume literature. To become steeped in imaginative modes of writing as both reader and author is to become rich enough to afford the price of verbal conceptualization.

As the thief to catch a thief, literature may be a key technique of liberation, but schools could and should teach youngsters the other techniques also—the other arts, crafts, sports, and survival activities— from the viewpoint of their relation to attentional self-control and mental balance, so that people can benefit from the abstracting power of language without being permanently distracted from the greater, silent knowledge from which it draws.

11

Reading and Writing as Meditation

Background

While editor of *Language Arts,* Julie Jensen of the Education Department at the University of Texas in Austin invited a number of educators, including myself, to contribute an article on the relationship between reading and writing. According to plan, these articles appeared first in various issues of *Language Arts* and then, under a grant from the National Institute of Education, were assembled as a book titled *Composing and Comprehending,* edited by Professor Jensen, reviewed by the National Conference on Research in English, and published by the ERIC Clearinghouse on Reading and Communication Skills (Urbana, Illinois).

I felt that it was time to relate reading to meditation, as I had already done writing, and thus to relate reading to writing through a third activity that might induce a viewpoint not likely to arise in the many research-based articles that I knew would also appear in the book.

————————◄●►————————

Reading and writing are ways of modifying inner speech, which comprises the more verbal currents of our inner stream. Reading and writing temporarily change how we talk to ourselves. Eventually this may change how we feel and think. The power to modify our stream of consciousness is something reading and writing share, something they do differently than do other activities, and something they do differently one than the other. A valuable way of approaching the relationship between reading and writing may be to explore these similar and different ways of influencing consciousness.

Consider what happens when we read. The text does not register on a blank. The inner stream of thoughts, feelings, and images that flows unceasingly in us virtually all the time, even in sleep, does not stop when we open a book, but it does adapt drastically to this act, because what comes off the page is another thought stream. What happens when one thought stream is integrated into another? Specifically, different things happen, of course, according to the nature and maturity of the individual mind, but generally, the text structures the stream of consciousness during the act of reading if the reader is attending to it with reasonable interest and incentive. (The text will usually influence even the mental digressions.) This means the text is in some measure supplanting some other structuring activity—socializing, working, or driving, playing a sport or musical instrument. Some activities influence the inner stream far more than others, because they require closer attention and permit less inner meandering. The less an external activity engages our thought and attention, the more some internal activity takes over the stream—recollection, reflection, fantasying, and so on. It is by no means idle to define an activity, precisely, by how it affects the stream of consciousness. What are the effects of reading?

Reading

Reading demands consistent close attention. It immobilizes you and holds both eye and mind—and commands the mind's eye. Though aspects of it become automatic, like driving, it engages imagination and intellect far too much to encourage mind-wandering, except during pauses, when the reader may ruminate over what he has read. Playing a sport or musical instrument or doing certain non-repetitive craft activities also controls the content and continuity of consciousness by imposing their content and continuity on the inner stream, which must cleave to these because of the concentration required. Reading differs from these other close-attention, structured activities by a critical factor; its content and continuity are the product of some other human being's inner stream, that is, a written composition. A text is structured by a mind, and the medium is symbols. The focus of reading, therefore, is very inward regardless of how external may be the referents of the symbols, the subject matter.

To arrive at the precise qualities of a thing one must winnow out what is unique to it (not necessarily superior). The uniqueness of reading emerges further as we pass on to a comparison of texts with other human compositions that move in time—films, music, dance, drama. These too differ from street scenes, chance encounters, and other unplanned activity in being compositions, which by their nature make us feel the presence of another mind. In this way a book and a film and a ballet are alike. But compositions in different media engage different faculties at play in the inner stream—sensory perception, imagination, emotion, memory, intellect. The "lively arts" like music, dance, and drama certainly stimulate our senses more and, by their powerful atmospheric effects, grip more our organism as a whole. (If you are participant, the performing arts affect you more as sports or martial arts do, whereas, if spectator, they affect you more as a book does.)

The sensuosity of the non-verbal media does not mean that they convey no meaning, nor is it true that language alone is symbolic. Forms symbolize inner things for us, especially the forms that make up a composition, and the sensory forms we witness in dance and music and art act as metaphors to "speak" to our sensibility. So non-verbal compositions also engage our memory and intellect and imagination, but to the extent that they present sounds and sights directly, they draw less on the imagination than does a text, which requires the reader to visualize and to play out action and setting for herself on the stage of the mind. And here is the real difference. Reading engages emotion and memory and imagination by means of the mind, because it is words not deeds or sights or sounds that elicit response. Imagery is conjured from words, emotion sprung by words, and ideas generated by words. Everything in a text is mediated by the reader's conscious intelligence, whereas the non-verbal media excite our faculties directly, as the natural forms and patterns of life itself do. Language symbolizes *concepts,* which the mind must *apply* to stored experience, whereas film imagery or dance movement or musical progressions stand for inner equivalents by some organic similitude, whether these inner equivalents are named and conceptualized or not. Consider the meaning, for example, of certain musical dynamics such as crescendo or staccato. It is this mediation by mind that distinguishes language and makes a written composition act in a unique way on the stream of consciousness.

When we read, we introject the text into our inner life and at the same time project our inner life into the text. This is a heady interaction. On the one hand, reading *supplants* our inner stream with someone else's to the degree that we do give ourselves over to it in rapt absorption. On the other hand, we also "read into" the text much that is not said there. Some of this reading-in serves the author's intention, inasmuch as a text can't say all and relies on the reader to fill in sensible implications. Some reading-in is distortion peculiar to a given reader—subjective "projection" in the psychologist's sense or biased selection and emphasis of an author's points or details. The reader may dialogue with the author or characters, kibitz, comment, cheer or jeer, and otherwise sustain a running response. The novice reader may—as we know from analyzing "miscues"when he or she sight-reads a text aloud—add, delete, or substitute some of the syllables, words, or punctuation marks, not to mention paraphrase and translate into his or her own dialect or idiom or understanding in order to ensure meaning. The scholar may annotate the margins with questions, exclamations, citations, glosses, and mini-essays. All of us may extend the text or spin off from the text by fantasying, recollecting, and reflecting—setting off trains of thought that may actually interrupt the reading but are in any case one way in which the text influences the inner stream. This interlarding, overlaying, or punctuating of the text constitutes some portion of our inner stream while reading, in addition to the rendering in the mind of the text itself with more or less fidelity or revision.

An interesting and valuable way to contemplate readers, reading, and texts concerns, in fact, the ratio between introjection and projection. Children between ages eight and twelve, for example, tend to open themselves to the text with unusual receptivity, holding ego in abeyance, with the result that the text very nearly *becomes* their inner stream, give or take some unconscious deformation or adjustment to fit their psyche. Not surprisingly, this is the same period (of "latency" before puberty) when people are most suggestible, most acquiescent in hypnosis (which is usually voice-induced, we note). Psychologist Ernest Hilgard made this connection with rapt reading while conducting research correlating personality variables with hypnotic susceptibility. This acquiescence corresponds, in reading, to the willingness to make someone else's inner life temporarily one's own. While it no doubt accounts partly for the fact that many people read more at this age than at any time later, it also characterizes how numerous adults habitually read or how they read certain kinds of books. The hyperbole of blurbs—"spellbinding,""enthralling"— expresses the state booksellers would like to see the reader in and which in fact does occur when we "suspend disbelief," silence our own inner voices, and give ourselves over completely to what authors have composed of *their* inner lives. Textual hypnosis may be a factor of the reader's personality and age, of the nature and art of the text, or of some mental set or reading process acquired from experience. It may also be a factor of the kind of discourse—whether fiction, true narrative, poetry, essay, informative article—in relation to a personality. What enthralls *you?*

The "getting lost in a book" represents one extreme of how reading structures inner speech or the total inner stream. It is like a benign "possession" permitted by the reader in just the way that psychologist Lawrence Kubie hypothesized that creative people let their unconscious take over for a while without fear that they will lose control or not return. Just as Kubie relates "creativity" to "regression in the service of the ego" so Hilgard connects rapt reading and hypnotic susceptibility to a strong ego structure that *knows* it will return after temporarily ceding sway to another force. Perhaps most important of all, "losing oneself" in a book or a surge of creativity makes a person feel liberated and happy, "beside oneself" with joy. The sensation of introjecting a ready-made inner stream—from an author or from the unconscious (perceived, precisely, as another)—is that we "get out of ourselves." This is understandable, because the feeling of being oneself is of recognizing one's inner speech, which repeats personal and cultural patterns. Alter the inner stream and we feel like someone else. So when we speak of reading for "escape," we must mean, as much as anything, escape from the closed circles of our habitual thinking, which reflects our troublesome outer circumstances in the form of worry and problem-pondering.

Even the margin-annotating scholar at the other, detached extreme of reading response partakes of this feeling as he or she gets "carried away" by ideas stimulated by the text. In approximating a co-author by so copiously amending and appending, our scholar is projecting also. The text has got hold of his mind, and he too is concentrating so intently that the subject-object separation is dissolving. Maybe he is not introjecting or projecting less than the ten-year-old but is interacting at a more verbal and conscious level. He is aware and can formulate his responses in words; he knows where the text ends and he begins, at least intellectually. But maybe his conscious, verbal responses do not cover all of his engagement with the text. Suppose his very intellectual excitement and professional commitment cause him to fall under a spell too—in addition to critiquing and extending the ideas he finds there. At any rate, while reading, his inner speech fuses the author's content and continuity with the responses they evoke from himself, and this interweaving forms a revised content and continuity inasmuch as text and response form a single inner flow. This collaboration between author and reader probably occurs no less between the rapt ten-year-old and his story but does not appear to do so because the child's responses are too unconscious and subverbal to manifest themselves. So we arrive at the fascinating paradox that introjection and projection are really the same thing viewed from different angles.

In stories for all ages, actual and fictional, we usually acknowledge that the reader's identification with key characters is paramount. This identification occurs as part of introjecting and projecting, of suspending for a while the demarcation between *I* and *he* or *she*. The concept and practice of bibliotherapy are based on it—that while we are "being" So-and-so we can expand our self and our experience to include those of the character in the story, who may change or find a solution that we still have not. Identifying helps people grow because we imaginatively incorporate into ourselves the needed features and experiences of the character that go along with the familiar part of him or her that permits the identification in the first place. This incorporation of character into reader corresponds to the way the reader assimilates a text into the ongoing stream of consciousness. And metabolism may be an apt metaphor because of its two-way action. Our perpetual inner stream compares to enzymes that re-make to a degree what is ingested so that our body can integrate this foreign substance into our existing system.

Again, through identification, the reader "gets out of himself." Too seldom do educators examine why stories have such powerful and universal appeal. Stories make up the largest part of popular reading, and identification is the key to much of this popularity, as authors, teachers, parents, and librarians all find out sooner or later. The personage in the story—real or invented—does not have to be like me if it resembles what I would like to be. Identification typifies the function of stories generally—to fulfill myself by letting me get out of myself for a while, to escape to the more abundant not-me and complete the potential me.

So all this is about growth, yes, but the *process* of the growth occurs specifically by *modifying inner speech*. We have to change— enlarge—how we think, alter consciousness, because anyone's life spells limitation. Children just admit this more readily. This is the real "escape," not from reality but toward it. So long as we are trapped within the circuits of our routine thoughts, confined to our ordinary consciousness, we remain arrested within the bounds of our necessarily limited experience. Quite without planning or realizing what we are after, we seek ways of getting out of ourselves, of eluding the re-runs, the self-haranguing, the re-cycled inner speech that perpetuates our limited and false notion of reality. Limitation is mental circling. We maintain by our old thoughts and feelings a dead world, false because restricted to a certain ego and culture. We want break-throughs, break-outs. But we don't know we do. We read for other reasons, we believe—for entertainment and information. But that is the same thing. To "entertain" means literally to keep a continuity going. Our inner continuity, left to itself, is too conditioned and habit-ridden. It needs intervention, we intuit—but of our own doing. Reading one does oneself, and one controls it (except perhaps in school).

Through reading we seek outside continuities from other people, to shuffle us up, restructure our consciousness, entertain us, continuities that give pleasure because they take us out of ourselves and release us a little at a time from our mental cage. Reading can do this quite well if we can choose the texts and the circumstances so that incentive stays rooted in this deep impulsion toward self-expansion and higher consciousness. Stories in particular are popular at all ages because they offer, besides personages with which to identify, the familiar continuity of time order and the concreteness of physical actions, objects, and settings. The plot of a made-up story or the chronology of actual events guarantees *enchainment*, that meaningful continuity that sustains us in place of the all too familiar patterns of thoughts by which we "entertain" ourselves. Stories surprise too. What happens next? As our minds mature, we find satisfaction in other, more abstract kinds of continuities as well—the logical and psychological enchainments of ideas and images that make up other discourse such as essay, poetry, theory. Adding these other continuities to chronology represents itself one way we expand original constraints. Trying on, trying out others' minds, hearing out the world, gradually enlarges consciousness to more nearly embrace the world.

Writing

Introjecting others' compositions into our inner stream is not the only way to modify it. Another way is to manipulate our own inner speech so as to redirect and transform it. Writing is such a way. In fact, we may perhaps think afresh about writing by regarding it so. So far I have mentioned composition only for its effect on the reader. Consider now the effect on consciousness of creating a composition. To do this we must define writing as authentic authoring, not merely as some sort of glorified plagiarizing, because it is the act of real composing—"putting together" for oneself—that modifies the stream.

Let's define writing, in fact, as precisely this modifying—as narrowing, focusing, editing, and revising inner speech. On the one hand, writing is just writing down inner speech, transcribing thoughts, self-dictation. But as stenographer to oneself, one does not write down everything and any old thing that pops into the head. Indeed, by setting some subject before herself at the outset, a writer directs her inner speech toward greater selectivity as compared with its more miscellaneous nature when left to the vagaries of random inner and outer stimulation. The writer then proceeds to develop the subject along some sort of chronological, logical, or psychological progression that provides the continuity or enchainment that carries the reader out of herself when she incorporates it.

Constructing that continuity does for the writer what following it does for the reader. But if the writer composes this out of his own innards, how can it be new for him, take him somewhere he has not been before? This is where the discovery aspect of writing, so much talked about today, comes into the picture. What is new in composition are *connections*. Composing connects. The bits and pieces of thought, memory, feeling, and imagery lie within already, it's true, but old habits keep turning these over in the same patterns or simply ignoring them. Without a special countering effort, these patterns are fixed enough by mental and emotional sets so that much of our rich store of material stays side-tracked because these valuable fragments can't connect with the current tracks our mind is shuttling around on. (Where there are thought trains there must be thought tracks!) The act of composing necessarily rearranges our store of inner material.

How does it do this? How is it that in transcribing inner speech we surprise ourselves and think thoughts we have not thought before? Don't we figure out what we want to say and then just write it down? Maybe, but this "figuring out" entails some very important processes that go on recursively, that is, by revolving among stages of jotting down ideas, reacting to these, reflecting on the subject when not writing, and revising earlier writing. This is how composing proceeds, and the heart of it—the inner equivalent of the recursive paper progress—is the focusing, editing, and revising of inner speech. In other words, the very features of a composition that any reader expects—coherence and continuity of content, or unity and development—do not characterize the ordinary movements of our inner speech. They represent, rather, a superimposition of a structure from outside the stream itself, from the will—that corresponds to the introjection of the text for the reader. The deliberate selecting of images and ideas, and of words themselves, not only breaks up routine and random inner streaming but *sustains the development of a subject beyond what we have thought or imagined about it before*. This is discovery. The composing process requires exactly the rearrangement of experience that jogs loose unused material and connects the heretofore unconnected.

Much of composing is for the reader's benefit, is rhetorical, for effects. In writing we do not merely put our thoughts in order, or get our story straight, we put our thoughts in order or get our story straight *for someone else, for a purpose*. This effort too, to use thought and language to act on others acts on the writer also, because it is a factor of contrivance that tends to meddle further with old inner patterns, which are as they are partly just from habits of privacy, or even solipsism. The writer puts herself in the shoes of the reader (gets outside of herself or introjects the "other"). What does the reader need or want? How can I surprise, awe, appall, sadden, amuse, arouse, lighten, enlighten the reader? The writer *casts about*, tries out, reworks—on or off paper, it doesn't matter—seeking ways and means. The composition evolves during the rhetorical process of getting it right for an audience and a purpose. The results show on paper, but the evolution takes place in the author and affects her consciousness as she works out ways to affect the reader's. Putting a version on paper aids memory and prompts revision. Writing down what one thinks acts reflexively to influence what one may think next. To this process of self-stimulation and self-cuing may be added feedback from a trial audience—advance reactions in order to sample the effects of one's composing so far. Incorporating this outside viewpoint may inspire further revision, not only of the composition but of the author's consciousness. Audience reaction at any point, in fact, can act as a powerful agent to break the inner monopoly.

Composing is also playing. The beauty of play is that it licenses the mind to frolic outside the usual constraints set for it by the consciousness-structuring of that fanatic, self-serving entrepreneur, the ego. A composition is always some more or less artful or unskilled creative plaything. Not just literary creations but factual articles, documentary narratives, and theoretical essays all raise for the author decisions about phrasing and fashioning, about balance and proportion, pace and rhythm, style and tone, dynamics and progressions. These are all toys to play with as well as utilitarian means to get the job done. They are elements of composing in other arts and media. Above and beyond fulfilling the logical and rhetorical needs, composing is crafting and constructing, kin to what children do when they make something just to make something. A writer sports with language, images, and ideas for pleasure just as an artist does with the elements of *her* medium—color and light, form and space, mass and movement. Composing, with words or otherwise, is playing to the extent that making anything has intrinsic gratification. Play is gratuitous, eludes determinism, and subverts ego. It plays a part in helping writing to liberate the inner stream.

But if writing is at bottom manipulating and modifying inner speech, can't it just be done in the mind without actual physical writing? Yes. Such a way is called meditation, which is composing the mind. The best way to appreciate the relation between reading and writing that I am developing here may be to relate them both in turn to another activity that *specializes* in transforming the inner stream. Various practices are lumped together under the concept of meditation, but I define them all as ways of raising consciousness by modifying inner speech.

Reading, Writing, and Meditating

Some meditation techniques simply slow down the stream so we can become aware of it and examine it without otherwise altering it. Even this consciousness of consciousness already resembles the reflexiveness, the introspection, the concentration required for writing. The writer has to feel her reality as a thinking reed having some power of control over thought. Other kinds of meditation resemble writing rather directly in that one assigns oneself a topic, focuses the mind on it, and develops it to a climax. This differs from ordinary cogitation by an extraordinary intensity of focus and by an equally unusual integration of all faculties of heart and mind—of emotion, perception, memory, imagination, and reason, which are brought to bear simultaneously on the topic in order to break through to new understanding of it. In the process of achieving this breakthrough, consciousness itself shifts into a more exalted state. The rarest form of meditation consists of entirely stopping for a while the flow of the inner stream. One slows it so much and focuses it so finely that it stops—becomes "one-pointed." Consciousness is altered indeed, and drastically in this case, because this meditation reaches the ultimate in "getting outside of oneself."

Whereas the first form of meditation consists of *witnessing* the inner stream and the second of *focusing* it, this last amounts to *suspending* it altogether. What happens when for a while we simply quit sensing, imagining, recalling, and thinking? This is something we should answer for ourselves by arranging the experience itself, but it is safe to say that in suspending inner speech one is bypassing ego and culture with their partial and conditioned conceptions of reality and making possible an unmediated attunement to the world resulting in revelation and ecstasy. The original and non-romantic meaning of "ecstasy" is being outside onself.

I see no reason, aside from convention, not to regard reading and writing as forms of meditation. All three are deliberate activities that a person initiates in order to meddle with his or her mind. Specifically, they modify the inner stream during the act itself, produce at their most intense an altered state of consciousness, and over the long haul liberate the patterns of perception and thought in the direction of expanded or higher consciousness. Reading assimilates one person's composed inner speech into another person's ongoing inner stream so that one's composition temporarily restructures the other's consciousness. Writing temporarily restructures one's consciousness as one focuses, edits, and revises the inner stream so as to act on another's. Reading and writing have other functions such as to instruct about mundane matters, but even these take their place in the bigger picture of transforming oneself, or raising consciousness; and the more reading and writing represent unforced personal choices the more this analysis is true.

All activities may occasion some modification of consciousness, the more so as they entail *single-minded concentration*. Reading and writing are not necessarily superior to some of these such as musical performance or martial arts, which certainly preclude mind-wandering or obsessing, but reading, writing, and meditating induce and sustain concentration to an extraordinary degree *on the inner world itself*. Reading and writing more nearly specialize than other activities in transforming inner speech and more nearly *avow* doing so. As the *most* specialized and avowed means of controlling and changing inner speech, meditation represents the archetype toward which reading and writing both tend. Reading and writing control inner speech by allowing a text to structure it or by structuring it to create a text. Meditation dispenses with the text in an immediate sense but may well follow the reading of one or lead to the writing of one. Practicing meditation may facilitate reading and writing and may benefit from them in turn.

12

A Pluralistic Curriculum

Background

Houghton Mifflin Company asked me to do an article for their 1983 issue of *Educator's Forum*, an annual publication distributed to education professors in all subjects. Though a form of advertising, since the authors of the articles are authors of Houghton Mifflin college books, the periodical aims to offer its readers quality essays on many educational topics, comparable to what professional journals might publish. I took advantage of the occasion to deal with a school problem affecting more than language arts.

Ever since 1974, when the *Interaction* program I had directed became the object of a schoolbook censorship dispute, I had been thinking a lot about the contradiction inherent in a standard curriculum for a pluralistic population. Parents living in different cultures or holding different values want their children to read or avoid different books. The exuberantly multicultural and all-embracing reading selections in the *Interaction* books angered many parents in the Charleston area of West Virginia, who felt such reading matter would subvert the minds of their children by giving voice to attitudes and values other than those they had instilled.[1]

Ironically, *Interaction* was designed to implement individualized reading by replacing the hard-cover class set with a paperback classroom library containing far more reading matter but only six copies of each title. Such a reading program would not require any child to read any particular selections but would enable all children to pursue their own agendas. This pluralistic approach—not created to head off book disputes and censorship but to invigorate learning to read—would, however, help avoid such problems caused by a pluralistic school constituency. And virtually every school district on this continent today services a community of mixed values and beliefs.

[1] For my account and analysis of this textbook dispute see James Moffett, *Storm in the Mountains: A Case Study of Censorship, Conflict, and Consciousness* (Carbondale, Illinois: Southern Illinois University Press, 1988).

Textbook disputes merely dramatize one way in which the standardizing of curriculum works against both the kind of education and the kind of democracy we Americans profess to believe in.

———————————◄●►———————————

"Out of many one," we read on our American coins—*E pluribus unum*. In our public schools we put this national motto fully to the test. They are expected to administer one education for all despite a great range of differences in student population reflecting all the ethnic, racial, religious, and social-class variety of American culture. Is this possible? How is it possible?

It may appear that our school systems have resolved the question inasmuch as they have for many generations functioned within this paradox of the one for the many. But events and trends of the last twenty years have rendered the always fragile unity of tradition impossible to sustain any longer, as we can hear in the crescendo of outcries rising against schools from all sides. In 1982 one of the programs in CBS's "Sixty Minutes"dealt with the increasing withdrawal of children from school by parents who object to the curriculum and prefer to teach their children at home. One of the two illustrative families was fundamentalist conservative and the other, intellectual liberal.

America is only an imperfect melting pot. In fact, the larger and more mixed the pot, the more the sects and factions eventually feel they must resist the general smelting and affirm distinctions. We have passed beyond that stage of nation-building where most people want to join an overall identity and where second-generation immigrants feel ashamed of the parents for speaking the old language. Only now, after the great assimilation of the nineteenth century and the super-growth of a society so vast and involuted that personal identification seems impossible, does our school system face the dilemma inherent but latent from our nation's founding, of educating a pluralistic populace by a single curriculum.

It is not the case, of course, that all school systems officially subscribe to a national curriculum, although standardized testing and federally instigated, state-legislated trends in accountability and minimal standards have made the curricula of local districts more and more resemble each other. Speaking just of a single school district, it is the case, however, that the curriculum is usually designed on the assumption that elementary students will follow essentially the same course of study and that the programs of secondary students will differ only to the extent that some choice in courses is available. Exceptions are interesting because they indicate that alternatives within a district may be managed at four levels of school administration.

Alternatives at Four Levels

To start with the largest administrative unit, a whole alternative school may be instituted on the basis of different concepts of curriculum. Sometimes such schools have their own sites, sometimes they have only separate organization within a shared site. Whereas the alternative-school movement of the late '60s and early '70s operated on special outside funding, thrived on curricular innovation, and catered to progressive and ethnic pressures, current alternative schools call for a voucher system, offer only familiar competing models, and cater to conservative factions.

At the next largest administrative level, tracking creates a kind of alternative schooling within a site by shunting some students through one set of courses and some through another. It differs from a real alternative sub-school in not having a separate staff or organization, in being not a whole curriculum but a variant program for part of the curriculum, and in placing students by school choice rather than family choice. Which track a student follows depends on test results in required or "basic" subjects, not on personal preference or family values.

Third, though less enthusiastically offered than ten or fifteen years ago, electives do function, as the name implies, by student choice. As alternatives arranged by subject departments, electives represent an administrative echelon between inter-departmental organization and the individual classroom. Thus a student may choose British poetry or science fiction, according to departmental offerings, while concurrently taking courses required of all or as a particular way of fulfilling a general requirement for literature or English.

Within the self-contained classroom, finally, alternatives are typically not very significant, though they could be. Despite labels of "individualized," few classroom managements, methods, or materials permit much educational variation or student choice. At the least, narrowly programmed materials allow only skipping or recycling lessons, according to scores, and amount only to everyone running through the same course but at different rates. At the most, some teachers let students choose from a broad array which books to read or which kinds of writing to do, sometimes on a "contract" basis. Several groups may be doing different projects at the same time, as in the truly "open" classroom. "Learning stations" and activity cards permit a working party of one or several to direct itself through an activity it has chosen or one selected for it by the teacher.

A truly individualized or, as I would call it, "student-centered" classroom is rare in secondary school, except in some junior highs, because of the imperatives about covering a certain content in common and in unison. Not only courses are required, but also particular topics, books, and activities within a given course.

The alternatives possible among these four levels of administration are impressive, but not all are used, of course, and some will not speak to our original problem of cultural pluralism. For example, tracking into rudimentary and advanced versions of a subject is done by the school on the basis of academic performance and so has nothing to do with differing values in the population. (Special programs for the handicapped do accommodate needs of that minority but are being cut back along with state and federal budgets.) Likewise, so-called "individualized" programming usually just distinguishes slow from fast learners in order to expedite certain learning required of all.

In other words, we have to ask which of the alternatives arrayed above will actually help to vary the curriculum so as to satisfy different families living in the same school district in an era when even the smallest community most likely comprises different factions, sects, or ethnic groups.

Presumably our very individualistic founding fathers did not intend for our schools to mint everyone alike but to create a framework, like the Constitution itself, flexible enough to apply at large and still give scope for local circumstances. For a district curriculum I think this means keeping people together as much as possible while still affording individual or family choice.

A voucher system will institutionalize and perpetuate conflict instead of reducing it, because it will provide choice only by dispersing people to different sites even when they might otherwise attend the same schools. At any rate, let's say that the larger the administrative unit offering choice, the less differing people can be kept together and the more alternative education will be bought at the risk of rift. Alternative sub-schools and electives at least accommodate differences on the same site.

But as we know from tracking, which often relegates ethnic minorities to the lower track, it is possible to grow apart in the same building. We also know that conflicts in values arise most in programs of required reading and writing, as in elementary schools, where electives are seldom offered, and in required high school English or social studies courses. Furthermore, parents may very well object to reading selections or ideas in elective courses as well.

Ideally, learning alternatives would occur in the smallest administrative unit, in the individual classroom, where the many might most effectively be one, learning about each other and from each other while learning with each other. This is most feasible for those programs or courses where pluralism can create the greatest problem for schools, namely, in the required classroom of language arts, reading, or English.

Textbook Censorship

Let's consider the direct way in which our pluralistic populace threatens public schools today. A case of textbook censorship that may serve as a cautionary tale occurred in 1974, in Kanawha County, West Virginia, a school district comprising both the sophisticated, affluent suburbs of Charleston and the poor, fundamentalist population of its urban center and rural environs. Severe conflict over a half-dozen language arts textbook series, produced by well-known major publishers, waged for a year and included violent demonstrations, school boycotts, school bus barricades, fire-bombing of schools, mine strikes, picketing of businesses, serious bodily injuries, suits and injunctions, and the resignations of the school superintendent and head of the school board.

The books were denounced by the objectors as anti-American and anti-Christian, that is, opposed to their values. This minority succeeded in getting the main series and some of the other books temporarily removed from the classroom and in intimidating the district and state into repudiating its own multicultural mandates in favor of decrees not to offend the values of any parents. A significant condition of the compromise stipulated that no student would be required to read any book objectionable to that student's parent on moral or religious grounds. Such a district decree could have the interesting effect of making way for individualized reading!

Censorship efforts increased steadily during the '70s and loom as a crisis for the '80s. The network of textbook censors has become extremely well organized and supported. Professional education organizations like the National Council of Teachers of English, which monitor the movement, report that the trend is approaching an epidemic. From Connecticut to California, frustrated citizens disappointed by governments that seem to ask a lot and yield little in return are starting to challenge public institutions more than hippies and radicals ever did.

In an editorial on censorship, the editor of *Phi Delta Kappan*, Robert Coles, wrote in the March, 1982 issue, "What are the schools to teach? It depends on which special interest group is speaking. Our once sound democratic consensus seems splintered and brittle." All the differences in values that the public let blur during the era of national assimilation and economic growth, have, under stress, become bastions for retrenching.

All of this spells a cultural conflict for which schools are not prepared. An essentially singular curriculum for all, especially in the most sensitive domain—required reading, writing, and discussing—will no longer do. Schools will have to be able to say in the future that no particular title or topic is required but that students will deal with many titles and topics relating to a general subject. The notion that an innocuous curriculum can be negotiated leads only to a blandness that irritates everyone. A majority rule cannot settle the matter because the culture is pluralistic, not merely dualistic like a two-party system.

Ironically, the sort of real individualization that some of us educators have strenuously advocated since more progressive times may soon be enforced by the strife of today. As factions insist on contradictory values, titles, and topics, it will become impossible to resolve conflicting directives except either by segregating students in different schools or by giving them different things to do in the same classroom.

The largest and the smallest units seem to hold out the best solutions. But, besides institutionalizing conflict, deliberately creating separate schools raises a host of nigh insoluble problems. Voucher systems are certain to run afoul of the First Amendment separation of church and state, since so many of the conflicting values derive from religious views. Also, can we really set up fundamentalists in their own schools, where they can teach "creationism" and literal interpretation of the Bible, and continue to refuse public funds for parochial schools? Moreover, many communities cannot afford to maintain separate schools, especially when some factions may number less than others. Other critics say school systems would become hopelessly politicized by community squabbles over sites and funds and overburdened by bureaucratic machinery for running the smorgasbord.

It should be much easier, as well as educationally more pertinent, for teachers to learn how to manage a class room in which small working parties are doing different things at the same time—as was done in the radical days of the one-room schoolhouse—learning to make their own choices of titles, topics, and activities. In this way, the original purpose of student-centering or the open classroom—to accommodate individual differences among learners—can be fulfilled, and at the same time parents can't claim that their child is being forced to do something in violation of home values. Youngsters, we know from experience, read, write, and discuss more when they choose titles, topics, and activities.

Conflicts of values force educators to re-examine the curriculum they require to see how biased or arbitrary or exclusive it may be. Can one syllabus for all be justified in a required course based on literature or social sciences or on mastering fundamental activities like reading, writing, and discussing?

When I taught at the nation's second oldest prep school, the English faculty of fifteen could agree to teach the classics but could not agree on what the classics are. No one was disturbed by this, although the students had to be prepared for the best colleges. The real aim was not for students to learn what the classics are but what a classic is.

The nature of the One that contains the many is something so profoundly human—or divine—that it can subvert a dilemma.

13

The Functions of Talk

Background

In 1986 the Committee on Oral Language in the Elementary School of the National Council of Teachers of English proposed to NCTE the publication of a book, *The Power of Talk,* to call attention to the importance of oral language in school, mindful of how neglected classroom talk has been. When the chairperson of this committee, Claire Staab of the University of British Columbia, invited me along with twenty others to contribute a chapter to this book, I felt this was indeed a worthy cause and was glad to help support these orphans of the language arts curriculum— speaking and listening. Compiled by Claire Staab and Sarah Hudelson, *The Power of Talk* was published in 1988 by NCTE and contains articles on research, theory, and practice aimed at teachers, student teachers, and administrators.

It is not hard to explain this neglect, which has persisted despite most educators' acknowledgment that talk is an indispensable base for literacy and social and intellectual development. Speaking does not lend itself easily and cheaply to testing. And, of course, what is not tested is not taught. Furthermore, as a spontaneous, interactive activity, talk is hard to control in a classroom. It is best done in small groups, which poses problems of management. Like writing, it is productive, comes forth from the learners, who may initiate subjects and take directions the teacher cannot foresee. The farther classroom activities get from texts, tests, and teacher topics the more students have to share control over both subject matter and the ongoing dynamics. Unfortunately, where students have most to learn, teachers have most to fear.

When we speak our thoughts we are translating inner life into outer life. While making the private public, vocalizing also renders the immaterial material. As ideas take on acoustical form they incarnate into the physical realm, condense out from mind into matter. This precipitation is an effect of socialization.

But when first learning the language, small children do not distinguish between vocalizing for themselves and vocalizing for others. This may be the main difference between pre-school speech and that of older children and adults, who talk to themselves but usually do so silently, aware at such times that what they are saying is not meant for others. Most children entering school are probably still learning to differentiate outer speech from inner speech.

The cycle of inner to outer and outer to inner is of great importance because each influences the other considerably. Outer speech occurs first, of course, as infants learn to speak from social interaction and from imitation. And even the shunting of some speech inward later occurs from social experience, which teaches a child to mentally separate itself from others and hence to differentiate talking to others from talking to oneself.

For a while infants rehearse their vocalizing in the crib. This practice then blends into prattle, which is the play talk that accompanies the child's other actions as it moves around among objects or manipulates toys. Playmates may be talked to and about in the same way as objects; subjects of talk may be no more distinguished from the audiences of talk than inner is from outer. In the oneness of childhood, people and objects, oneself and others, subjects and audiences, are only gradually differentiated.

One effect of this indiscriminate behavior is that we learn to talk to ourselves—to think—in very much the same way we vocalize. This can be enriching and impoverishing, depending on the environment. After some speech becomes silent and inner, by stages of subvocalization, it retains the qualities and limits not only of language itself but of social interaction. Profound as this effect of speech and sociality is on thought, it does not determine it alone, inasmuch as thought develops also from innate reasoning structures as well as from other, nonverbal experience.

Talking to Oneself

Some functions of language for children are not, then, social though socially influenced. One is solo play, which includes prattle. Children relate to objects as though they were people. This is a natural effect of acquiring speech, whereby one develops a concept of "other," with whom one exchanges and whom one internalizes along with the language. Prattle mixes talk addressed to dolls and other toys with a kind of self-accounting of what one is doing. In the typical way of children, though the play is for pleasure, for its own sake, it also is work, an important practice in vocalizing and verbalizing.

As children start learning how to do and make things, play talk expands into work talk, prattle into self-direction or what psychologists call "task mediation." Children talk themselves through something they are learning to do, like putting on certain garments or operating some kind of machine. They may repeat more or less some original instructions someone else gave them, recalling the words to recall the actions, or they may simply be describing what they are doing to reinforce or accompany one kind of action with another.

Adults also will sometimes mediate a task verbally, either to help get it right or just for "company." Though more usually we internalize these self-directions, we can recapitulate them if we need, for example, to pass the know-how on to others by word of mouth or in writing. School children may more easily than adults cast this task talk back into outer speech in, say, giving how-to directions to others for something they have mastered doing.

Talking to oneself, then, has both play and work functions aside from exercising vocal and verbal powers in preparation for other functions. Talking silently to oneself becomes a form of verbal thinking that will merge with nonverbal thinking and hence play a crucial role in the inner life manifested through these other functions.

Talking with Others—Dialog

The more socialized children become, the more the parallel prattle of playmates becomes real dialog, in which speakers heed and respond to each other. Of course, interacting with adults builds a model for this if adults do in fact heed and respond pertinently to the child. As children truly influence each other, so that what one says owes much to what another says, they develop dialogs of different functions, though often mixed.

Human communion

Some dialog arises just for the sake of social interaction itself, as a kind of affirmation of fellowship or verbal shoulder-rubbing. The prototype for this very important function occurs when infants first learn to talk, which they do primarily not for communication but to join the human race, for communion. So children often generate talk, like adults, as one way to be with other people, in addition to touching, looking, and doing activities together. "Small talk" is a form of this. The content of what is said amounts to little; what counts is the act of talking together. The function of this sort of talk hardly differs from other social relating and needs to be allowed and regarded as such.

Verbal play

A lot of dialog combines human communion with play. It is sporting and gaming. Children joke, tease, and banter. Many exchanges are just verbal play—mock insults, for examples, or pretended dialog between invented characters. Witty repartee like the black game of "doing the dozens" is an adolescent development of verbal play. And, of course, theater improvisations grow out of spontaneous pretended dialogs. Jumprope jingles, counting rhymes, and game songs are verbal play made up to accompany other play action. Like adult sea chanties and other work songs, some of these establish a necessary rhythm for some body movement or, like square-dance "calling," direct and synchronize certain actions of play. Though the versions of game chants, jingles, and songs that are passed on through oral lore may not appear dialogical, they are usually made up originally and constantly revised as collective improvisation accompanying other play.

Storytelling

A large proportion of school children's dialog consists of exchanging stories. Stories are paramount because they usually make statements, though indirectly and perhaps symbolically, like dreams. In fact, for children, stories are the main way, and sometimes the only way, of making statements, because their thinking tends to represent generalizations by concrete tokens rather than explicitly to formulate generalizations.

Some of these stories are accounts of events that actually happened to them or to others they know. Much "news" circulates this way, either fresh or retailed. Often an anecdote by one child prompts a listener to tell a similar incident or experience—about, say, getting lost or losing something valuable—and thus an informal group ends by generating spontaneously a "thematic unit," the stories supplying instances for orchestrating the theme. Such a session produces in effect a kind of collective oral essay that serves as a model for writing such an essay.

Other storytelling sessions amount also to collective composition. Sometimes play partners make up a story together by pooling their inventions, selecting and building ideas of characters, setting, and action as they manipulate dolls, puppets, or other objects, or simply as they imagine a story in purely verbal terms. Gradually props become less important as visualization develops in tandem with verbalization. Stories then are played out more in the theater of the mind but initiated and sustained by the interplay of dialog.

Some storytelling is re-telling. In the oral culture of children many stories are twice-told tales exchanged to keep stocking the individual's repertory from the group repertory. Adult influence can of course be especially strong here. Not only do many elders introduce stories into the children's oral culture by telling them or reading them aloud, but they also set an example of storytelling art so that children will indeed pass them around. Hearing and relaying oral stories prepares children to follow stories in books and to put stories into writing. Because so many of these stories come from elders or books, they infuse children's lore with maturer language, conceptions, and narrative technique that they can imitate and circulate.

Showing-and-telling

Show-and-tell often appears artificial in school because it's done in too large a group (usually the whole class) and because the teacher directs it. Actually it's a very natural kind of dialog that children engage in on their own. In fact, no talk comes more spontaneously among children than talk about what is in hand or at hand. The more concrete one's thinking, the more talk is tied to objects or actions in the here-and-now. Children playing together or visiting one another's homes find many occasions to talk about objects they're using or examining. They explain how they got them or made them, how they work, and what they mean to them. So show-and-tell can move orally across areas of discourse that in writing would be called narrative, exposition, and essay.

Often it is questions that start the telling or that keep it going (too often missing in classroom show-and-tell). The playmate's curiosity may invite an explanation or may cause the teller to fill in his or her initial remarks. The great cognitive value of questioning by peers is that they usually ask for what can't be seen—the function or purpose, history or significance of an object—which forces the explainer to move into more remote or abstract domains. Because children start by assuming their audience can fill in for itself all the details that they are mentally holding before themselves as they speak, they tend to speak too compactly. Questions make evident that the audience wants more detail and connection and so prompt the speaker to elaborate.

Getting and giving information

Questioning may in fact be generally the most valuable trait of dialog. Children's curiosity makes them great questioners, but interactions with adults are especially important here. For one thing, if adults honor their questions and are patient about the volume of them, this licenses children to ask freely of peers and elders both. But adults should ask honest questions of children, especially about things they don't know the answer to. This both sets an example and causes children to elaborate. Since children often assume that their peers know no more than themselves, they may not ask them many sorts of questions that they believe only adults can answer. Good parents and teachers will show children, by asking honest questions and by getting them to ask each other, that they know very different things and have a lot to exchange.

A primary function of dialog, then, is to get information, which will include giving it. In fact, the less developed one's literacy is, the more one must rely on conversation to get information. (In the case of illiterate adults we can see the extreme of this dependency on others, which accounts in part for the deep shame many of them feel.) Nearly all of this oral information has parallels in reading matter—the history of people and places in the environment, how to do and make things, etc. But some gregarious children become so adept at getting information orally that they don't look to printed matter for it. Eventually, though, if their curiosity and motives mature at the same time that they enjoy plenty of access to dialog, they will discover that it is an exhaustible source for all they want to know.

How-to information may be first in piority for children, because they want to know how to do for themselves, to master the processes and procedures that get things done, to locate or make items they want, to operate the technology of their world. This is all a big part of growing up and achieving independence. So getting and giving directions provides a practical motivation for much dialog, which serves to stand in for or supplement the written directions posted around or affixed to objects and machines or printed in brochures, periodicals, and books. But many directions never get written at all ordinarily—for getting to So-and-so's house or for fixing such-and-such an item. And oral directions partake of the general advantages of dialog. One can fit them to what the receiver does and does not already know. Questions can be asked about details, comprehension checked, and misunderstanding headed off. Objects involved can sometimes be examined and explained in show-and-tell fashion.

Task collaboration

Working together on something naturally generates dialog. The task might be building an object, organizing an activity, taking care of a plant or animal, or doing some investigative project. Task talk helps partners figure out how to proceed, remind themselves of details, coordinate individual efforts, troubleshoot problems, and evaluate progress. It's a most valuable kind of talk for several reasons. Not only does it make possible collaboration to achieve something that individuals might not be able to do alone, task talk exercises social cooperation and thinking ability.

What the group accomplishes together or thinks through collectively enables members eventually to do similar things by themselves. Pooling know-how, creativity, and problem-solving ability enriches each mind. The nature of the task tends to structure the talk and give an occasion to use logic and imagination on concrete, practical matters. Many children not given to chattering will talk more, and often well, when speech is a necessary concomitant of getting something done.

A task can be academic but still practical, as when partners discuss a text they have read in order to do something with it afterwards. Maybe they have gone to books or articles for information they need to carry out a project and now they want to talk about what they understood and can utilize of what they read. Deciding how to perform a play script or dramatize a story entails interpretation of the text as part of task talk.

Similarly, the task talk of writing partners centers on how to turn up and work up material and how to revise drafts and disseminate final versions. Various investigative projects require task talk about where to observe, whom to interview, and what to research for background. Children will find task talk about academic projects natural if these are set up to extend the familiar dialogs they engage in when playing or working together out of school.

Mental development

While fulfilling playful and practical functions, dialog develops the mind by the very nature of its verbal and conceptual interaction among minds. When children talk, they are exchanging everything from vocabulary and sentence structures to information and ideas. But more important, conversation is a growing process itself whereby initial plans, plots, incidents, instances, concepts, and generalizations become refined, related, complicated, and concatenated. As a processs of amending and appending, dialog carries forward enormously children's thought and speech.

Discussants try out ideas and ways of saying things and get immediate feedback in a situation conducive to ongoing revision. It's the constant trying and finding out the results that furthers any growth best. Dialog does this for verbal thinking. By means of it infants first learn not only to speak but to grasp the concepts to which words refer. It's not surprising that it continues to function as the supreme teacher if allowed to flourish.

Unfortunately, schools have not appreciated this and have traditionally regarded peer talking as bad behavior. Furthermore, even when dialog has been acknowledged to have learning value, it has been ignored or slighted because it does not lend itself to cheap scoring and tidy management systems. But talk may be passed over also because it seems too familiar and homely, and inexpensive, to be regarded as a serious means of learning. After all, children can talk out of school. But school can turn dialog toward reading and writing. It can also improve the quality and range of it far beyond how it might be practiced by some children on their own. Dialog can be limited and negative, as when it's used to consolidate an in-group by slandering outsiders, or ineffectual, as when members shy from important issues out of politeness or lack of trust.

A good conversation, as we all recognize, goes somewhere, somewhere quite distinct from where it started. The participants build on each other's contributions so that unforeseen ideas emerge. The best of this sort of dialog may not occur habitually out of school, where the emphasis may be more on socializing or gaming. But the process is similar, and schools can foster dialogs of the more cognitive sort without losing spontaneity or introducing a strange activity. The beauty of dialog is that mental development can occur as a by-product even of its playful, social, and practical functions. Children do not see themselves as doing something for a cognitive or intellectual function. Fine, they don't need to. The intrinsically mental interaction of dialog will incidentally function to develop thought and speech even though the avowed purpose is something more obvious and tangible.

Personal development

One of the most important of these other purposes is personal development. People of all ages spend a lot of time talking about themselves—their problems, their relationships, their activities, and their desires. They use partners to reflect themselves back, to sound out others' feelings and conjectures about their life, to get advice and fresh points of view, or to receive confirmation of perceptions and validation of selfhood. Besides the whole array of professional counseling, adults create almost ritual occasions for this personal sort of dialog—luncheons and coffee klatsches, bar meetings and locker-room sessions. The teenagers' telephone soul talks serve this function. Pre-adolescents too are searching for themselves, finding where they stand among peers and adults, sorting out feelings and perceptions, and confiding hopes and fears. Conversing with a trusted few helps shape identity, make decisions, and construct one's model of the world.

Again, such a vital function can be continued and even more fully realized in school, where resources can be greater than on the streets or in homes. Besides more peers, and some more adults, the school offers, it's to be hoped, a staple small-group process by means of which to take advantage of the human resources. Children soon find that they can trust and confide in, or at least utilize, other people than just certain "best friends." Furthermore, if the classroom lets students supply the content of language arts activities instead of jamming the channels with prepared fodder, children discover also that many of the concerns they felt were peculiar to them are shared by many peers and so do not have to be pursued so confidentially.

Here is where another asset of the classroom plays a big part, the culture of literature. From reading and reacting together to literature, children learn that many of their feelings, experiences, and wonderings have been written about by people now adults. They can feel they are joining the broader fellowship of universal human experience and that this is the major subject matter of literature and school. Each person's experience is unique, but it's a great help to the young to learn that their quest for understanding and meaning and personal development can be carried on in a framework that makes the most of dialog and combines it with the adult colloquies of literature.

All this joins with their own writing. Sharing their experiences and thoughts with writing partners and then classmates furthers powerfully this personal exploration of themselves and the world that is the function of much conversation. In a climate of reading and writing about experience children can advance this sort of dialog by including what they read and write in such discussions and by creating organic connections between actual experience, the vicarious experience of classmates and published authors, and their own efforts to write about real and imagined experience.

Realizing the similarities of one's own and others' experiences reassures children and widens their circles of identity. Becoming aware of differences helps define uniqueness, dissolves some egocentricity, and enables children to sketch some maps of the world and their place in it. Dialogs with all types of other peers, in this classroom culture of literacy and literature, fills in tremendously the whole chart of similarities and differences that we all start to make early in life—on which so much thinking is based—and that help us deal with the tensions created by perceptions of kinship and strangeness. Working all this out becomes inextricable, of course, from the playful, social, and practical functions of talk.

Talking to Others—Monolog

Dialog engenders monolog. From the duets and colloquies arise the arias, the solos. Launching solos is a major function of conversation. All that has to happen is for a participant to take over for a while to tell a story or explain something. Some things one has to say require length—elaboration, chaining, detailing, or other kind of development that goes beyond a sentence or two. Such a continuity, spun out not from the group but from some individual, is a monolog, which follows the time order of chrono-logic or the order of some other logic.

Dialogs not only generate monologs on a given occasion but also teach people, across occasions, how to sustain alone a continuity of thought and language. All the dialogical actions we have been surveying so far model kinds of continuities that individuals may emulate. Collectively telling a story, explaining how something looks or works or is done, giving instances of a theme or generalization, or reasoning through a problem or argument—all these kinds of continuities created by groups in which one has participated may become internalized as models for future monologs. As a group does, so eventually may an individual do. From the give-and-take, question-and-answer of dialog children may learn to elaborate detail in describing or narrating, illustrate an observation with examples, and prove an argument with reasons or evidence—without listeners having to prod and probe for these. A monologuist has to foresee what listeners will need or want, whereas the dialoguist relies on the questioning and other prompting of partners to find out or get out ideas.

Of course, we often don't know what we have to say until we've talked a while. This opportunity to work out thoughts out loud with others exemplifies the way dialog teaches monolog. Being both interpersonal and intellectual, dialog affords at once the social experience a monologuist must have to foresee listener needs and the elaborated thinking necessary for sustaining verbal continuity alone.

As group talk underlies solo talk, solo talk underlies reading and writing, which are usually monological. That is, any text that is not a script or transcript is the extended utterance of a single speaker, the author. As participants in group talk take turns listening to each other and speaking to each other, they gain experience similar to following a text and to creating a text. The longer the monologs children spin out for each other, the more easily they fit into the stance of readers and writers, because comprehending and composing texts entails precisely the predicting and elaborating and enchaining of events or ideas just described.

Following someone's talk by ear is enough like understanding a text to provide valuable preparation, especially as the monolog embedded in conversation is less perfect, not carefully planned and phrased, and may thus require considerable alertness and active interpretation to follow successfully. This makes for a strong reader, one *expecting* to have to fill out and connect the text. Soloing within a conversation is enough like writing to develop allowance for an audience and the forging of a purposeful continuity. In other words, insofar as comprehending and composing texts depends on social, verbal, and cognitive development, children are learning to read and write as they talk. Like general mental and personal growth, literacy does not need to be an avowed purpose of oral practice for talk to function as its base.

Interviewing

An interviewer tries to get access to what a certain person knows by asking some prepared questions and usually some spontaneous questions as well that are prompted by some of the interviewee's responses. So an interview is a special kind of one-sided, question-and-answer dialog that invites monologs from the interviewee, who therefore usually does most of the talking. Part of the art of interviewing is to think up questions that will most successfully elicit from the subject what one wants to find out. This requires thoughtful formulation and sequencing of questions before the interview and alert, flexible questioning strategy during the interview.

To the extent that interviewers plan their talk and may transcribe and edit the interview afterwards, they approach the role of an author composing a text. Though still speaking spontaneously, the interviewee is pushed also in the direction of authoring by constant elicitation. Each question calls for some monolog, and the series of questions prompts a series of monologs that the overall pattern of the interview structures into a master monolog. Interviewing is an interesting case of an audience drawing out a monolog by periodically prompting and therefore co-authoring the content and organization.

Summary

The functions of children's talk are social, playful, practical, and personal (or psychological). These various sorts of toy talk, task talk, and topic talk constitute a rough progression from speech anchored to objects or actions present while conversing, on to subjects more removed in time and space, such as problems or projects that are concrete but not necessarily limited to the occasion of the talk, and then on to longer-range, more disembodied subjects such as certain generalities, conditions, or issues. Some of talk is for oneself, uttered aloud at first then gradually subvocalized into inner speech as one distinguishes self from other, inner from outer. Talk shifts constantly between, according as it is meant to act on the speaker or on others.

All these kinds of talk build on and influence each other. As inner speech grows from outer, monolog evolves from dialog, but in the long run influence is circular. All also develop thought and speech. This great side benefit owes to the very nature of talk as practice in how to take things and how to put things, that is, in interpreting what others say and in putting one's own inner life into words for others. Listening exercises attention and inference. Speaking exercises the faculties of conceptualizing and verbalizing.

Since how to take and put things corresponds to what we call in school comprehension and composition, talk necessarily teaches children in some measure how to read and write. Furthermore, this experience teaches the most difficult aspects of literacy—the social and cognitive, as contrasted with the lexical and linguistic facts of literacy.

All of these functions together further the main goal of any individual—overall self-development. The social, playful, practical, and personal functions combine so as to bring along at once the growth of relationships, emotions, intellect, and creativity. It is a measure of the power of talk that it can do so much at once if allowed to play out its possibilities. Such a claim should seem credible when one considers all that is involved in materializing our inner life for others to engage with.

14

Liberating Inner Speech

Background

College Composition and Communication published in October, 1985, a talk I had given at the annual conference of that organization in Detroit the year before. I used the opportunity of addressing college composition teachers to parlay the idea of writing as controlling inner speech into the idea of writing as liberating inner speech. In this talk I attempted to spell out more fully than before how, through composing, language can serve as its own counterspell. For oral delivery it seemed somehow appropriate to draw on some personal experience and on some human examples from literature.

At the end of one of Truman Capote's earlier short stories, a character in bad emotional straits says to himself, "Think of nothing things. Think of wind." There are times when thinking does us no good because it is compulsive. At an extremity when thoughts can only be few and dire, it is better to hold the mind still, as this character is trying to do. What he needs is a new thought coming completely from outside the state of mind he is in, but that's exactly what's impossible, at least for the moment. In acute form his plight represents the self-limiting situation of inner speech most of the time.

In James Jones' novel of the peacetime army, *From Here to Eternity*, certain soldiers given to doing stockade time learn how to stop thinking when placed in solitary confinement, to keep from going berserk. They pass this art on to others who bring onto themselves this strange version of the anchorite's life. Prison has in fact shown more than one street-violence criminal how to discipline the mind when the soul is on ice. Many inmates have become "committed" readers and writers who couldn't be bothered with that sort of stuff in school. Well, what else is there to do on ice? True, but true too is that many prisoners really want to have new thoughts.

175

In 1960 I co-taught a weekly class at San Quentin Prison with a counselor there. Inmates attended voluntarily and spent most of each Saturday doing with us various kinds of what later came to be called encounter groups and discussing with us something we vaguely called "semantics." Criminals behind walls have the advantage of *knowing* they're obsessed. They came to class to liberate their inner speech, to have new thoughts that would enable them to stay out of prison once they got out. One thing some of our inmate students began to see was how each's own kind of crime symbolized his particular mental arrestation. Armed robbery means something very different from safecracking, passing bad checks, or molesting children. Seldom do the rest of us have such a good chance to see, crystallized before us, the clear shape of our mental incarceration.

Extremity is instructive. The case of the criminal brings out something true for most of us most of the time—that, left to itself, without guidance of conscious will, our inner speech tends to repeat itself in the direction of obsession. We have habits and limits. We recycle the same ideas and images, ride on the same trains of thoughts, and reach familiar conclusions. By means of redundant inner speech we maintain a whole world view of reality, a sort of sustained hallucination, usually shared to some degree by family, friends, and compatriots.

But we don't really like this stale fare and so go to a lot of trouble and pay a lot of money to put ourselves in the way of outside stimuli over which we have no control—new people, places, and events that can direct our thoughts in ways they would not have gone on their own. We travel, take courses, give parties, subscribe to magazine or book clubs, go to performances or sports contests, watch TV or movies, and play videogames. The comedy of Sinclair Lewis' satiric short story "Travel Is So Broadening" is that the character monologuist clearly drags along his old mental baggage on his trips and so never has any new thoughts, however far he travels. Like compulsive criminals insisting that society lock them up again and again, he is self-imprisoned, as represented by the monologue form itself in his case.

Many professional writers understand that obsession drives their work. The last words of John Irving's *The Hotel New Hampshire* are " . . . you've got to get obsessed and stay obsessed. You have to keep passing the open windows." Since Irving has already made clear that passing open windows means not jumping through them, he is saying here we need obsession to keep us from suicidal despair. Bears, motorcycles, Vienna, the cozy coherence of family life smashed beyond repair. Critics often point out that novelists retell the same story across all or most of their books. But the novelist's mental hygiene consists precisely of *varying* his inner speech through writing, of playing out the obsession but at the same time of *surprising himself*.

I would say that we don't have to *get* obsessed. We *are* obsessed in the sense of limiting ourselves to knowing only what we can afford to think. "Think of nothing things. Think of wind." Stopping thinking, thinking of nothing things, or getting obsessed all aim to hold the mind still, because, as the yogis say, the mind is a drunken monkey. What some people come to through extremity has been for a long time practiced deliberately in the form of meditation meant to hold the mind on a good focus.

In other words, out of these observations we may distil two possibilities for offsetting the compulsive and hence potentially destructive nature of inner speech. One is to try sometimes to suspend it altogether, by blanking or fixing the focus, which may be done positively or negatively. Meditation is positive. Stonewalling or obsessing is negative. The other is to ride out the obsession as far as you can, as Irving suggests. This can be done by all-out acting out, which may land you in prison, or by writing out all the way. Meditation and composition require will and conscious direction. The writer's way seems to indulge fully the obsession but actually forces it to grow into something else. The key here is "fully." Scope is necessary to make this work—a range of form and of subject matter.

Those of us not criminals or novelists may understand from what they commit to public view how it is we ourselves go about enacting or offsetting our own repetitive inner speech. We want adventure, novelty. We want things to come up that we can't predict, that are out of our hands, and heads. To the extent that we repeat ourselves when we talk to ourselves, we are good and bored. We want to be *surprised*. But we are timid adventurers. We want something new *and* familiar, to be *safely* surprised. From within the routines of our mental self-imprisonment we look to other people and things outside to shake us up, restock our mind, and redirect our thought trains. All these common stimuli that we often seek under the name of entertainment really aim to remodel our monotonous inner world.

One might think that surprise cannot be a bootstrap operation. If we look to other people and things it is because we cannot predict what they are going to do, especially if they are unfamiliar. You don't know what turn of events the daily news or the plot of a movie is going to take, what play a football team is going to run next, from which direction the invaders are going to violate our space next on the screen of the video game. A good lecture or essay also tells us what we did not know or had not thought, or at least recasts our information and ideas.

But is it really true that the mind can't surprise itself? Obviously we have new thoughts all the time, but aside from those prompted rather directly by outside stimuli, how do we get these new thoughts? What is the inner process whereby the recirculating inner speech rejuvenates itself and takes a new track? The heart of this discovery process, I believe, is *development*, the sustaining of a line of thought far enough to allow combinations of inner material to occur that one has not so combined before. Anyone's mind is a huge storehouse of imagery, information, concepts, and experience that could be permuted many different ways.

The problem is that dominant emotions, motives, and fixed frameworks—partially inherited—keep chaining or clustering all this into the same trains or constellations of thoughts. What we need are new organizational forces to recombine our inner treasury and to make room for fresh outside material. It's not impossible for this to come about if we just sit and cogitate, but spinning out a continuity long enough and rich enough to surprise oneself may prove too difficult for most people unless they symbolize the thoughts outwardly so that they may be reviewed, recast, revised, and resumed. By now you will have realized that I have sneaked up to the composition process by a backdoor. Why a backdoor? Because I want to identify composition with composure.

Like all of us, students are thinking only about certain things, and those things only in certain ways. Their patterns of limitation have been laid down by their own fear and desire, on one hand, and by social inculcation, on the other. This is what I call obsession. To think of new things, and of old things in new ways, they will need to start with something familiar and go somewhere with it they haven't been before. The composition process can be this kind of mental trip, a development of ideas not merely determined by one's limitations but conditioned, rather, by some ongoing circumstances not easily commandeered by that censorious monomaniac, the ego.

As the criminal may epitomize destructive fixation, the novelist epitomizes the creative exploring of fixation. The writer lets the composing process act on his or her mind. Because the process has some conditions of its own, and to some extent a mind of its own, it can act to alter our inner speech very much as outside stimuli do. This is what novelists mean when they say, as they constantly do, that the characters take over the story as if they have a life of their own independent of the author's mind. A part of our self that wants growth and change finds a way to subvert the inner establishment.

How does composing differ from just musing? If I the writer envision an audience upon whom I wish to work certain effects, I compose under the influence of that audience and thus modify my inner speech from what it would have been had I just been talking to myself, musing. In other words, to the extent I truly think *for* that audience I think *like* that audience. I must role-play the other. That's one big difference between writing and musing.

Second, I compose in some form or mode of discourse that has characteristics independent of me. Suppose I write a dialogue. That requires simulating two or more minds, which means a dialectic, not just one monopolistic ego holding forth. Suppose I write up an interview I recorded or a scene I witnessed. In so doing I put in my own words what someone else said and thought or what occurred before my eyes that I did not stage-manage. Reportage causes me to modify my mind to do justice to outside sources, which I incorporate or assimilate. The same for other research. But take even an inner source—memories. In composing a memoir that others will comprehend and respond to I must recall details more clearly than I would usually for myself alone, select and ignore aspects according to the effects I wish to produce, shape a salience, formulate the experience in language that I have not previously cast the memory in, make clear a significance that I may not have clarified or made explicit before for myself. A memoir often induces new understanding of a memory.

Consider in this way the other conditions that different forms impose—letters and journals, the chronological ordering of narrative and the logical and psychological ordering of various expositions, arguments, and personal essays. Traditional poetic forms such as limericks, haiku, or sonnets; the spectrum of fictional techniques; the folk forms such as myth, fable, and parable; the variety of performing scripts—all these likewise subject my inner speech to conditions not of its own making and hence cause it to alter itself.

Third, contemplating a record of what I have verbalized so far, I look back over it and change order and organization, phrasing and tone, pace and emphasis—very difficult things to do if one is merely *thinking* the continuity. The crux of it all—development—requires holding all the parts in place in the mind to assess the concatenation of ideas, images, language, feeling, cumulative effect, and the impact of climax and ending. This recursive scanning too alters thinking, not only while one is composing but sometimes for the future also.

Part of revision involves other people. Myself at a later time acts of course as a kind of other person, but if I the author also "field-test" a preliminary version of my composition on a trial audience of individuals separately or members of a group together, my original mind-set will usually undergo change. Professional writers commonly do this, and students should be allowed the same opportunity. Assimilating the feedback may not only influence the final version of the composition but may also enlarge the author's mind.

Finally, a composition is a *construction*. When you make something from some materials, the materials have to change. A composition structures the mind while the mind is structuring it. Construction has its own laws, some of which govern any composing in any medium, some of which pertain only to language. In writing, one parcels out, rearranges, and reformulates the inner life in ways that change its native state.

Making something is playing. Besides accommodating the logical and rhetorical needs of the subject and purpose, an author tinkers with the medium as a child fools around with physical materials to find what you can do with them and to create for the sake of creation. Putting ideas and words together to make a composition gratifies play urges at the same time that it does the job of communicating. Play eludes determinism and hoodwinks our singleminded censor.

All these factors of composing surprise our habitual thought patterns because they have life and laws of their own. This is how writing may loosen obsession and redirect inner speech. The ego is nothing if not partial and very much needs these influences toward impartiality. As these terms "partial" and "impartial" indicate, real objectivity is not impersonality but wholeness, the filling out of personality to more nearly match the width of the world. Like the novelist, the student needs to get going a continuity of thought that rides him or her right out beyond the confines of personal inner speech, to self-surprise. In keeping with the homeopathic principle of treating in kind, the remedy is to parlay the obsessiveness of inner speech into its own solution by copious and various composition experience. The self-incarcerated can liberate themselves if shown how they maintain the walls themselves. It is this expansion toward wholeness that is the connection between composition and composure.

15

Ways of Teaching Literature

Background

By the late '80s some educators had begun to realize that literary criticism, research in reading comprehension, and the response-to-literature movement in pedagogy had a lot to offer each other and should be brought into closer contact. Among these were two Canadians, Stanley Straw of the University of Manitoba and Deanne Bogdan of the Ontario Institute for Studies in Education, who invited some specialists in these areas, including myself, to contribute a chapter each to a book aimed at such cross-fertilization.

Usually invited to speak or write on composition during this era, I was pleased to have a chance to talk about literature once again and took advantage of the occasion to bring together for the first time in such succinct form the various ways in which I would go about teaching it. I tried to qualify those ways that could be abused to assess all in relation to issues of interpretation and appreciation, touching on theories of literature as a framework. A very crude notion of reading comprehension underlies the teaching and testing of it in schools, which at the same time place reading comprehension at the center of the curriculum in accordance with the predominance of reading itself over the other language arts. The notion that texts bear only one meaning, which can be tested as the right answer, like other factual material, would enrage most literature theorists today and is carried over from "practice readers" and "skill builders" into literature, by implication if nothing more, whenever teachers interpret for students, manipulate their discussion toward the "right" meaning, or test them against some definitive interpretation. An authoritarian approach to meaning defeats a fundamental purpose of literature—to help us see life in more depth and breadth.

Like literary criticism, the teaching of literature varies according to whether one emphasizes the author, the reader, or the text. This is not surprising since these three parts or parties represent nothing less than the basic communication triangle formed by the first, second, and third persons (*I, you,* and *it*). So the fact that the criticism and teaching of literature seem parallel may owe no more to university influences, although these have often been very strong, than to the nature of discourse itself, which is characterized by interplay among a speaker, an audience, and a subject. Schools of thought in both criticism and education keep shifting focus from the meaning the author deliberately or unconsciously gives a work, to the meaning the reader awarely or unawarely takes away from the work, to the meaning the text may have independently of either author or reader by virtue of constants in certain structural relationships in language and symbols.

But literature differs, we feel, from other written discourse, though it may never be defined except in reference to a particular society. Poems, plays, and fiction—mythic, figurative writing—usually constitute what our society deems literature, but we often include in it certain essays, autobiography, and history—nonfiction—that are artful enough and profound enough to hold up across time, whereas we exclude some verse, plays, and fiction that we regard as ephemeral entertainment of no great creative value. So we seem to define literature partly by genre, partly by sheer quality. It is as if we expect literature to correspond to mythic and figurative writing but acknowledge that genre is no guarantee of creative discourse, which may crop up in other forms. Anything good enough may qualify as literature. *Moby Dick* defies discursive classification. Thomas Carlyle's *The French Revolution* became a literary classic because of its ornate style and dramatic narrative rhetoric, which made it more than history (or less).

For school purposes, definition need not pose a serious problem anyway, since it seems best not to distinguish strictly between response to literature and response to other texts. All kinds of reading entail matters of comprehension and appreciation, and the distinguishing of one kind of text from another ought to remain an issue across various reading experiences, not seem to be settled in advance, precisely because the definition of literature is relative. That is, the *nature* of the text in hand should be something students think about all the time along with the *subject* of the text. Deciding what is literature is too basic a process to exempt students from. Why does one author pursue a certain subject in fiction and another the same subject in nonfiction? Or can we really say the subject is then the same? Why do the language and structure of some texts seem to have a life and purpose of their own somewhat independent of the subject? When is the interplay of author, audience, and subject not just communication but, well, *play,* esthetic sport?

If literature existed only to be comprehended, we could regard "response to literature" as merely a subclass of "reading comprehension," since literature is only one kind of reading matter. But literature exists not only to be understood but to be undergone. So actually for literature the case is the reverse: reading comprehension is a subclass of response to literature. Meaning is only part of the story. Serious fiction, plays, and poetry, or certain essays and true stories, are meant to act on our whole being—to astonish, decondition, purge, exhilarate, or dismay us, for example. Some Ancient Mariner collars or charms us and puts us through an experience that makes us feel some of the same things real experience might. It is to these effects that the term "rhetoric" applies, to this acting on others through words.

If we want to call this experience that literature puts us through part of its meaning, that's all right so long as we acknowledge that this meaning of meaning goes far beyond common school notions of "reading comprehension," which can be tested by paraphrasing or by citing passages in the text for proof. The meaning of a literary experience cannot be "objectively" tested because it is not a merely semantic matter unless we apply "semantic," as Susanne Langer does, to all the arts. The cumulative and holistic effect of a great literary work is, significantly, nonverbal, like that of music, dance, painting, and the other "semantics." This is so partly because much of the meaning has the same experiential impact on us as in the other arts but partly also because even the meanings in the ordinary sense can be so numerous, overlaid, and interwoven that their totality becomes *ineffable,* unutterable, as critics have said of *King Lear* and *Moby Dick.*

By contrast, school efforts to teach and test "reading comprehension" constantly betray the assumption that texts have but one meaning and that anyone reading correctly will discover that meaning. Most current literary theory would vehemently denounce this. It is no doubt part of the very definition of literature that it means on several levels at once, intended or not, and that different readers will come away with different meanings, many or most of which may gibe perfectly well with each other. So the schools' conventional pedagogy for "reading comprehension" actually conflicts in part with the purposes of literature, for which the concept is ill-suited but which the concept of "response to literature" should include.

As I enumerate various ways of teaching literature that may be used in school—but too often are not—I will try to assess them as I go and at the same time suggest connections between pedagogy and criticism but without referring to literary schools by names. What is important are some principles and perceptions common to both.

Ways of teaching literature actually involve, besides reading, the other language arts—listening, speaking, writing, and, let's add, acting. In fact, one might proceed by grouping literature methods according to which language art predominates. But since actual classroom activities often combine them—or should—it may be more practical to start with some key questions of teaching method and then go to particular activities.

The first question I raise is often by-passed because the answer is assumed. How is the text chosen? By whom and what for? Whether an adoption committee, a department head, a group of teachers, a single teacher, a group of students, or an individual student chooses will make considerable difference in which teaching methods are possible. A basal reader series or high school literature series contains its own method—often in the form of prep talk before reading and detailed questions afterwards. It is through these series that most American youngsters have become acquainted with literature. The comprehension quiz dominates commercial literacy programs that lead into literature programs and establishes a read-to-test mentality that begins with indifferent passages written just for the program and continues into the anthologies of literature by famous authors.

These programs or series are most often chosen by adoption committees at the school, district, or state level, fairly political levels where rank-and-file teachers may not be well represented. In high schools, decisions are usually made in the English department, more or less autocratically or democratically, but choices may have to be made from a narrow range decided above. At both elementary and secondary levels the critical choice of whether to buy a textbook series or sets of trade paperbacks or individual copies of trade books rarely falls to classroom teachers. Purchasing policies can rule in or out different teaching methods.

Let's look a moment at the most common school purchases, hardcover textbook anthology series. Prepackaged literature curricula lock in a certain sequence of reading and a certain organization based on genres or themes or general social history or on periods, figures, schools, and influences. Here is where a prevailing theory of literature may exert great influence on the presentation of literature—and hence where structuralism or contextualism, for example, might skew the pedagogy, since it's not very feasible to build into such a package a variety of approaches, and since a personal-response or deconstructionist approach, say, does not lend itself well to predetermined organization. Actually, what filters down into textbooks, as with linguistics, is usually some concepts that are familiar and simplistic, that don't count on teachers knowing much about literary theory and can be easily formated.

Thematic organization pre-interprets the texts, we note, besides tending toward moralism and truism. Chronological organization may teach history more than literature. Genre provides the most neutral and useful organization, since it can teach literary forms simply by giving examples of each while leaving subject matter wide open and sampling any number of periods, styles and authors. Even literature arranged by types, however, leaves methods more open if the books are straight anthologies containing no directions, questions, or other pedagogical paraphernalia. Clean compilations organized by types of writing are the only sort of school books I have ever published. The less textbooks of literature differ from trade books, the better for teaching purposes. Selections may be arranged so as to bring out relationships among the types of writing, but the order of printing does not have to be the order of reading.

Because commercial publishers center on state and district adoption agencies, which are very political, they favor conventional thematic and chronological organizations and sanitize subject matter by anticipating censors' objections. Selections may be didactic and moralistic or include too many old chestnuts that parents can recognize and that teachers are used to teaching. Most literature courses in high school are nationalistic—American or British—or internationalistic—World—and so have the mission of "covering" a corpus produced in a certain time span. Although this mission may actually leave open the means or methods, as I believe is the case in most schools, and may well not spell out which texts shall represent the various periods to be covered, once a course is embodied in textbooks, choices vanish. Buying curriculum in a package is asking for trouble. Though putting together reading materials locally, in a school or department, may be less convenient and can also be narrow, this approach avoids at least the severe strictures of corporate practices, which put, after all, other considerations ahead of education.

Text-by-text selection opens up more teaching possibilities, because texts are not locked in a certain way and interlarded with editor-written directions or interpretations embodying a particular approach. Moreover, when a group of faculty or an individual teacher puts together a syllabus he, she, or they must think much more about their choices. Why this and not that? In what reading order? This makes teachers deal with some of the issues literary theorists take on, such as the nature and value of literature and what happens when authors write and readers respond. What experiences can or should students have with literature? And selecting texts while thinking about teaching methods then raises the issue of whether or when students should select texts.

The ultimate flexibility in choice occurs when students themselves are let in on just such deliberations by being permitted to make decisions about what they are to read, at first perhaps in small groups and then individually. Individualized reading enjoys more support in elementary school, where the chief issue is making readers out of students, than in secondary, where literature is singled out and made a sort of content subject like social studies and biology. This shift from student-centered to subject-centered characterizes the whole transition from grade school to high school and accompanies the fragmentation of the school day into specialized subjects, teachers, and locations. But if we are to aim for a complete array of ways to teach literature, we must consider individualized reading as possible in the later grades, when "literature" succeeds "reading." Individualized reading can be introduced into the more difficult situation of secondary school by preceding it with independent reading by small groups. The fact is that too many valuable teaching methods have not penetrated schools very much because they require that students play at least some role some of the time in choosing texts (which will then very often have to be in trade books).

Discussion of methods must consider not only who produces the texts and who chooses them but also who, finally, interprets them. Just as texts may be chosen by groups of adults, individual teachers, groups of students, individual students, or some combination of these, texts may be interpreted for students by a community or individual teacher or by students themselves, alone or together. Indeed many ways of teaching literature vary essentially according to who is interpreting and in what circumstances.

This preamble has been necessary to make sure that neither the choice of texts, the chooser of texts, nor the interpreter of texts is taken for granted. This openness makes available a full repertory of classroom dynamics that best utilizes the human resources on hand. Now let's look at the methods themselves.

1. Partners take turns sightreading aloud to each other, discussing the text along the way.

At worst, such "reading groups" have been misused to let the teacher hear and coach individuals—to the boredom of peer listeners and to the mortification of the unaccomplished reader. For such checking and coaching it is far better to run one-to-one sessions while the rest of the class is working in other sorts of small groups. At best, group reading can be a fine social way to read a text together, help each other, and check one's own understanding. Not now obliged to coach in this group session, the teacher can leave the group alone part of the time and sit in occasionally to role-model a good participant—take a turn reading aloud and take part in discussion without leading it.

The main point is that partners do collectively what individuals might do alone some time. They read the text while giving oral interpretation and personal responses in the form of spontaneous questions and commentary. Members are encouraged to read aloud as they imagine some person might speak the words but not to regard this as performing. Anyone may remark on the text while reading or while someone else is reading. These remarks may be about what the text makes them think or feel or remember, what they think is going to happen next, or what they don't understand.

Conversing while reading not only gives a text a social setting but helps individuals pay attention to their inner responses when they are reading silently alone. This method externalizes and dramatizes the usually unnoticed stream of responses that goes on in us as we read. Pooling understanding spreads it, and hearing others' responses to a text stimulates one to think more about it.

This is a basic method that prepares for many of those to follow here. How well it works depends, as with the others, on how involved students become with the text. Better if partners choose it or work out a choice with the teacher.

2. Partners perform a text after rehearsing it.

This method may grow directly out of the preceding, combining as it does voicing and discussing of a text. While the goal is some kind of prepared performance, this activity should not be regarded as a specialty called drama but as a staple process for experiencing *any* text. The point is not to perform only scripts but to regard all texts as scripts, not to mount a few time-consuming spectacles but to make possible many more commonplace enactments of texts. A group selects a text they already know or scouts and sifts for a text. Then members work up a rehearsed reading and render it, text in hand; or, more rarely, they memorize and stage a text. A group may perform live or record for others to witness later.

This method may begin like the first, as turn-taking sight-reading interspersed with discussion, the way professional actors run through a script before rehearsals. Discussion deals with anything from punctuation and factual references in the text to tone of voice and overall point or purpose. The effort to work out a just rendering forces participants to analyze and interpret the text as a self-contained creation, but this effort may also make performers feel they need to learn more about the context of the work. Some of the best textual discussion possible in school occurs in preparation for performing, because the practical goal and social means ground it, direct it, and motivate it.

Specific techniques have been developed for public theater and schools that students may be introduced to. In Story Theater some participants mime actions while others read narration and others read lines of characters. Chamber Theater is a way of dramatizing any narrative by placing the narrator on stage amid the characters. Readers Theater favors voice over action so that actors may hold scripts and concentrate on evocation through language. All three in fact dispense with stage trappings, permit rehearsed reading without memorization, and consider any kind of text as potentially performable. (For further treatment of these and related activities see *Student-Centered Language Arts and Reading: A Handbook for Teachers,* James Moffett and Betty Jane Wagner (Boston: Houghton Mifflin, 1983). The performing of texts works best when accompanied by related activities such as improvisation and the writing or adapting of texts to be performed.

Performing poems may well be the best way to study them. Consider what is involved, for example, in deciding with partners how a poem is to be voiced, that is, lines or parts of lines assigned to single or choral voices and the whole orchestrated. Interpreters understand that a new voice may be used to represent any shift of time, tone, point of view, and so on, not just a changing of "characters." I have had adult students compile a collection of old and modern poems, discuss and rehearse readings with partners, and submit a final audiotape of the anthology.

A side-effect of this method is that it results, precisely, in performances that others can witness live or on audio or video recordings. The
effect can be a stunning knowledge explosion as whole classes become
acquainted with works that some students have not read but that others
have. Such dissemination alone would justify letting students work in
small groups and choose different texts. This method also increases expo-
nentially students' sophistication about textual interpretation and technical virtuosity in the literary arts. Performers study a text with both unusual involvement and detachment, because they have to enter farther in
and stand farther back, draw more on personal response and yet objectify
it so that their audience can understand what they have understood.

3. Students listen to and watch performances of texts.

A major way of experiencing and understanding texts is to witness
both professional and amateur renderings. For a school program of independent reading that I once directed (*Interaction* Houghton Mifflin,
1973), I persuaded the publisher to get some professional performers to
audiotape some selections so that students could follow the text with
their eyes while listening. This not only enables weaker readers to gain
access to texts they are mature enough for but not able to read alone but
also brings out for good readers some depths and resonances of works of
other eras that they might not otherwise attune to. I used to do some
Shakespeare plays with excellent prep school students by just playing
records or films of them and giving them a chance from time to time to
comment or question between scenes. Sometimes they had read the text
or were following it for the first time; sometimes they never saw the text.
Professional actors make many footnotes unnecessary by rendering
through voice and body much meaning that students could miss reading
alone.

A literature classroom should allow for students to know the same
text in different ways and different texts in different ways. But viewing
and listening should always include interludes for spontaneous questioning and exchanging of responses. Performances can be powerful stimuli
to accustom students to discussing texts. When performances of the
same text contrast with each other and with one's own imagining of the
text, students can see how widely interpretations vary. Performing oneself, and witnessing the performances of classmates, helps considerably
to assess and appreciate professional performing, including commitment to an interpretation.

4. Students write an extension of the original work.

A fine way to enter further into a literary work is to make up scenes
that were not in the original but that are consistent with it—a conversation referred to in a play but relegated to offstage, or an incident that

could have happened given what a novelist, say, has already established about a character or theme. Parody is a form of extending a work that one has read. Students might agree to stop at a certain point in a short story or poem and write their own ending before knowing the author's. Or they might cast the text into another medium—adapt a memoir for stage or film, illustrate a poem or short story, rewrite a folk tale as a ballad (or vice versa), and so on. Many Readers Theater scripts have been created by editing and splicing together excerpts from diaries and letters, transcripts, memoirs, documents, and all sorts of other texts so as to make a statement or connect disparate things thematically in a kind of collage. Sometimes the script-makers, usually the performers too, write further text as introduction and continuity.

Any sort of extension might be written collectively by a small group as well as individually. That is, partners compose together one story, play, essay, or whatever by pooling ideas and taking turns scribing the ideas as they are contributed around the table. Composing and revising alternate in the same session. This process can naturally elicit perceptive discussion of texts as partners recall, interpret, and extrapolate the text together.

This is a more intuitive approach than writing *about* a text, though, like performance, it *entails* analysis. Such activities induce the perceptions one needs in order to have something worthwhile to say about literature and at the same time help make the perceptions explicit enough to verbalize. Imagining an extension to a text, however, allows the reader to parlay responses further along the same level of phenomena that the author created in. It's a way of identifying with and collaborating with the author.

5. Members of a small group discuss a text without the teacher.

Choosing or accepting a text they really want to read makes an enormous difference here. This method assumes that the group members are capable of reading a text at home alone and are interested in sharing their responses to it without having an immediate practical aim such as performing or extending, although those activities and reading aloud together will prepare for it. After choosing what they want to read, partners agree on a time to meet to discuss it. To facilitate discussion, they understand that they are to jot down questions that arise as they read and note down any other ideas or feelings or memories that the text stimulates. The teacher can role-model this when sitting in sometimes by giving personal responses as a fellow reader not as a senior person trying to make points about the text. In this way the teacher can help students heed and value their spontaneous responses as a basis for sharing reading experience.

Questions can be about things students didn't understand or about matters they simply want to hear their partners discuss and give opinions on. A group might then want to ask the teacher what he or she thinks, or seek factual information about the author and context of the reading selection. Without the teacher leading or testing their comprehension, group members can freely admit any puzzlement or incomprehension instead of having an investment in hiding them, which ends by hiding uncertainties from oneself.

Such sharing validates subjectivity on the one hand but also gives learners a chance to match it with others' subjectivity and so find out what is private and what is public. Comparing responses with peers is the best way to discover how differently individuals can interpret the same text. This difference cannot be shrugged off as a generation gap or a peculiarity of English teachers. Contrast is the great teacher, and peers are the perfect ones to do this sort of cross-teaching. Adult leadership in this case would spoil the process. The interplay of personal responses brings out consensus where it exists and the universality of some feelings and experiences. It directs attention to specific features of a text as partners explain the feelings or interpretations these gave rise to.

6. Students take notes of their responses while reading alone.

This method consists of keeping a reading journal by jotting down as notes for oneself all kinds of responses to the text—memories, observations, feelings, associations. Such a journal leaves an ongoing record of reading experience that students often enjoy rereading later and sharing in various ways, one of which is to make reading recommendations to classmates if they've been reading different texts. An excellent activity for its own sake when students have acquired at least the beginning of the habit of reading silently, this will also provide rich material for the small-group discussion just described or for performing, extending, and otherwise dealing with texts. It can serve well whether students are reading the same text or going separate ways.

Students can discuss with the teacher and each other how best to capture responses in notes without breaking involvement with the text. Actually, consciousness of responses can increase involvement. Reading can strongly stimulate the mental life, but students are so habituated to anticipating oral or written tests after reading that they ignore their own responses in order to concentrate on what they think they will be asked. Constant comprehension quizzing engages students' minds more with authority than with the text. This backfires because when asked to interpret or play literary critic for themselves, students then have little to work with; the personal insights and connections that would make for interesting criticism have been repressed beyond access. Ongoing reading notes raise responses to awareness, fix them for later retrieval, and establish a habit to counteract the amnesia caused by incessant comprehension testing.

With teachers themselves I have tried an interesting variation on the journal that actually might be a good way for students to prepare for keeping one. I photocopied a number of poems, essays, and stories that I thought they would find stimulating, leaving an unusually wide margin around the text on each page in which they could note down their responses to specific passages. This annotation could include underlining, circling, arrowing, linking, and any other graphic way of indicating reactions besides verbal notes. In the case of my class, a composition course, all these annotations became fodder for their own writing, with the understanding that they did not have to write about the text as such but about ideas prompted by the text (another kind of extending). They chose one text at a time, by the way, from the dozens I gave them to pick among.

Students need not annotate a text for composition purposes only, but also for the same reasons they would keep reading journals. Some experience annotating special wide-margin copies will no doubt help to keep responses specific and anchored to particular items in a text. This is an especially useful method for poems. (In an undergraduate course I was fortunate enough to take with Archibald MacLeish, he had us keep notes on our responses to every poem we read in the full-year course, and he read these notes and responded to many of them.)

Reading responses don't just pertain to reading. They constitute an invaluable part of a student's mental life and can be used not only to enhance comprehension and appreciation of texts but to fuel thinking, talking, and writing on the many subjects to which reading experience contributes.

7. The teacher leads discussion of a text by questioning students and parlaying the responses.

This method presupposes that a whole class or some subgroup of it has read a text in common (or heard or seen it performed). The size of the group makes considerable difference, since the larger it is the less each individual can participate and the less each can influence the direction of discussion and maintain interest in it. Teacher-led discussions can serve to establish models for thoughtful interaction, but the more the activity centers on the teacher the more difficulty will students have eventually learning to discuss on their own. This is a method that teachers do very differently. Results vary from very positive to very negative.

I used to enter my secondary-school classroom armed with a list of what I thought were penetrating questions that would lead students to the heart of the story or poem or play. My students, who were very bright, seldom let me finish the list, because their answers pulled us in directions I hadn't foreseen or advanced prematurely by another route to my climactic questions. I had to adjust my list so much that I finally took to just playing to their responses as the best way to further their understanding of the text. Teachers who lead discussions of literature usually want to monitor comprehension or provoke thinking beyond what occurred during silent reading. But if they prepare questions to which they feel they know the answers, students try to guess what they have in mind and don't think for themselves. They bypass their native responses, which are what needs to be worked with if they are to develop. They look to the teacher for the definitive interpretation and learn that literature has right answers.

One possibility is for the teacher not to prepare a list of questions but to ask a few open-ended questions or simply ask for responses to some event or character or passage in the work. This sets up the chief learning activity, which is the parlaying of initial responses into a rich interaction of ideas and points of view: both the teacher and the students ask follow-up questions in response to responses. This refines thought and feeling and sensitizes participants to the *totality* of cues in a text. Connections thicken.

As teacher I would play my own opinions into the discussion only to the extent that I felt this would not short-circuit students' thinking or close down discussion. If my students had acquired a lot of experience with the activities described above, they would probably be able to consider my personal observations as just so many more stimuli for their own thinking without feeling they had to hew to a party line. But this is a delicate issue, and teachers used to an authoritarian role or simply prone to asserting their own views may easily deceive themselves about what is beneficial for students.

If students feel free to ask questions of the teacher, on the other hand, the teacher's expertise might be drawn upon in valuable ways. They might, for example, feel that more biographical or historical background would add interest or understanding to the text. Or they might feel puzzled about something in a text that discussion has not resolved and want to know if the teacher can satisfy their curiosity.

8. The teacher lectures to students about a literary work.

In the wrong hands this method could be fatal to the independence of student thought, especially if it were the only or nearly only method used. But let's consider the possibilities even though the method has been much abused. Let's assume, first, that it's only one of several or many methods in the teacher's repertory and so is not a routine activity forcing out the others described here. Suppose also that students have had the previous benefit of those activities described above that foster peer learning and independent judgment.

Some lectures situating a literary work in the life of the author and his or her society and literary traditions might be welcome and valuable if students are truly interested in the work. Courses surveying American or British or world literature may make such lectures even necessary to the extent that such courses are predicated on cultural continuities or on structural connections between works of different periods and cultures. The use of lectures to present more or less factual context need not risk pre-interpreting the texts themselves, though that can easily happen, or at any rate can give a historical or technical emphasis to literature that students may believe to be what they should cleave to.

A more serious danger arises when lectures consist of direct interpretation through close textual analysis. Such explanations can easily cause students to leave meaning to the teacher and just memorize the given interpretation until the test is over. But even an *explication de texte* by the teacher can actually help develop independent interpretation if done only occasionally as a sample of how close textual attention can enhance understanding and enjoyment. For such exemplary performances the teacher would do well to choose a text students themselves are not working on and make the lecture a good show—do an expert job on it and ask nothing from students about it then or later. Make it a gift. Such a lecture becomes strictly a learning aid, a demonstration of possibilities. To increase its value, however, the lecturer might allow students to ask questions about anything in the text or the analysis of it.

Seeing what an expert can see in a text may well increase what a student can see the next time she or he reads. An astute analysis by the teacher may show specifically and memorably just how diction in a poem or point of view in a short story or juxtaposition of scenes in a play can convey meaning. A very few such performances scattered over the genres could considerably enrich student responses and sharpen comprehension. A teacher might also use such lectures to illustrate various basic literary critical approaches—emphasizing in turn, for example, social-political context, textual independence, archetypal structure, deconstruction, and so on, without necessarily naming the approaches or introducing special terms. Occasionally applying such approaches to the same text would especially contrast them and could help remind students that no single interpretation, no matter how brilliant, exhausts a text or rules out other lines of perception.

Finally, students themselves may work up their own interpretation of some literary work and present it to the class, in some cases supplying as well some background information of a biographical or social nature. The text could be one familiar to the class or one the student lecturer presents in some way as an opening.

9. Students write essays about literary works of their choice.

The preceding activity can prepare for this one and might sometimes constitute an oral draft for it, especially if classmates and the teacher discuss the lecture afterwards. Because writing literary criticism is difficult and requires unusual motivation, it may be especially important that students choose the works they want to write essays about even if they're only choosing from a required reading list. It would be much better if they chose a work not assigned in the course, one that means something to them personally.

One way to ease into formal essays on literature is to write first about personal meaning, perhaps by making connections between the experiences of characters in a novel or play and some experiences of oneself or people one knows and observes. Reviews provide familiar examples of an excellent sort of literary criticism that also bridges from personal essay about one's reading to formal analysis. By way of assessing a performance or text for a consumer audience, students can write reviews on the models of those in periodicals. These often include background information, story summary, analysis of technique, comparison with other works on the same theme or in the same mode, and appraisal of the work leading to a recommendation.

At some point many students might really want to take a literary work that attracts them strongly and do an all-out interpretation of it, replete, where pertinent, with close textual analysis, social background, and comparison with other works. This gives young people a chance to share their perceptions and show others what this work means to them. But even the very advanced prep schoolers I taught did not like to write frequently about books. Using literary critical writing as a way of testing literature does a disservice to both literature and composition. Essays on literature should come only after much experience with the other activities described earlier here and should be done only occasionally, not routinely. Ideally, they would be expressions of strong and honest interaction between a book and a student after discussion, performing, extending, and other more implicit ways of studying literature have had plenty of opportunity to develop her literary sensibility and ground it in independent judgment.

10. Students write in the literary forms they read in.

This is a long-range method—hardly less than a total curricular approach. It means that in addition to writing extensions of literature and writing about literature, youngsters write literature itself, at least in the sense of practicing fiction, plays, poetry, autobiography, and personal essay. Without setting up a mechanical correspondence, teachers can arrange for students to read and write in a certain form at about the same time. To write in traditional forms like fables, parables, limericks, and haiku one indeed must read some examples first. But this is really necessary for all kinds of writing, not perhaps to get a definition of the form, which may be very common, like the short story, but to discover the possibilities of it and how professionals make use of it. We needn't get into strict "model writing." The point is to immerse oneself in reading of the sort one is trying to write—investigative journalism, memoir, poetry, how-to, or whatever.

All the professionals do this. One reads more perceptively and writes with a better grasp of techniques in that form. Students who have made up dialog understand better what Shakespeare and Ibsen are trying to do in a certain scene or concatenation of scenes. Just as writers must role-play readers to compose well, readers must role-play writers to comprehend well. Many artful things a playwright, novelist, or poet does are wasted on readers too passive to notice what these literary craftsmen are doing. This loss affects not only comprehension but the impact and import of a work. Writing in the forms one reads obviates a lot of formal analysis that would otherwise be necessary to call most students' attention to textual dynamics that should be affecting their responses. Along with most of the other methods set forth here, this one affords an alternative to the vivisections and postmortems on texts that have turned so many youngsters against the study of literature. Their instincts rightly tell them that literature is not written so much for cerebration as for celebration. (Thinking, yes, but in the mythic, figurative mode.) Because this last method can apply to a whole course or curriculum, as a principle for relating reading and writing, it may in the long run attune students more than any other single method to what is happening in a piece of literature.

Students need to experience eventually all the modes of discourse and all the literary types and become sophisticated about what forms in fact exist and how they relate to each other. Literature is better understood in the context of other discourse—nonfiction, scientific, utilitarian.

To conclude this summary of methods of teaching literature, let me make a few observations on the relation between this pedagogy and literary criticism? Is it necessary to teach theories of literature and introduce the concepts of various literary critical schools? Well, to do justice to the numerous movements of today would require a course in itself. Can we justify taking time for it away from literary works themselves? To limit students to one literary school of thought is arbitrary. No teacher has a right to bias students' education, especially since directions of thought in literary theory really amount to fundamental philosophical, even metaphysical positions.

My experience has been, moreover, that youngsters will pick up the jargon and approaches of a literary theory and feel modish but substitute those borrowed terms and concepts for their own responses, which can remain undeveloped beneath the glamorous patina. The brighter the student the more serious this problem may become. Students will learn more if they have to cast about for their own terms and concepts for what they perceive. Even old, apparently innocuous academic descriptions like plot, character, and theme usually prove more of a liability than an asset by stereotyping thinking if taken too seriously.

Insight into literature will be better served if students unwittingly recapitulate literary theories through their native efforts to engage with works in the variety of ways outlined here. These methods shift emphasis around from text to context to subjective response just as competing literary schools do. If the theories asserted in the various literary movements are worth their salt, students will recapitulate them in some form as they work with literature from the varied stances entailed in these ten methods, which do not derive from any particular theories but accommodate all.

Now, although a teacher may, when participating in discussions with students, feed in ideas from these theories so that they are all eventually absorbed into the classroom culture, it is unnecessary to teach them systematically, replete with rubrics and respective terminologies. But it does follow that the best literature teachers would benefit from knowing something about the various schools of literary criticism, which, if nothing else, at least show us all the ways in which literature can be thought about. This eclecticism should very much help a teacher lead these ten methods, which foster pluralistic, multi-dimensional response to literature, in keeping with the holophrastic nature of literature itself whereby a single set of words speaks simultaneously on several levels at once.

Theorists differ in emphasis on the writer's processes, the internal integrity of an artistic text, or the reader's responses. Some feature the meaning the author intended, some the self-contained meaning of the text as a thing in itself, some the archetypal meaning that works remote in time and space share because of certain universal structures they share, some the meaning that individual readers find for themselves, some the skewed meaning that the culture surrounding the work has imbued it with, and some the unconscious meaning that constitutes a secret text within a text—or an infinite regress of such texts. All these meanings can be present in a single literary work. So most texts offer opportunities to come onto all these meanings or viewpoints if the teaching methods themselves rotate students among all of the discursive stances generated by the wheeling trinity of persons.

16

Hidden Impediments to Improving English Teaching

Background

By the time I was invited to speak at the 1984 conference of the International Federation for the Teaching of English in East Lansing, Michigan, I felt compelled to analyze why changing the language arts curriculum in U.S. public schools is so difficult despite the advent of many new ideas and innovative movements. I felt discouraged. It seemed that teachers were still talking about ideas proposed in the '60s but never actually instituted. I felt I had been not only working in vain but that I had been talking to the wrong people: educators were not hard to convince but were caught in forces coming from beyond the professsion. Real improvements in curriculum would have to involve the broader society that schools merely reflect.

The emphasis of the IFTE conference on the social contexts of learning suited my drift splendidly. I was concerned, however, that my analysis would seem negative and be unwelcome. Actually, it made sense to many people, and the talk was well received. Judging from some equally favorable response to its publication in the September 1985 issue of *Phi Delta Kappan*, a lot of educators were beginning to feel that it was time to acknowledge the "hidden impediments." In 1985 Boynton/Cook reprinted the talk along with the other IFTE papers in *Language, Schooling, and Society*, edited by Stephen N. Tchudi.

————————◄●►————————

For the last 20 years, I have sought to help reform the language arts curriculum. During these years, both applied research in teaching methods and basic research in verbal and cognitive processes have increased substantially. We know much more today than in 1964 about how people use language and how they might be helped to improve their use of it.

But more classroom innovation was taking place in the 1960s than is occurring in the 1980s. And most of the advances made during that progressive era have since been erased by regressive trends that began in the mid-Seventies. If greater knowledge leads to better action, why are most schools moving backward, retrenching into materials and methods long since tried and found untrue? What are the obstacles that thwart efforts to improve discursive learning and that flout the knowledge accumulated from research?

I know; it *seems* that exciting change is breaking out all over. If you were to judge from what you read in the professional journals, hear at professional conferences, find in the goal statements of school districts, and encounter in some preservice training or inservice workshops, you would think that the joint was jumping. (It may actually be jumping, but more often from institutional agitation than from curricular innovation.) But once you leave this hubbub of bright shop talk and go into the classroom itself—once you ignore what the adults are saying and look at what the youngsters are doing—you will find little of what you have heard about. It is as if teachers and language arts consultants must check their understanding at the classroom door.

Educators know far more about language learning than their actions show. And many teachers are doing things that they do not believe in because they are not free to do otherwise. Resigned to their plight—or just thankful to have a job—many usher their charges through an insultingly robotic reading program or a grammar/composition textbook series that they despise and that its own publisher scorns (even while deftly plugging it into tidy managerial systems and the back-to-basics mystique). Other teachers, wanting to believe in what they are told to do, try to rationalize; you don't think deeply about what you have no power over. When I recommend individualized reading and writing, small-group process, and a broader range of oral and written discourse, teachers commonly say, "I think you're right, but I can't do those things in *my* school."

Even fired up by a summer institute in the National Writing Project—the best curricular movement I know of—all too often teachers wistfully put aside the exciting activities they have learned about because certain required things must be done instead—the competency tests taught to, the Warriner's books used. And somehow, the means and the occasions for using what they have learned in that summer institute never materialize. True, a few remarkable educators have done what is mostly just talked about: got children to write and revise with the self-concept of professionals or started up small-group discussions or a writing workshop. But too often these teachers are operating in specially arranged situations, often experimental. When the person, the funding, the other special circumstances disappear, so does the exemplary activity, for nothing in the school organization or philosophy makes certain that it will endure.

Educators today commonly regard research as the key to curricular change, but what is holding up the improvement of the language arts curriculum is not lack of knowledge. Those teachers who had been enfranchised as well as enlightened found ways to teach reading and writing successfully long before research attempted to show them how. We don't need a laboratory to see how people who read and write well become involved and adept. We don't need special studies to tell us that the language opportunities offered in school are almost invariably inferior to those of an optimal learning environment or that if teachers would shut up and let children talk both groups would learn more. We already know perfectly well that such oral activities as small-group discussion and improvisation will pay off for reading and writing.

John Mellon and I spent a good part of two years during the 1960s trying to prove that cognitive development would result from small-group discussion—an impossible task because there is no one-to-one correspondence between thought and language that would enable improved thinking to show scientifically in transcripts. Then I realized that we weren't trying to *discover* something that no one knew; we were convinced already, as anyone would be who had spent much time teaching or observing children or observing his own discursive processes. What we were really trying to do was come up with scores that would embarrass schools into instituting and honoring serious oral-language activities. The experts in research quantification whom we consulted said, "Why sweat it? Just tell us what you want to prove, and we'll show you how to make the figures come out right. It's all bull anyway." Actually, no amount of proof would have made effective oral-language activities a staple of the language arts curriculum, even in the Sixties. There were reasons other than a lack of evidence that prevented this sorely needed implementation. Then as now, if it's not tested, it's not taught. The matter partakes more of politics than of science.

The current reliance on research distracts us from the true causes of ineffectual and irrelevant methods of teaching. Partly, this preoccupation with research is a kind of whistling in the dark to keep up our courage. Partly, it simply supports some educators and researchers who depend on it for funding, academic recognition, and career advancement. I say these things with considerable sympathy; some of my best friends are researchers.

University-based educators may find that, unless they scientize their work by casting it as research, they may not be able to stay long in an academic setting. This is especially true in the field of composition, which has seldom been regarded in universities as more than a menial trade that—lacking the body of content characterizing such fields as history, literature, or physics—cannot be staffed (as these subject fields are) with tenure-track faculty members. It is some comfort that much of the research in composition has shifted in recent years from statistical experimentation to case studies and ethnography—approaches more congenial to the nature of composing. But we need not await the results of even this research to institute a fine curriculum in writing—no more than we need to hang suspensefully on the outcome of research comparing the efficacy of one school reading method with another when schools still don't practice the most efficacious methods often enough for them to show up on the research scoreboard.

If lack of knowledge or evidence is not what blocks curriculum improvement, then what does? It's something that no one rushes pell-mell to examine—a set of attitudes and emotions in both the public and the profession that is mostly unconscious.

Generally, the larger society places certain constraints and demands on schools that conflict with the learning activities advocated by most thoughtful educators. A majority of the public wants schools to control the content of reading and writing. But so long as students do not find and choose the content of reading and writing for themselves, they remain essentially unengaged with schoolwork and never learn to make the decisions that lie at the heart of composing and comprehending. Furthermore, both laity and educators fear the liberation of thought and behavior that students would achieve if talking, reading, and writing were taught most effectively—that is, if these powerful tools were freely given to youngsters for their personal investigation. Parents and teachers are unconsciously hedging and stalling on implementing a successful language arts curriculum.

Let me try to analyze this formidable obstacle in some detail. First, most parents still want schools to reinforce home training by inculcating their values, heritage, and modes of behavior. (By the way, *inculcate* derives from a Latin verb meaning "to grind in with the heel.") This creates a conflict with educators. Whereas most parents want their children to stay the way they made them, most teachers regard learning and growth as change.

The public wants schools to prepare youngsters for jobs and roles such as it grew up among. It wants to perpetuate a world it understands, a world limited to a particular era and culture. This is, of course, the real meaning of "back to basics." Consequently, when the public asks schools to teach its children to read and write, to think and create, it does not entirely mean it. At least, it doesn't mean it as educators might, who know that growth entails change and that you can't both indoctrinate students and teach them to think for themselves.

Most laypeople believe that reading and writing should be taught by informing the students of something they do not know, that is, by filling empty vessels and by correcting errors. Let's note in passing how well this fits the assumption in our profession that as research better informs us we will be better able to solve teaching problems, which must result from mere lack of information. From the assumption of an information deficit, it follows that learning to read and write need not disturb cultural values, which the schools are expected to reinforce.

But reading and writing are, in fact, very dangerous—at least as likely to transform as to transmit culture. Everyone knows this, however subterraneanly. Literacy bypasses the local oral culture of family and may acquaint youngsters with ideas and ways of life that their parents either ignore or abhor. As a way of carrying one's thought beyond received ideas, writing too may change youngsters. *Composing*, after all, means putting together. Composing is *making* sense. An authentic author is not a plagiarist or a paraphraser but someone who puts things together for himself or herself.

Reading and writing *are* dangerous and have always been so regarded, which is why literacy was restricted until the printing press made control of manuscripts impossible. Ruling classes in the past always tried to prevent their subjects from acquiring such powerful instruments. In today's democracy, members of the ruling class are the adults, who are also obliged, however, to pass on these instruments to the next generation. And so we do, but with half a heart. We think doublemindedly about reading and writing because our contrary motives place us in a double bind.

Parents who fear losing their children—and the majority do in some way—want the content of reading and writing to be controlled or made indifferent. Teach my children to read, but I don't want them to read this or this or this. Teach my children to write, but they don't need to delve into that or that or that. Just teach them to read and write so they can get good jobs. Such an attitude, steering ambivalently between the necessity of literacy and the threat it poses, ultimately delivers to schools the message that they should teach youngsters to read just well enough to follow orders and to write just well enough to take dictation.

The content of reading is controlled by limiting reading to textbooks, which adoption committees and publishers make certain do not contain anything that most parents don't want their children to think about. Efforts to censor books in public schools and libraries have increased at a shocking rate since the mid-Seventies. It is well-known that U.S. publishers put out only material that will be adopted in such lucrative markets as Texas.

If parents and educators conflict on the issue of change in students, they also unwittingly conspire to control content. Many schools prefer a heavy emphasis on phonics in teaching literacy, along with an atomistically programmed treatment of reading comprehension, because these are easier to administer and evaluate than an individualized reading program, which permits choice of subject matter, activates the intellect, and fosters a far greater quantity of reading.

For years I marveled that laypeople ordinarily unconcerned with pedagogy should take up cudgels for the literacy method called phonics. Then I realized that they value it precisely because the drills with word particles or isolated words constitute the most meaningless approach, the one most devoid of content. (I don't say that *teachers* are necessarily attracted to phonics for this reason.) In other words, a contentless method seems an ideal way to render reading innocuous. A heavy emphasis on phonics is preferred because it appears to teach reading while crippling it.

The U.S. is full of children—and adults—who passed the so-called reading tests but still can't read, because those tests are really just *phonics* tests; who passed the comprehension quizzes with their snippets of indifferent content; who plodded through all those disinfected textbooks controlled for everything from vocabulary and sentence complexity to topics and ideas—but who won't read now unless they're flogged into it. They never saw reading as a personal resource with which to do what *they* want to do.

But what about books outside of school? Won't *they* rob us of our children's minds and alienate their affections? Well, if you choose the right teaching methods, youngsters will never want to read outside of school and will do so only when the next boss down the line forces them. Most of the time, people read for content, for what the text is about and can do for them. To the extent that teaching methods and materials neutralize subject matter and mobilize anxiety, they fail to engage the mind and the will. Then, of course, nothing works, even when 12 years are squandered on it.

Don't get me wrong. I do not think that parents and educators are deliberately undermining reading and writing even as they extol them and give them top priority as so-called basic skills. But all adult parties have reasons to fear reading and writing that we do not generally acknowledge. This causes us to deal with reading and writing in a double-minded way and hence to sabotage our own professed goals. Laypeople fear loss of control over the minds of the young, from which would seem to follow rejection of adult values and consequent change in the social and moral order—revolution.

But if adult society as a whole fears losing the minds of the young, teachers in particular fear losing their own minds if they try to teach the way they know they should. They fear the loss of classroom control and of status if they allow youngsters to choose the content and form of what they read and write. Making students active and teachers reactive seems like a gratuitous relinquishing of power. *But empowering others is the teacher's job.* How many teachers, though, have been trained to decide how to teach decision making, how to liberate instead of to infantilize? Even those who do try are eventually stymied by requirements and edicts decided over their heads. You see, we have all been infantilized too.

Two main alternative methods for teaching literacy and reading are the language-experience method, whereby learners dictate what they have to say while looking on, and the read-along or lap method, whereby children follow on the page as someone reads something to them that they want to hear and eventually to be able to read for themselves. Content is uncontrolled because the learner chooses what to say and what to hear. The aide merely acts as a temporary intermediary between learner and text until, through massive experience in simultaneously seeing and hearing the language, the learner takes over this role for himself or herself. In combination with plentiful small-group talk to develop the oral base, such methods foil completely the traditional scenario that casts the teacher as the star of the show and makes the pupils an audience. These alternative methods all call for a decentralized classroom management permitting individuals to work either in small parties with one another or in pairs with aides, while the teacher circulates among them all.

Let us move now to writing. Here, too, the schools have a powerful reason to thwart all the best expert advice, research, and up-to-date understanding. Parents have not needed to crusade for censorship of writing, because U.S. educators have not asked students to do much writing at all and, when they have, have usually supplied students with the subject matter they wish them to write about.

The negative feelings toward writing acquired early from Prussian handwriting exercises, plus the generally mechanistic literacy practices already referred to, insure that learners no more choose to write on their own than they choose to read on their own. On the many occasions when I have asked teachers to recall learning to write, most have said that the positive experiences occurred out of school and that school writing was associated with pain and failure.

Some lucky elementary school children may be allowed to write about material they choose and in the forms they choose. But most are still licking their wounds from learning handwriting and spelling when they begin the first of the endless writings about given topics, about what they were told to read, or just about what they were told. It begins with the paraphrasing of reference sources (called "reports") and the plot summaries (called "book reports"), which are really just checks on the directed reading. It continues through the "critical papers," "research papers," "term papers," and "essay questions" of high school and college and runs on through the "review of the literature" section of the doctoral dissertation. What all this writing has in common is that it monitors assigned reading and tests coverage of given content. Inasmuch as the reading material is controlled, the content of the writing is automatically controlled as well.

Only rarely in their entire academic careers do students do other kinds of writing, and then such writing is usually only marginally related to the classroom. Most universities don't give a hoot for composition courses other than as a way of servicing the testing practices of other courses. Consequently, writing has rarely been taken seriously and taught for its own sake, in all its variety of forms and purposes, as a central humanistic way of knowing—which is how it would attract young people.

Instead, reading and writing are brought into a stupefyingly negative relationship to each other that makes students want to avoid both. Every time you read, you have to write something about it to show you got the point. That is, the punishment for reading is having to write. Both are something that someone else wants you to do for their purposes, not something you want to do for your own.

Writing that tests can at least be real writing, some sort of essay, even if the content and purpose constrain it to a given topic and a very limited type of essaying. Worse is the conversion of writing into a downright fraudulent set of exercises called "composition" that are not writing at all but a kind of *de*composition—an atomizing of the writing process into pieces that can be studied and tested like any other factual content. Isolated dummy sentences and paragraphs are analyzed, ticketed, combined, sequenced, or edited.

The College Board test called "composition" has lent respectability to this fraud and set a terrible example of what you can get away with by converting a squirmy verb into a placid noun, by reifying the writing process to fit it to cheap, multiple-choice tests. Again, as with reading, writing becomes safely eviscerated and decorticated. Not only is the content of writing preempted by assigned reading and required topics, but even the act of writing itself is converted to content.

Reading about writing, like writing about the reading, burlesques the ideal of integrated learning. Killing two birds with one stone is hardly desirable if you want the birds to thrive. So in writing, too, we educators have reinforced that part of the public psyche that secretly tries to sabotage the key learning activities that help people to think for themselves.

A solution to this problem calls for a new covenant between school and home. Educators will have to take the initiative and enlist the laity in the teaching of those very processes of inquiry that they distrust. For one thing, becoming involved in school reading and writing may keep parents from feeling that they are losing their children. For another, literacy should be taught socially, through other people, in the way initial speech is taught, as a kind of incorporation into the human community, not as isolated drills with materials and machines.

Language-experience and read-along methods are best suited to such an approach and would insure that hearts and minds are engaged in reading and writing from the outset. To serve best, these methods require pairing a learner with an aide who takes down the dictation and reads aloud until the learner can decode and encode for himself or herself. These aides can be any literate adults, including senior citizens, but older youngsters from other grades make fine aides, too. Children must feel that literacy is a powerful gift that all elders are freely and gladly passing on to them.

Beyond literacy itself, truly successful teaching of reading and writing and speaking and thinking requires a drastic redeployment of human resources that only far closer collaboration between the laity and educators can bring about. The three keys to improving the language arts curriculum are 1) *individualization* of the learning tasks, so that individuals are frequently doing different things at the same time; 2) *interaction* among individuals for oral-language development and the benefits of small-group dynamics in all the language arts; and 3) *integration* of learning across subjects, media, and kinds of discourse, so that individuals may continuously synthesize their own thought structures. Developing a curriculum based on individualization, interaction, and integration depends on a far greater involvement of the lay community than is now usual—for several reasons.

One reason is economic. The schools are going broke, but their economic crisis could turn into a good thing in some ways. Schools will have to use paraprofessionals, and teachers will have to welcome them. As the public refuses to increase school funds, on grounds that schools just need to use more effectively what they already have, it will become apparent that, in lieu of money, many people will need to help out in schools in order to keep them going. Many underemployed workers or overeducated homemakers may find great satisfaction in becoming volunteer classroom paraprofessionals. Such a shift of human resources would end once and for all the dominance of the nervous-hostess model of classroom organization, whereby a lone teacher tries to direct two or three dozen children through a unison activity.

Once the laity begins to play an *overt* role in schooling, it will have to share accountability for the results—instead of holding teachers solely responsible for the success or failure of schools while at the same time not according them the decision-making power commensurate with that responsibility. Moreover, I feel sure that this direct involvement in the schools will help the public become disenchanted with our current testing practices. Perhaps these school volunteers will come to realize that what in school is called "reading" is often not real reading, that what is called "composition" is often not real writing, and that this fraud has arisen partly from the double bind in which the schools have been placed.

Then I think we may see not only an end to the practice of scapegoating schools for social ills but also a beginning of realism in the teaching of reading and writing. As representatives of the public, paraprofessionals can break the double bind, all while providing the human resources needed to make the alternative work. Literacy needs to be taught in the same organic social way that children are taught to speak at home. Literature should be an endless extension of bedtime stories. The writing curriculum should reflect what adults write in all their various vocations and avocations and should recapitulate the processes that characterize writing outside of school.

Students who have mastered literacy and are exploring all the kinds of discourse and the various disciplines need access to the people who practice these disciplines: scholars, government officials, journalists, lawyers, scientists, case workers, merchants, and so on. By role-playing adults in various occupations, young people not only prepare realistically for joining the adult world but also become familiar with the whole range of utilitarian, literary, and scientific discourse. Whereas younger pupils learning literacy need outsiders to come into the schools to help them, older students need to be able to go forth from the school to observe or to apprentice at other sites.

The community should help students arrange experiences that will allow them to investigate the larger world they are expected to join and eventually to take over. As it is now, schools worry about liability suits because they are held responsible for students during school hours. But that is precisely the sort of difficulty that can be worked out with the community. Both school and community have to be willing to let students find out what is going on in the world and not try to control the content of what they will perceive, discuss, reflect on, and read and write about.

The worst of our joint hypocrisy has been to worship critical thinking—even to the point of biasing the whole national curriculum toward the climactic production of so-called critical essays as tests in university courses—while never inviting students to cut their intellectual teeth on their own environment. We cannot do all the selecting of subjects and topics and frameworks that students are to think about and still honestly expect them to become independent critical thinkers. High-quality education requires that students circulate freely through the society they will one day run and critique it under the auspices of those who are currently running it.

Economic hard times may result in another boon: dropping textbooks. Aside from the fact that all textbook programs are political footballs by virtue of—I should say by "vice" of—the need for the approval and financial commitment of some level of government, textbooks pervert the teaching of the language arts in particular by working against individualization and interaction and against the integration of the language arts with each other and with other subject areas. Basal readers, literature series, and so-called composition or rhetoric textbooks merely get in the way by overcontrolling the reading matter and by converting writing into just one more thing to study *about* instead of to *do*.

In addition to what students write themselves, which in a good program should provide a considerable amount of reading material, the community can easily supply more and better reading material than textbooks ever offered. Teachers, specialists, laypeople, and librarians can help students to organize all these materials physically, for easy access, and mentally, for individual reading programs.

Of course, straight anthologies of literature have often been compiled for the schools, but even anthologies are often thematically organized or include additional material to direct thinking. Though certain compendiums of information created for young people may be useful in the natural and social sciences, the language arts are not empirical subjects but rather *arts*, activities, practices—not fit objects for required study by youngsters. For these reasons, I have never myself consented to create books for schools other than anthologies of readings.

Furthermore, it is extremely dangerous to buy curricula, especially since they are packaged by large corporations, which, in today's business world, are increasingly amoral. Just as state and local school boards implement the public's hidden fears of learning, the publishers enshrine these fears in materials that, in turn, mold the public's notions of curriculum, because everyone experiences them as children.

In combination with economic crisis, the increasing pluralism of communities also makes imperative some new covenant between the home and the school. Just as financial hard times could actually improve education, so could the staggering diversity of ethnic, linguistic, national, and religious groups with which the schools are flooded. No longer will it be possible to pretend to educate well by a single, standardized curriculum. A pluralistic society must have a pluralistic curriculum, which is to say that the individualization that should long ago have determined the main organization of schooling may now be forced upon us. Learners are different and need different things. Their parents differ about what they think schools should do; individuals differ by both personal make-up and ethnic background.

Voucher systems would prove more, not less expensive and would institutionalize rather than eliminate conflict and social fragmentation. If everyone is broke and has to share the same resources, we will have an opportunity for an extraordinary educational enterprise. All groups will have to cooperate in order that their own differences may be served.

In accommodating group differences out of necessity, schools will finally be able to allow for individual differences as well, because once we abandon our insistence on standardization, we will see how to organize resources for learners to be doing different things at the same time throughout a community that has become a large school. One reason for standardizing was to make evaluation easier, so that educators would be accountable to the public. But the more that hard times force laypeople to participate in schooling and the more that this pluralistic public gives schools conflicting ultimatums, the more the fiction breaks down that educators alone are accountable for learning outcomes.

Instead of pretending that as research findings come in we will improve our teaching, let's begin to acknowledge that we will improve our teaching when we stop colluding unconsciously with the public to thwart our own awesome goal of teaching youngsters to think for themselves and begin instead to initiate a deliberate collaboration with the public. Neither the public nor educators need fear the loss of power and identity. Things are out of control *now*. And one reason young people are so hard to handle is that they feel that we are not doing what we profess but are using the schools as mere holding tanks to keep them from exploring a world they never made but will some day have to live and work in. Thus they build up enormous resentment and suspect that adults are frauds and hypocrites. Then indeed are their minds lost to us. We must give them reading and writing as *theirs*, as human rights, not give with one hand and take back with the other.

Broaching this problem with the public means laying out for it something like what I have tried to say here, though probably with more tact than I felt was needed in talking shop with my professional colleagues. Most educators already have a good idea of how learning stands to be improved and deeply long to make significant changes. Inasmuch as the obstacles involve our relationship with the society that commissions us to teach its youth, it is with that society that we must work out solutions.